ULTIMATE
FRESHWATER
FISHING

ULTIMATE
FRESHWATER
FISHING

JOHN BAILEY

DK PUBLISHING, INC.

TO THE JOY OF MY LIFE

A DK PUBLISHING BOOK

PROJECT EDITOR EDWARD BUNTING
ART EDITOR KEVIN RYAN
US EDITOR RAY ROGERS
MANAGING EDITOR FRANCIS RITTER
MANAGING ART EDITOR
DEREK COOMBES

DTP DESIGNER MATTHEW GREENFIELD
PICTURE RESEARCHERS
TOM WORSLEY, ANGELA ANDERSON

PRODUCTION MANAGER
RUTH CHARLTON

Note on underwater photography

Acknowledgment is made to the various sources of
underwater photographs for this book. Many of
the images, including all those of fish approaching or
taking bait, and fish being released, are the result of
highly specialized photography by Kevin Cullimore.

Note on fish welfare

The author and publishers are glad to confirm that
no fish were severely injured in the course of writing,
photographing, and preparing this book for press.

Note on weight charts

Records listed in the charts serve to give an
approximate indication only and are subject to change
as fresh records are set. A "trophy" means a weight
that an angler can be proud of or could consider as a
target weight to aim for.

First American Edition, 1998

2 4 6 8 10 9 7 5 3 1

Published in the United States by
DK Publishing, Inc.
95 Madison Avenue
New York, New York 10016
Visit us on the World Wide Web at http://www.dk.com

Library of Congress Cataloging-in-Publication data
Bailey, John M. 1951-
    Ultimate freshwater fishing / by John Bailey.
      p. cm.
    Includes index.
    ISBN 0-7894-2866-0
    1. Fishing. 2. Freshwater fishes. I. Title.
SH441.B28 1998   98-7551
799.1'1--dc21   CIP

Color reproduction by Colourscan, Singapore
Printed and bound by Butler & Tanner Ltd, Great Britain

CONTENTS

FOREWORD

ALL MY LIFE I HAVE BEEN A FISHERMAN, and I have never had a single, solitary regret about it . . . no matter how cold, how wet, or how fruitless the day has been, I've never even considered wanting to do anything else with my time.

I've been lucky. My rod has taken me into some of the most magical places on earth, and I've fished in the Himalayas, the Rockies, the southern Alps of New Zealand, the Volga Delta, the wilds of Mongolia, the lush valleys of Europe, and another thousand secret and breathtaking places that I never would have dreamed of visiting had I not been an angler.

I have had elephants push through my camp at night, brushing against the skin of my tent. I've been watched by panthers and even been roared at by a tiger. I have had hooked fish snatched by crocodiles and watched a black bear investigate my bag while I fished for steelhead. I have been blessed with the greatest of fishing pals around the world – gillies, guides, or just inseparable friends. Among them are Johnny Jensen from Denmark, Simon Channing from Australia, and Pete Smith from Wales. I have come to appreciate the magic of water: the way rivers sing to you or how still waters present that mysterious face that challenges you to woo, to investigate, and to devote your life to their shores. But it is the fish, above all, that make the angler's life, and every fish has its own special appeal.

Though I have been fishing for 40 years or more I have still completed only 10 percent of the adventures I mapped out for myself as a child. So, just as I learned to cast a line almost as soon as I could walk, then, God willing, I'll still be flicking out my fly, my bait, or my spinner right to the very end!

John Bailey

HOW FISH LIVE

FISH LIVE UTTERLY FASCINATING LIVES,
and, although we know a great deal about
them, there are many aspects of their
world and their experience that remain,
to a greater or lesser degree, unknowable.
Nonetheless, as anglers we must try to
know our quarry as well as we possibly
can. If we regard fish as objects rather
than complex creatures, we simply won't
catch many of them: the angler is a
hunter, and knowledge of the quarry
is the foundation of success.

There's more to it, though. The more
we learn about the lives of our fish, the
more we marvel at them and realize how
special they are: the respect and
consideration that this brings help
make us caring anglers.

A MOMENT IN THE LIFE...

This is a view beneath the surface of a woodland pond in spring.
A stirring pike, rising up slowly from its cradle of dead branches,
observes a school of passing prey fish with a cold, calculating stare.

Lifting the Veil

The surface of any river, lake, or stream is like a veil that hides the mysterious world below it from our gaze as we stand on the bank. It is a world that we long to understand. The sport of fishing, and the experience that it brings, can lift that veil by teaching us about the fish and their ways, about the water itself, and about every detail of that strange and magical habitat in which fish live.

Tackle, rigs, and bait are important considerations for the angler, but they are secondary to a thorough knowledge of the fish being pursued. Where does the fish live in the water? What can its body language tell us? How, when, and on what does a fish feed? A hundred questions of this kind are on the mind of the true angler on every visit to the waterside.

How to watch fish

To catch fish, you need to understand them, and that almost always means observing them and building up some idea of their habits, fears, and fancies. To watch fish successfully, you must first be able to see them! Polarizing glasses are vital for taking away the glare of the water surface and allowing you to see clearly into the lake or river that you are intending to fish.

Binoculars are also essential. Even if a fish is just a few yards away, the magnified view they provide will help you identify any distinguishing marks and may even show you what it is eating. Thigh boots, or even chest waders, can be useful too, allowing you to get into shallow water, approach a fish, and merge with its environment. Camouflaged clothing is also important: you must always remember that a fish is a wild creature that may well see humans as its major predator.

Do not worry if, on your first attempt, you don't see any fish at all. Fish watching is an acquired art. You simply need to relax and go with the rhythm of the water. This sounds vague, but once you are totally at one with the water, at peace there, you'll find that the secrets seem to come. At first, you may see just a few indistinct shapes. Learn to focus on these. Soon they will become clearer, and you will marvel at what you see.

The more you learn about your fish through watching, the more confident you will become about catching them. For example, you will soon learn where a rainbow trout has its patrol route, which might tell you exactly where to place your fly to catch it. You might see whether a bass is eating worms, hunting small fish, or snapping at fluttering mayflies: then you can be sure which bait to put before the fish of your dreams.

The more you watch fish, the more aware you will become of how the water itself behaves. You will soon begin to know how the current scours the bottom and how the force of the water can be diverted by a rock or fallen tree. You will also start to appreciate the complex and varying effects that wind action has on a body of water. On lakes, watch the birds. A swan feeding on weed in winter is proof that there is still a stand of underwater annual plants even at the end of the year. Such vegetation can harbor small fish, and these may well attract pike. If a grebe is regularly diving in a particular area, schools of prey fish may be present, and these will pull in bass, zander, or perch.

The majesty of fish

To the thoughtless angler, fish are simply objects, commodities even, that are there simply to provide us with occasional amusement or diversion. However, to the angler who watches and understands them, fish take on a new and majestic quality. Once the veil has been lifted, fish may be recognized as fascinating, wild creatures with complex lives that are constantly changing and can never be fully understood. The beauty of fish is also enhanced when you see them in the water: a caught fish can indeed look wonderful, but in its natural state it is even more glorious. Anyone who has seen a steelhead trout lying in the shallows, washed by the gin-clear waters of a mountain stream, or a silver salmon leaping the falls in a glowing sunset, will know exactly what I am talking about.

The more that we know about the fish and the waters that harbor them, the greater will be our desire to cherish fish and not to harm them in any way. We might begin to feel that it is sufficient simply to watch some fish and not even bother trying to catch them at all. Perhaps we will try to outwit a serious specimen if we see one but think it better to let the average ones swim free. Above all, we will inevitably choose to protect our waters from pollution, vandalism, and litter. The thinking angler who has seen beyond the veil is the best guardian that the streams and lakes of this world can ever hope to have.

▲ THINKING LIKE A FISH
Their element is not ours, so we tend to think of fish as alien creatures. Move the veil aside, try to see things the way fish see them, and you will be a more understanding angler.

◄ NATURAL FOOD SUPPLIES
To select the kind of bait you should be using, try wading out into the river and investigating what food is actually available to the fish. Here I am looking at some stonefly larvae.

► MERGING IN
Always wear undramatic colors and a hat to take the glare of the sun off your face. Crouch down, avoid rapid movements, and tread lightly.

RESPECT FOR NATURE

I N 1990 THOMAS DAHL, the American environmentalist, issued a report called *Wetland Losses in the United States, 1780s–1980s* to the US Department of Fish and Wildlife Services. Dahl had concluded from his research that the 48 contiguous states (the whole country except Alaska and Hawaii) had, over two centuries, lost half their original wetlands. This amounted to 1 acre (0.4 ha) of wetland lost every minute of those 200 years. The worst cases were California, with 91 percent of wetlands gone, and Florida, where 9.3 million acres (3.8 million ha) had been lost (Florida's original wetland area could not be calculated, hence no percentage). Almost all this wetland loss was due to drainage done for the sake of creating farmland.

THE VISIBLE COSTS

Similar wetland losses have occurred the world over, and, as a result, huge areas of fish habitat have been lost. Many of the once sparkling steelhead rivers of British Columbia have been all but destroyed by the logging industry, by hydroelectric projects, or by ill-advised mining. Lowland rivers throughout Europe have been hopelessly degraded by the insidious practice

▲ LETHAL NETS
The driftnets that are laid at sea are indiscriminate killers. The invisible mesh, often many miles long, ensnares all manner of wildlife, including seals and dolphins as well as valuable fish stocks. Migrating salmon are particularly hard hit.

▼ CLEAR MOUNTAIN STREAMS
Unpolluted and unexploited, rivers like this one in New Zealand still run sparkling and clean. Thankfully, such streams are being preserved for the stocks of trout that they hold and for the pleasure of generations of anglers and naturalists.

of dredging, which turns meandering waterways into straight and featureless canals. Pools and ponds throughout western Europe and America have been filled in, concreted over, and built upon. The abstraction of water for agriculture, industry, and domestic usage threatens both the flow of rivers and the groundwater supplies throughout the developed world.

In parts of Scandinavia, lakes and rivers have been denuded of their fish by rain that has been made acid by the industrial gases released from western European factories. Throughout India, the deforestation of upland slopes allows the monsoon rains to wash away the valuable topsoil and silt up the rivers. And river waters virtually everywhere are polluted: the mighty Volga is not safe to drink from, and swimmers in the Thames in London risk poisoning from the water.

CARING TO PRESERVE

In every single country where there has been any protest at the destruction of the waterways, it is the anglers who have stood up and clamored for the return of our pure water systems, highlighting pollution and opposing damaging developments. And such protest can be effective. In India, the government has heard the plea, and sanctuaries have been created to preserve the mahseer in badly affected rivers.

As individuals, we must all do whatever we can personally, for example by reporting pollution and by keeping the river banks clean and free of litter. In New Zealand, conscientious anglers now voluntarily limit their visits to wild-water streams, knowing that too much fishing can destroy a small and fragile ecosystem. Through the care and respect that we show, and by preaching the marvels of fish to others, anglers can be true ambassadors for the natural habitat and for fish the world over.

▲ INDUSTRIALIZATION OF THE RIVER
Factories, warehouses, and increasingly heavy shipping all lead to pollution and the gradual degradation of water quality. Industrially utilized waters such as these may hold just a few very tolerant fish species, or no fish at all.

HANDLING FISH WITH CARE

The first consideration of every angler must be for the welfare of the fish. In the water they look strong and powerful, but the effect upon them of being lifted out of their natural element can be traumatic. Remember, too, that dry hands or a landing net can easily dislodge scales and remove the protective layer of mucus.

1 LANDING A CHUB
This chub is now exhausted and ready for landing. But do we need to remove it from the water to be admired and then released? Bringing it onto the bank will cause a certain amount of stress.

2 UNHOOKING
If you use a barbless hook, as many thoughtful anglers now choose to do, there is no need even to use a net. Lower your rod to take the tension off the line, and slip the hook with your fingers.

3 REST AND RECOVER
Now ready for release, the fish has still not broken the surface. It is still tired, though, and needs time to recover its strength before swimming away into the powerful current. Hold it facing upstream until you feel its fins begin to pulse and the muscles flex. There is now no danger of it rolling over in the deeps and being unable to right itself. It is ready to go.

LIFE IN FRESH WATER

THE RELATIONSHIP BETWEEN fish and water bears similarities to that between birds and air: the water supports fish and enables them to move. Water can be kinder than air, carrying food to the mouths of fish, but it can also suffocate fish when oxygen levels are low. There are two aquatic worlds, fresh and salt water. Migratory salmon, trout, sturgeon, and eels can live in both, but most freshwater fish will die if placed in the sea.

HOW FISH BREATHE

HUMANS, IN COMMON with other air-breathing animals, live in an atmosphere with an oxygen content of about 20 percent. As we breathe, air is taken into our lungs, and there the oxygen enters the bloodstream to be carried throughout the body by hemoglobin in red blood cells.

For fish, taking in oxygen is a slightly more difficult business. For a start, there is much less oxygen in water than in air. The content of oxygen dissolved in water varies from 1 to 5 percent: clearly a fish needs a very efficient breathing system.

Gills answer this need. They are the vital organs that recharge the fish's blood with oxygen. Each gill is a piece of tissue in which the fish's blood vessels divide and divide again into tiny capillaries, in a feathered pattern. The fish takes in water and passes it across and between its gills. The blood in the capillaries is separated from the water by only the thinnest of membranes. Oxygen passes from the water into the blood, while carbon dioxide and other waste products pass into the water.

How does the water get from the mouth to the gills? Briefly, a fish that is breathing opens its mouth to take in water. Once a mouthful is obtained, the lips are closed and sealed off by flaps on the inside. The floor of the throat is then raised so that the water does not go down the gullet into the stomach but is pushed out through the gill arches. The gills themselves hang on gill flaps that are located on the outside of the gill arches. After use, the water is expelled through the gill flaps.

VARIATIONS IN WATER CONDITIONS

Fish are more at the mercy of the elements than we humans are. Air readily supplies us with oxygen almost everywhere we go, and in normal conditions only high altitude prevents this. However, water can prove much less friendly to fish, and there are many times when they will not feed because there is not enough oxygen in the water to invigorate them. A salmon swimming up a river in summer, when the water is low, clear,

and warm, will avoid pools in the river that contain little oxygen. That is why an experienced angler looks for them in shallow, fast-running stretches that are better oxygenated.

Carp can also run into oxygen shortages. They often live in shallow ponds; in summer, the sun can warm a pond and cause much of the oxygen it contains to come out of solution. At times like this you see carp swimming along the surface with their mouths in the air, gulping in oxygen direct from the atmosphere. Don't be fooled – they still can't breathe air: a little oxygen is dissolved back into the water in their mouths, to be extracted by the gills in the normal way.

The experienced carp angler knows that at times like this feeding is going to be irregular, because the carp can do no more than fight for oxygen, and in effect for their lives. All this changes once windy, wet weather sets in, the temperature falls, and rain puts freshly dissolved oxygen back into the water. The fish are reinvigorated and begin to look for food again.

WHERE TO LOOK FOR FISH

Knowing how a fish breathes can often help an angler pinpoint its location. Take, for example, a grayling and a barbel in a fast-flowing river. The grayling takes oxygen most readily from the faster-flowing parts of the river. As a result, it will be found in the waters close to the head of a pool, where the flow is very quick and "streamy." Barbel breathe more easily in slightly slower water and as a result will be found in the lower regions of the pool, where the water has slowed down.

Different fish species have different oxygen requirements. Char, salmon, and most trout demand well-oxygenated water, and that is why they tend to inhabit the colder rivers, often at high altitude, where the water is cleaner, clearer, and richer in dissolved oxygen. Carp and catfish can tolerate lower levels of dissolved oxygen and flourish in slow-moving rivers, often at lower altitudes and often with warmer, dirtier water.

▲ AIR AND WATER

Ice-cold water from a glacier cascades down a mountainside in Kashmir. Though thoroughly oxygenated, the water is not warm enough to support a great deal of fly life. Insects blown into the water from bankside foliage are important items on the menu.

▼ SMOTHERED POND

Ponds in the lowlands are usually so rich in nutrients, both from the natural fertility of the surroundings and from farm fertilizers, that many are covered with floating weeds like this. Only stillwater specialists like carp and tench like to live here.

◀ STARVED OF OXYGEN

A summer drought has shrunk this rainbow trout's pool and starved the fish of the oxygen it needs. The trout has been struggling for two days and is now very weak; it will not survive another day unless it is rescued.

▼ BREATHING EASY

These rainbows are lucky. Their river is not low and they have made their way to the head of a pool in a cold, streamy stretch, where they are enjoying the plentifully aerated water.

HOW FISH EXPLORE THEIR WORLD

EVERY ANGLER NEEDS to understand the wondrous ways in which fish have developed over millions of years to fit their habitats. We are trying to catch animals that are perfectly adapted to their environment and that are proven survivors.

Fish are totally at home in their aquatic world, and they learn over the years that they spend there. A carp that has lived in a lake for 50 years has built up an exact knowledge of its surroundings. It will know exactly what the skyline should look like, and any angler appearing on it is immediately noted and avoided. The fish will also follow familiar paths through the water, and any tackle blocking those paths will be immediately obvious. The fish will know all the usual sounds and vibrations of the day, and anything new will represent a threat.

THE SENSE OF SIGHT

Without addressing the intricate biology of the fish's eye, let us consider its eyesight from the standpoint of the angler. First, it must be said that the idea that fish are short- or partially sighted is complete nonsense. Most fish have vision as good as their particular habitat allows, limited only by the light and the turbidity of the water.

Most fish are actually long-sighted, and most predatory fish can see particularly well in front of them. The eyes of prey fish are adapted to detect the movement of any predator to the sides or to the rear – and that, of course, includes you.

Although much of the water surface above a fish acts as a silvery mirror, reflecting the bottom and impenetrable to its gaze, in the center of its visual field a fish can, in fact, see very clearly through the surface layer. Moreover, that "window" is greatly enlarged by refraction at the surface. The message here is obvious – if you are standing upright and uncamouflaged on

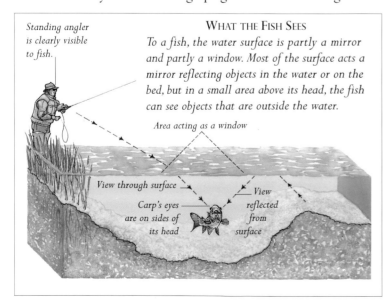

Standing angler is clearly visible to fish.

WHAT THE FISH SEES

To a fish, the water surface is partly a mirror and partly a window. Most of the surface acts a mirror reflecting objects in the water or on the bed, but in a small area above its head, the fish can see objects that are outside the water.

Area acting as a window

View through surface

View reflected from surface

Carp's eyes are on sides of its head

▲ EYES OF THE PREY
Needing to be constantly on the lookout for predators, the roach has excellent vision that allows it to see in virtually all directions.

◀ EYES OF THE PREDATOR
With its hunting lifestyle, the pike sees best above and in front, but the superb sensitivity of its lateral lines and nerve endings would enable it to survive even if blinded.

a steep bank, then there is every chance that fish, especially those near the surface, will detect your every movement. Even outside the area acting as a "window" *(see illustration on previous page)*, the surface will at times be choppy and give the fish a chance to spot you through the tilted edge of a ripple or wave.

Contrary to many opinions, fish can see in color, so it does pay to experiment with the color of your baits, flies, or lures, especially at depth or if you are pursuing suspicious fish.

The pike has an added refinement. In clear water, it can probably see its prey up to 60 ft (20 m) away, but it also has two sighting grooves that converge toward the tip of its snout, which helps explain how the pike can track a moving fish so precisely, even over fairly large distances.

OTHER SENSES

Given the acute senses of smell and taste of many fish species, we should take great care in preparing our baits. We can hardly imagine the sensory power of the seagoing salmon that can detect the particular scent of its own river, or the eel that can pick up the smell of a dead fish half a pond away at night.

Think, too, of those bottom-feeders that have barbels around their mouths. These are covered with sensitive taste organs that help the fish detect bloodworms in the mud and also to home in on your own tasty little minnow deadbait.

Hearing has an important part to play, too. Members of the carp family have an arrangement of vertebrae that forms a bony connection between the inner ear and the fish's swim bladder. This accentuates their hearing and allows them to hear other fish swimming nearby, as well as detect your footfalls.

The lateral line is yet another sensory system that helps protect the fish. On most fish you can see it as a line of scales, pitted with tiny pores, running along both sides of the body. The lateral line is really a series of special sensory cells that

THE FISH'S "SIXTH SENSE"

The pike's lateral line is a marvel. As well as picking up information that the pike needs, it also discards data that are not essential. The *pike can distinguish, for example, between the vibrations made by a school of prey fish and those caused by surrounding water plants.*

Lateral line

detect changes in pressure around the fish – a vital tool that gives the fish a precise knowledge of what is going on around it in the water. Couple the lateral line with the millions of nerve endings that pick up signals of many different kinds from the water, and you have a truly sensitive creature.

Virtually all the fish that we hunt also have a strong sense of touch. Many of them like to feel pressure against their bodies, as any angler who has watched carp sheltering against the dead branches of a submerged tree, or a salmon cradled in a crevice among the rocks, can testify. Eels demonstrate their tactile nature by the way they love to lie inside any pipes that may open out into the water they live in. The eels lurk in this neat hiding place, gently scratching their backs on the inside of the pipe whenever they like. They also lie inside old pipes in builders' debris on the beds of gravel pits, lakes, or rivers.

FISH HAVE EARS

The success of a lure can depend on vibration, and even sound, as well as sight. The right lure, therefore, will have a good action, the right color for the day, and perhaps some clicking ball bearings to appeal to yet another sense.

CORDELL RATT'L SPOT AUDIBLE LURE

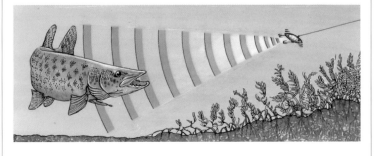

SENSITIVE ANTENNAE
The "cat's whiskers" are essential for sensing and probing out food at night, when most feeding takes place.

▲ KEEPING IN TOUCH
Living in very turbid water and being largely nocturnal, this great catfish has small eyes. Rather than relying on vision, it uses its extraordinary probing whiskers to test and taste every possible food source.

HOW FISH FEED

A FEEDING FISH IS A CATCHABLE FISH, so this is the point at which fish and angler come very close together. You can sometimes persuade a fish that is not feeding to change its mind, but 99 percent of the time, your first important job is to identify those fish that are hungry.

In most cases, this is not too difficult. For example, many bottom feeders, such as carp, bream, and even some panfish, will send up bubbles as they root among the bottom debris. They will also frequently color up the water. Predators also betray themselves, and even more dramatically. The bow-wave on the surface, and the scattering school of small fish, could not be clearer signposts for the lure fisherman!

FEEDING TECHNIQUES

Every species has its own characteristic feeding techniques, and these can vary with the food source. Most fish eat more than one food type, and members of the carp family are perfect examples of this. In warm weather, groups of carp are frequently seen drifting slowly just below the surface, as though they were simply enjoying the sun. Actually, they are grazing on small aquatic crustaceans and daphnia that float in the water. As the carp breathe, they filter these tiny creatures out of the expelled water with their gill-rakers. Obviously, at these times carp are much more difficult to catch than when they are rummaging around in the mud looking for big baits such as worms or mussels. That is what the angler wants to see – great clouds of mud, and big fish feeding hard.

Let us look now at the way that fish take insects from the surface, for many species have a liking for terrestrials that fall from the surrounding vegetation. To some extent, the way in which food is taken depends on the insect in question, but the observant angler can also learn a lot about the fish from the form of the rise. For example, grayling, dace, and bleak usually drag the insect down and devour it underwater at their leisure. Chub tend to catch swimming insects by suction, and you will often hear a loud smacking kiss from some distance away. The behavior of asp and trout is distinctive, and with big insects, such as mayflies, both species will greedily snap them up, often leaping right out of the water to do so.

Predators, too, differ in their feeding, and the form of attack can often label the species precisely. For example, if only one hunting fish seems to be involved, then the chances are that a pike is responsible. If predators are striking into a school of prey fish in a group, then zander, walleye, perch, or even asp are the more likely species. If a single fish is pursued over a number of yards, then perch are the likely culprits. The asp is especially dramatic in its feeding habits and generally tends to

FOUR STYLES OF FEEDING

The way in which fish feed depends on their mouth shape, on whether they have mouth teeth or throat teeth, and on the principal food items that they take. Some fish adapt their forms of feeding to suit different kinds of food.

◀ SEIZING
The pike is a great "seizer" of its food. Approaching its prey with lightning speed, it opens its jaws, sucks in the food with a rush of water, and bites down on the hapless victim. Not even eels can escape from this kind of attack.

◀ SNATCHING
Many species, such as black bass, panfish, and trout, will come to the surface to grab a terrestrial insect that has just entered their world. Often this is done violently, with a splash and perhaps a little fountain of water.

◀ SLURPING
Members of the carp family enjoy slurping food down between extended lips. Floating baits are simply drawn down into the vortex that the carp creates. Sometimes bubbling and audible sucking sounds accompany the slurping.

◀ SUCKING
Many fish vacuum bait up from the riverbed by telescoping out their lips, creating a vacuum and allowing water and food to rush into their mouths. Debris is expelled through the gills, and the food passes down to the stomach.

attack bleak, rudd, and roach in the surface layer of the water, where it comes at them like a shot from a gun, making a tremendous splash in the process.

Before leaving predators, a word on catfish is in order: we always tend to think of them as quiet bottom feeders, but this is not always the case. Especially at night, they will come to the surface and hunt schools of fish very noisily, thrashing through the surface layers and sucking in the fleeing fish. It is an eerie, primeval sound – once heard, never forgotten.

It always helps to know exactly how a predator seizes its prey. For example, a pike will generally take a fish across the back before swallowing it headfirst. A deadbait, therefore, should have a large hook somewhere halfway down the body, so that an immediate strike can be made.

Most fish species are highly adaptable and have learned to survive on whatever the food chain offers them. Often the relationship is extraordinarily complex. The famed ferox trout of European glacial lochs provides a vivid example, surviving solely on a diet of small char. Without the presence of those char, and their food sources, there would be no ferox trout.

Very few fish are totally herbivorous, but the rudd of the Elbe Basin in Bohemia seem to have developed an almost exclusively vegetarian diet, existing on pondweed, duckweed, and anything easily digested. Another notable herbivore is the grass carp, and I can truthfully say that the first one I ever caught was on a floating thistle flower! I followed that one up with a second fish that slurped in a piece of floating lilypad.

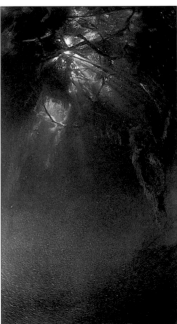

▲ ENERGETIC FEEDING
A hunting predator will often break the water surface altogether to reach its prey, and trout frequently take large insects from rocks where they might have felt they had sanctuary. Perch have been known to pursue small fish onto the tops of lilypads and even up the bank itself.

◀ FOOD FOR FREE
Here we see a great curtain of drifting daphnia, tiny water organisms that no member of the carp family can resist. They devour these highly nutritious creatures by the countless millions, and you will often find fish so totally preoccupied with daphnia that they are utterly heedless of an alternative bait.

SCHOOLING

I
T WAS THE MONTH OF APRIL and I was in a boat on a large, deep loch in the Highlands of Scotland, watching the screen of the echo sounder in front of me. I had located a school of char some 40 ft (12 m) beneath the surface, stretching down another 50 ft (15 m) to a depth of about 100 ft (27 m). The image suggested that these fish were packed tightly together. The school was around 500 ft (150 m) long before it tapered off, and it stretched about 250 ft (80 m) out toward the middle of the loch. The school of fish, therefore, must have filled a volume of water of over 6 million cu ft (more than 180,000 cu m). Imagine it. There must have been literally millions upon millions of small char grouped together in this enormous school in that great, deep, black water. But why does this happen? Why do fish school at all?

DEFENSE

To some extent, fish come together because of a food supply and, of course, when it is time for spawning. But one of the major reasons for schooling is for defense. Living in schools provides protection, especially for young or small fish such as the char just mentioned, and nearly all fish live together in groups when they are young, even if they become solitary once they are adult. Some small fish, such as minnows and dace, remain in schools throughout their lives. Schooling protects them in many ways, most importantly because in a school there are many pairs of eyes and sets of defense organs at work, rather than just the one set of a single fish. This increases the

► PREHISTORIC SCHOOL
This fossil shows a school of fish that died together. Generally, school fish stand a better chance of escaping a pollution kill. Some fish die, but the survivors are alerted to the danger and move off in search of cleaner water.

chances of detecting any oncoming predator early on. Also, the individual members in a big school are constantly changing their position and shimmering in the light. This bewildering array of reflections makes it difficult for any predator to home in on one particular fish. Confusion tends to set in, and the predator may be discouraged. Finally, if a predator does make a determined charge, then the school scatters in front of it, wheeling away in all directions and again making it difficult for the attacker to pinpoint a single target.

For many years I had an aquarium in which I used to keep several species of freshwater fish. Among them were perch, and it was noticeable that if I put in a single minnow the perch ate it almost instantly. The solitary prey offered an easy target. If, however, I put in some 20 minnows at the same time, then the average lifespan of any individual minnow was much longer. In fact, by belonging to a school, the minnows easily lasted two months longer. Despite a large number of attacks by the perch, their numbers were whittled down only gradually.

▲ DRAWN TOGETHER
Very occasionally you will find a carp that leads a solitary life, joining up with others only at spawning time or over a particularly rich food-bed. This is usually a big fish that has outlived its fellows.

◄ SPAWNING CARP
At spawning time, all the carp in a lake or stretch of river will gather together in a vast frenzy. Individual members may even be thrown out of the water and onto the bank!

A LIFE TOGETHER

You will often find that big, old fish are members of a very small school. In all probability, such a school may once have been much, much larger, but the numbers have been reduced by predation, disease, or simply by old age. Over a 15-year period I witnessed a school of bream decline in number from around 30 down to just three. Finally, for one last sad season, I watched a lone wandering survivor until it, too, died. Interestingly, the bream in that diminishing group did not go and join any other school in the water but kept to themselves.

Occasionally a school of a particular species will meet up with another one, but it is very rare that intermingling takes place. School members seem to know each other, and each school tends to keep its integrity. Perhaps as anglers we ought to keep this in mind: if we put too much pressure on a single school of fish we can cause it acute stress and damage.

▲ EVER WATCHFUL
Even when a school of small fish becomes excited during a feeding spell, it never totally drops its guard. There will generally be some school members watching out for any possible lurking danger rather than joining in the feast.

▼ MASS MIGRATION
When the urge is upon fish to migrate, they come together in massive groupings. This surge of sockeye salmon is turning the river red. The fish lose all sense of identity and merge into one common purpose, in this case reproduction.

SURVIVAL

Half a century ago Dr. Henri Gillet, the renowned French fisherman, wrote about aquatic life in the rivers of Africa. He noted that the four main predators living in the Congo — crocodiles, Nile perch, tigerfish, and Goliath tigerfish — all had an insatiable craving to eat each other. Tigerfish gobble up young crocodiles with great zest, and the crocodiles return the compliment. The Nile perch help themselves to crocodiles and tigerfish . . . when they aren't serving as victims. So, as Dr. Gillet pointed out, what you have in the Congo is a "mutual devouration society," but one that is probably not too different from freshwater life everywhere else in the world.

CAMOUFLAGE

The basic motivation of a fish's life, as with any other animal, is to survive long enough to breed and therefore give life to a new generation. To accomplish this, fish have evolved all kinds of tactics that help them find food and living space and also ensure that they avoid being eaten themselves.

Camouflage, the first of these, is a tremendous bonus if you wish to avoid attention! Some fish adopt fairly obvious forms of camouflage: the common barbel has a sandy brown back, which enables it to blend in perfectly with the type of bottom make-up that it prefers. Flounders, which are found in the brackish

▲ BARRED SIDES
You can't beat the camouflage stripes of a perch as a survival aid! So well does the perch blend with the reeds that it is unlikely to be seen by the small fish it is pursuing or by any big predator that might be after it. The perch wins either way.

▼ ALMOST INVISIBLE
An overhead view of a rainbow trout in a shallow chalk stream shows how well the trout blends into its setting. Despite the strong light, a passing heron could barely spot this fish — although on a very sunny day its shadow might possibly give it away.

▲ EVASIVE ACTION
This tiny carp was being pursued by a pike (see p. 40) and hopped onto this lilypad until the danger had passed. After two minutes it flipped back into the water and was gone.

◀ SAFETY IN NUMBERS
Small fish cluster together, and when a predator strikes into them they flee in all directions. This has the effect of confusing the predator, which loses the focus of its attack.

waters of every continent, are adept at looking like mud, gravel, and sand, and only their swiveling eyes give them away. The silvery fishes that are so common in all the world's freshwater habitats have dark backs (actual colors range from greenish brown to dark blue), but these fade to silvery white on their sides and bellies. Seen from above, their backs merge with the colored water of lowland rivers or even the blue of crystal lakes. Seen from below, their undersides are lost against the mirrorlike reflections of the water's surface.

Many fish have the ability to change their coloration to fit in with a change of environment. Put a European dace in a white bucket for 10 minutes, and it becomes paler than when it was lifted from the river. Trout that live over a chalk bottom are paler than ones living perhaps only half a mile downriver, where the bottom is more consistently gravel.

Camouflage is just as important for the predator as it is for the prey. Muskellunge, pike, perch, zander, and walleye all do their best to blend into the background as inconspicuously as possible to increase the efficiency of their ambush attacks.

AGE BRINGS EXPERIENCE

There is no doubt that fish learn by experience, and the longer a fish lives, the less likely it is to make mistakes. If a young trout is alarmed, the chances are that it will scuttle off upriver, close to the surface. There it presents an outline that is easily noticeable from above or below the water line. An older trout will simply sink down to the bottom of its pool and even drift into bottom weed or under a rock or stone. This is a far more effective defensive measure. The ability to learn is increased if a fish is a long-term resident in a water or even in a particular lie. Carp are extraordinarily quick to detect the presence of

any alien being around their pond, and they know how to take appropriate evasive action. Fish have the intelligence, too, to learn from observation and can "read" the evasive actions of other fish that come under attack. Danger does not need to be experienced first-hand for fish to be alerted.

A LIFE UNDER THREAT

Prey fish have other enemies to worry about besides predatory fish. Seals, herons, cormorants, otters, mink, bears, martens, and a whole host of other animals and birds have a liking for fish flesh! Add to this the constant threat of disease and the activities of man – water extraction, pollution, and deoxygenation – and you begin to see how very imperiled is the life of our fish stocks. Any fish, large or small, that lets its guard slip for a moment can easily end up a dead fish. As anglers, we do well to remember this at all times.

LAMPREY ATTACK
No fish is safe from enemies. I caught a pike in the Baltic Sea that had a huge sea lamprey stuck to its flank, sucking out its body juices. It was only with difficulty that I separated the two. Below are my photographs of the lamprey's sucker mouth and sharp, conical teeth — and the wound that the lamprey had left in the flesh of the pike.

MOUTH OF LAMPREY

WOUND INFLICTED BY LAMPREY

BODY LANGUAGE

IT WAS AUGUST IN DEVON, England, and the weather had been so warm that the tiny river that ran down from the moor had shrunk to a series of small pools connected by thin trickles of water. In one of these pools, surrounded by trees and overhung by rocks, rested a small Atlantic salmon weighing about 6 or 7 lb (3 kg). The fish had run up from the sea some two months before, on an early summer storm that had swollen the river. Now that the water was low, the salmon found itself imprisoned. Its body language spoke volumes about misery: it lay motionless on the stream bed, comatose for hours on end, with its eyes just occasionally rolling in their sockets.

Then it rained, and the river started to rise. The salmon's fins rippled, its body pulsed, and finally it literally leapt from the water, droplets sparkling from it: the fish was on its way.

NEGATIVE SIGNS

A frightened fish is easy to read, because it will bolt through the water, often sending up clouds of mud or debris as it crashes blindly along the bed. Stressed fish are equally easily to recognize, especially once you have watched fish in a net or in an aquarium before they have had time to acclimatize. The fins work very slowly, and the eyes frequently move rapidly around the socket, a sure sign of distress. In some fish the eyes become bloodshot or discolored. Over a period of time, scales begin to

▲ JUMPING FOR JOY
Here we see a tiger fish leaping out into the African sunlight. This could indicate fear or might be an attempt to escape a pursuing predator, but the most likely explanation is that the fish is simply showing exuberance in the form of an unfettered burst of energy.

SIGNS OF TRAUMA IN A FISH

This freshly caught carp was photographed while being kept in a tank for a few days for scientific purposes. Its appearance speaks of unhappiness: it moped in a corner of the tank, not moving, and two days passed before it took any interest in feeding. Let us not forget, carp are regarded as the most adaptable fish!

WILD EYE
The eye of any traumatized fish will seem to roll rapidly around its socket.

GAPING MOUTH
A stressed fish often breathes very rapidly, its lips literally gulping in oxygen. The gill covers will be working equally hard.

LOWERED DORSAL FIN
A drooping dorsal fin really testifies to a fish's state of mind. It signifies stress and unhappiness with the current environment.

LIMP TAIL
The tail fin of a fish in distress is rarely held outstretched but is limp and provides no real thrust.

DROOPING BODY
The entire body of a stressed fish appears lifeless, with very little positive movement.

drop off, or the protective mucus hangs off in threads. Very frequently white spot will set in, the flanks and fins of the fish being covered in tiny white pinpricks. Tense fish will often fight among themselves, and trout especially will snap at their companions. Fish in trauma eat very irregularly and start to lose both weight and condition. It is not long before illness sets in, often signaled by advancing patches of fungus. A sick fish often finds it difficult to maintain perfect balance and will swim with a wobbling, ungainly motion.

Lack of oxygen is a frequent cause of trauma, and fish will come to the surface and begin to gulp raw oxygen. Fish that swing over onto their backs, exposing their stomachs, are particularly vulnerable, especially in bright sunlight when they frequently suffer from sunburn on the unprotected flesh.

POSITIVE SIGNS

A happy fish will generally move constantly but confidently, in total command of its movements. Some fish, and especially members of the carp family, will simply hang among lilies and quite obviously enjoy the warmth of a summer's day. Stretching the fins is a sure sign of this. The fins, especially the dorsal, of a contented fish will almost always be erect, and the pectorals in virtually all species will constantly fan the water. The sight of a fish leaping can often be a good indicator of *joie de vivre*.

▲ HUNTING POSTURE

Here we see a pike coming out of its torpor and proclaiming its mounting hunger to the world! Look how the fish is beginning to tilt upward, its fins beating and its eyes moving slowly around, taking in all the features around it.

▼ "NO-THREAT" POSTURE

Minnows often provide the bulk of a chub's diet, but they can read the predator's body language and they know that they are safe — for the time being. The chub is satiated and happy to hang in the current, its fins just holding its position.

SPAWNING

Reproduction is the one great purpose in the lives of all fish species, and in order to spawn they will undergo any hardship, any length of journey, and any danger. Anglers should surely bear this in mind. Even when it is legally allowed, should we pursue fish that are at such a climactic period of their lives? Shouldn't we rather just marvel at what is happening? Shouldn't we put aside our rods and watch what is happening in the water before us? The sight will never be forgotten.

THE DRAMA OF SPAWNING

To witness the spawning of even relatively small fish can be a thrilling experience, but just imagine being present to watch beluga sturgeon lay their eggs! Can you imagine the scene? We are looking at the Ural River in the shadow of the mighty Ural Mountains themselves, way, way north of the Caspian Sea, where the river is still deep, broad, and swift-flowing over endless gravel. The great fish, weighing anything from 300–3,000 lb (150 kg to 1.5 tonnes), are there in numbers. Colossal fish. Fish like submarines. Imagine sturgeon of this size laying and fertilizing eggs, thrashing the water to a foam. Could there be any more thrilling sight in the natural history of the world?

Can there be anything more noble than the sight of salmon in winter, fish that have given every ounce of strength to fight their way to the headwaters of the rivers, hundreds of miles from the sea? The salmon are close to death, but they summon their last reserves of energy for the future of their species.

And there is so much mystery involved in it all, even today. No one really knows where eels breed in the Sargasso Sea, or even how. Who has seen Goliath tiger fish or the Nile perch spawning? I feel that as anglers we must take an interest in the fish we hunt. To ignore this most vital aspect of their lives is to strip them of the respect and admiration they deserve.

▲ BROWN TROUT SPAWNING
Brown trout spawn from autumn through the winter, the eggs being laid in a shallow nest by the female and then fertilized by the male. The eggs hatch within a couple of months, and the fry then live in the gravel for another month before moving off to feed on small crustaceans.

PROTECTING THE EGGS

The fish described in this book all reproduce by laying eggs, generally over weedbeds or stony bottoms. Muddy bottoms do not make good spawning sites, since the eggs may become buried in the mud, which has poor levels of dissolved oxygen. Eggs are generally adhesive, so they stick to plants or stones and are not washed away in the current.

Some fish, such as bullhead and stone loach, lay their eggs in crevices under rocks. Others build nests to protect their eggs. Salmon and trout spawn in a hollow in gravel *(see p. 93)*. Sticklebacks make nests of plant matter cemented with mucus from the male's kidneys. A male will shepherd two or three females into the nest, and once the eggs have been laid and fertilized the brightly colored male will guard the nest until they hatch.

There are variations on this theme. The female bitterling has an egg-laying tube that she inserts in a freshwater mussel. The male releases his sperm close to the mussel's breathing inlet, to be sucked inside. The eggs develop inside the mussel, and the young fish escape through the opening from the mussel's gills.

◄ SPAWNING CARP
This photograph was taken in June at an English pond. After a mild night, the morning sun warmed the water to the critical point, and the gathering carp began to spawn in earnest. Rolling and tumbling in the shallow water, they made a noise that could be heard half a mile away! So energetically did the fish spawn that females were lifted bodily out of the water, and one fish was hurled so far up the bank that I had to rescue her from the undergrowth.

MORTALITY OF EGGS AND YOUNG

Once laid, the eggs of fish lie in the water, so the rate at which they develop will depend on the temperature of the water. Trout eggs are laid in autumn and can take up to 160 days to hatch in cold hill streams, whereas bream eggs, laid in the spring, hatch within a week or so. When the fry hatch they will die unless food is available for them, so the timing is critical.

Successful spawning is always going to be as arbitrary as a lottery, with a multitude of factors all playing a part. A warm spring may mean that a higher than average number of bass or pike eggs hatch. However, the warmth could stimulate any resident eel population into awaking from the torpor of winter to make a feast of these very eggs and fry. Perch lay their eggs on sunken marginal branches and inshore weedbeds, and a lack of rain over the three-week incubatory period could result in a fall in the water level, exposing and destroying the eggs.

The appearance of an otter on the redds *(see pp. 89, 93)* of a salmon river can wreak havoc, especially if females are taken. A winter downpour can scatter any eggs that the salmon manage to lay and fertilize. The young that survive could fall victim to a glut of cormorants on the river. Never let us forget that the life of all of our fish is very much at the sway of fortune.

▲ NEWLY HATCHED FRY
Fry and fingerlings (juvenile fish) inhabit the shallows in the summer, staying close to reeds and plants both for shelter and for food. They present an irresistible target to all prey fish, especially to perch schools and small pike and muskellunge.

▼ SALMON RUN
Salmon must be the most lion-hearted of fish. Nothing will bar their way to the spawning grounds. Undeterred by drought, flood, or waterfalls, they like to run in shallow water at night to give themselves some security from predators.

FRESHWATER HABITATS

THE FRESHWATER ANGLER will learn to catch fish in tiny streams, small and medium rivers, and massive watercourses such as the Mississippi, Danube, or Ganges, and in pools, lakes, reservoirs, and inland seas. The nutrient content of waters varies from rich to poor, and there are many other factors that affect the life of fish. Therefore, before describing the fish and how to catch them, I shall discuss their five main types of habitat.

HIGHLAND STREAMS

O F ALL THE FRESHWATER HABITATS of the world, the most beautiful must be the highland streams that gush and sparkle at high altitudes on all the continents. Because they are remote, highland streams are nearly always quiet, serene places where the angler can forget civilization and embrace nature. The fish here may be small, but the wise angler knows that the setting, not the size, is what counts most.

TYPICAL FISH, PLANTS, AND INSECTS

Highland streams are extreme environments subject to harsh winters and the drought of summer, not to mention the ravages of acid rain. Thunderstorms are common, causing flash floods that can sweep stones and boulders before them. The highland stream is a hazardous habitat if ever there was one.

The highland stream is often referred to as the trout zone of a river, and trout of various types tend to be the predominant species. Providing that the river lower down is not dammed or too severely polluted, there may also be salmon parr and, in autumn and winter, spawning adult salmon. Other fish species present are smaller ones – minnows, bullheads, or loach, but nothing to interest the angler.

The trout themselves are also likely to be on the small side, and anything more than ½ lb (0.23 kg) can be a fish to be proud of. Size, however, is not the issue. These tiny fish are often spectacularly beautiful to look at, with distinct, vivid markings, and they will generally be energetic and muscular. They are also extremely hard to outwit in the crystal-clear water that is often only a hand's span in depth.

The aquatic plant community is usually restricted to mosses and liverworts. Waterweeds (aquatic broadleaved plants such as water crowfoots) are unlikely to find enough soil to form roots or be strong enough to withstand the rapid current, for this can often exceed 2 ft (60 cm) per second. The invertebrates that inhabit fast-flowing waters are specifically adapted for clinging onto the rocks, mosses, and algae-covered surfaces. The friction of the water against the stream bed creates a layer of slower-flowing water in which insects can just about survive. Some of the insect nymphs (aquatic larvae) have evolved a flattened shape that enables them to cling on even in the faster-flowing currents. Many of these insects also have tiny claws with which they can cling onto moss or streamside lichens and prevent themselves from being swept away downstream.

The breeze is almost continual in these upland areas, and it serves to bring a constant supply of insects for small trout and salmon parr. Countless midges and horseflies will be swept into the pools, and craneflies may join them in late summer.

FINDING THE FISH

As every real estate agent knows, the location counts for a great deal when choosing a home! A trout lie – the place in which it rests in the water – must satisfy the fish's need for comfort. The trout needs oxygen, an agreeable temperature, and shelter from the main current. Safety is important, so cover must be available. Food matters a great deal, so the trout will prefer an area close to some stones or larger rocks, among which it can hunt for small fish and invertebrates.

A small brown trout will usually choose to lie in relatively slow water moving at 6–8 in (15–20 cm) per second, coming out to feed in faster water moving at 12 in (30 cm) per second or more, in which drifting food is to be found.

Riffles – areas of fast, broken water studded by boulders or large stones – hold good populations of aquatic insects, and the quick water is always likely to sweep them away to a fish waiting behind a rock. The course of a highland stream will also be punctuated by slower, deeper pools, some of them fed by miniature waterfalls. Larger fish will congregate here, enjoying the deeper, cooler water, which offers them protection from predators and shelter from storm and drought.

TYPICAL FISH OF A HIGHLAND STREAM

The water in a highland stream is quick, clear, and shallow, and only fish of a streamlined, athletic build can survive there. Typical inhabitants are small, lithe trout. Salmon parr will also be in residence, and at spawning time the adults will ascend to water barely deep enough to cover their backs. There may well be smaller fish hiding in the stones – minnows, perhaps, with various loaches and even a tiny bullhead or two.

◄ SMALLER WATERS
Some populations of Atlantic salmon and Arctic char migrate all the way up the rivers and into the remotest mountain tributaries to spawn.

BROWN TROUT
Heading upstream to find turbulent water in which to hunt insects and fish.

ARCTIC CHAR
Still in nonbreeding colors; it has only just arrived from sea.

CHAR PARR
Young Arctic char aged approximately 18 months.

MALE SALMON
Ready to fertilize and defend eggs.

RAINBOW TROUT
Holding a good position for catching water-borne food.

FEMALE SALMON
Lays mass of eggs in a rough trench (redd).

GRAYLING
Waits for a chance to steal salmon eggs.

SMALL LAKES

SMALL LAKES ARE FREQUENT features of landscapes. Some are created by faulting in the earth's crust or by glacial action, or they may be the result of human activity, having been created for ornament, recreation, or more practical purposes. Farmlands, in particular, are studded with ponds for irrigation and for watering livestock. However, over the last 50 years or so, a huge number of small waters, especially in the developed world, have disappeared – filled in as part of land reclamation programs for the development of housing and industry, or drying up as water tables fall.

Where small waters do remain they tend to be very rich in nutrients. Manure from livestock can help cause rapid growth of algae, leading to pea green water and organically rich bottom mud. Midge larvae, or bloodworms, absolutely thrive in these conditions. All cyprinids – carp, bream, and tench in particular – specialize in picking bloodworms and tiny pea mussels from the silt. Tench will also pick up water lice and fly larvae from plant stems. There really is no end to the food variety in such places – damsel flies, dragonflies, water beetles, leeches, water snails, water boatmen . . . It really is no wonder that these small waters can support vast stocks of fish.

TYPICAL FISH OF A SMALL LAKE

The common inhabitants of small lakes include roach, carp, eels, bream, tench, bass, and panfish of all sizes. In Europe and North America, catfish, although often not very large, will also be found. Small lakes tend to heat up rapidly in the summer, resulting in oxygen deficiency. For this reason, trout and other salmonid species are generally absent unless the water is fed by cold springs or plentiful inflowing streams.

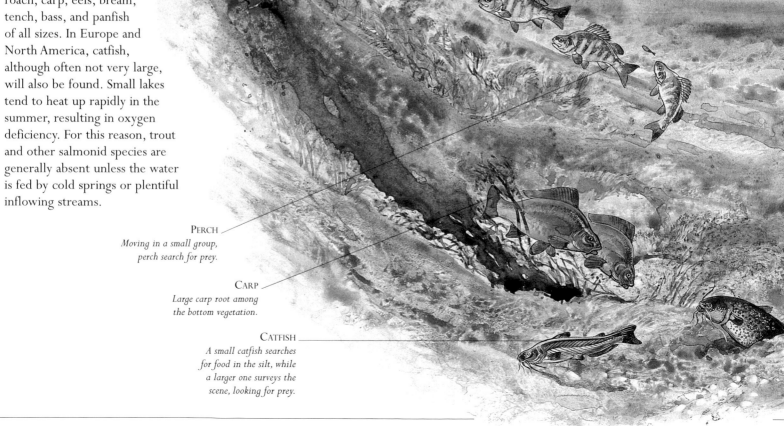

PERCH
Moving in a small group, perch search for prey.

CARP
Large carp root among the bottom vegetation.

CATFISH
A small catfish searches for food in the silt, while a larger one surveys the scene, looking for prey.

◄ A MAN-MADE POOL
Nature quickly heals the rawness of a hole cut in the ground and cloaks the banks with grasses, reeds, and weed. Ponds created for fishing become havens for wildlife.

Small bodies of water tend to have an equally rich variety of aquatic plants. Milfoil is common, and hornwort flourishes in the autumn, along with all types of pondweed. In sheltered bays, luxuriant growths of duckweed can choke the water surface. Waterlilies of various kinds will also grow in dense patches, and in the shallows you can expect to find reeds, spatterdock, yellow flag, cattails, and pickerelweed, all fighting for space.

OVERPOPULATION

Many small ponds, especially old ones, are surrounded by trees. These protect the water surface from breezes, allowing the pool to warm up quickly in the summer. Spawning, therefore, is generally successful, so there is a constant tendency for most fish species to overbreed and for the individuals to become stunted. Sensible fishery management, or a good number of predators, is important if trophy-sized fish are to be found.

Expect to find predators, such as pike or perch, sticking to the margins, lurking under fallen branches, or resting in the shallows under lilies and among stems. Carp have regular patrol routes, and tench stick to their own comparatively confined territories. If bass are present, once again look for them in the daylight hours, hiding close to structures of any sort. An old boathouse or boat jetty will attract bass, pike, and perch.

FRY AND FINGERLINGS
These make a perfect meal for perch and pike.

PIKE
A good specimen lurks menacingly among the bottom weed.

BASS
Leaving its shelter, a bass looks for food.

BREAM
A solitary bream tips its body and goes down to feed.

TENCH
A tench cruises, possibly filtering daphnia from the rich water, while another rises from the silt, where it has been searching for food.

▲ A LOST HABITAT
It is a sad result of modern-day development that we are losing many of our small lakes. This one dried up after the farmer on the adjacent land began to pump water from the ground to irrigate his crops. A lake drained is seldom, if ever, refilled.

SMALL RIVERS

EVERY HIGHLAND STREAM GROWS UP. Having gushed from the uplands, each one moves across less steep terrain and becomes an obvious, meandering river. There will be more trees along the riverbanks and possibly some deep pools where the water is almost still. Livestock will be grazing, and there might even be an abandoned watermill. In this somewhat slower, richer environment, the fish will grow bigger than those found in small, barren, upland streams. It is here, on the small river, where angling really does begin in earnest.

HUGE VARIETY

The water will still be flowing swiftly, and it is generally cool and well oxygenated, even through the hottest summer months. All this gives rise to a great variety of fish. Grayling and trout are still present, providing the water is not polluted. Barbel, chub, perch, and pike will be making their appearance, along with various cyprinids. Eels enjoy the water, too, and there may even be a few bass happily hunting schools of small prey fish. There will be far more plants, especially in the alkaline waters of chalk streams and limestone rivers. Ranunculus will flower in the summer, sweeping in great green drapes along the gravels. You will also see starwort, and even watercress. In the slower, more silty margins of the small river there may be beds of cattails and arrowhead.

The water quality and abundant plant life support a much more diverse invertebrate community than is found in the highland stream. There are water lice, midge larvae, snails,

◀ STREAMY REACHES
Here, the river has just left the mountainous areas and is beginning to slow down in its journey across the plains. Fish life is still dominated by trout and grayling, but cyprinids will soon begin to make their appearance in pools and deep holes.

alder fly larvae, and many types of caddis larvae. In the silt you will find mayfly nymphs, bloodworms, pea mussels, and even larger mussels. There are crayfish under the stones – perfect food for bass, chub, and larger trout – and the surface is alive with skating insects. In short, the fish are in for a real feast.

In the faster-flowing stretches, look for trout and grayling, especially over gravel. If there is a watermill, expect to find them in the pool itself and in the quick water that leaves it. Bass or chub will almost certainly be under any trees that overhang the water, especially among tree roots that grow out from the bank into the stream.

Perch will take position in deeper, sheltered water for weeks or even months until a flood comes to move them downstream, but don't make the mistake of thinking that pike are always in the deep slacks. When they are hunting, they will often go into streamy water, looking for schools of roach and grayling or an unsuspecting trout.

◀ LOWLAND RIVER
If ever there were an angler's paradise, this must be it – early morning on a truly beautiful lowland river in the fall, with the mist still clearing and the golden leaves reflected on the serene surface.

▲ ONTO THE PLAIN
Small rivers can be very susceptible to drought conditions, and some virtually dry up in the later months of a long, dry summer. There are almost always deep holes, however, where fish can shelter and survive.

TYPICAL FISH OF A SMALL RIVER

The small river absolutely bursts with life and can easily house more than a score of different fish species. Some will grow large in this very fertile environment. Predators will abound, growing fat on rich pickings. As well as resident fish, there will be migrants passing through, intent on spawning in the upper reaches but often spending several weeks or months sheltering behind a bridge or in a deep pool until conditions change.

EEL
The eel loves to shelter among rubble and fallen brickwork.

PIKE
Look for the pike just out of the main current.

BROWN TROUT
The brown trout loves a quick, streamy glide.

SALMON
Passing through on their way upstream, salmon will sit at the tail of the pool.

GRAYLING
You will find grayling in slightly slower, deeper water.

YOUNG ROACH
The fry prefer shallow water, where they feed on tiny flies.

BARBEL
These strong fish really enjoy a good flow of water.

ROACH
Look for roach in slack water over a clean bottom.

PERCH
These predators can be found anywhere, marauding among schools of small fish.

◀ **THE MINI-FISH**
Among the gravels will be a whole host of tiny fish. Look for minnows, sticklebacks, loach, and bullheads, all hiding there until the light fades and they can hunt with a little more confidence. If the water is pure, there will also be crayfish.

LARGE LAKES

MOST LARGE LAKES, wherever they are in the world, are in the mountains. They have been formed by the movement of glaciers, by faulting in the earth's crust, or both. These huge waters are very deep and cold. Streams run into them across volcanic rocks, such as granite, which are acidic. The lakes are therefore acidic and not very fertile, though the water is clean and clear. Plants are scarce, supporting little invertebrate life. In terms of school fish, the food supply is adequate to support only small, slow-growing trout, char, or whitefish.

The only types of fish that can grow large are those that predate on these schools. In Scotland, ferox trout *(see p. 115)* start to feed on these schools at an early age and consequently grow to weights over 30 lb (13 kg). Large specimens of pike, muskellunge, and perch are similarly found in mountain lakes.

Locating fish in such huge waters can be difficult, since there are few visual features above the waterline. However, there are a few clues: shallow bays entice muskellunge and pike in the springtime, when they come in to spawn in the reedbeds.

TYPICAL FISH OF A LARGE LAKE

The deep, dark waters of a large lake contain far more life than you would expect. Apart from trout, char, and lake trout, there are very likely to be pike, and perhaps even muskellunge. Despite the cold, eels can grow to a considerable size over many years. Salmon tend to swim in the surface layers, rarely deeper than 10–13 ft (3–4 m), and they are caught frequently by anglers trolling for them. The fish populations of such waters tend to be ancient ones, and no human stocking has ever made any significant impact.

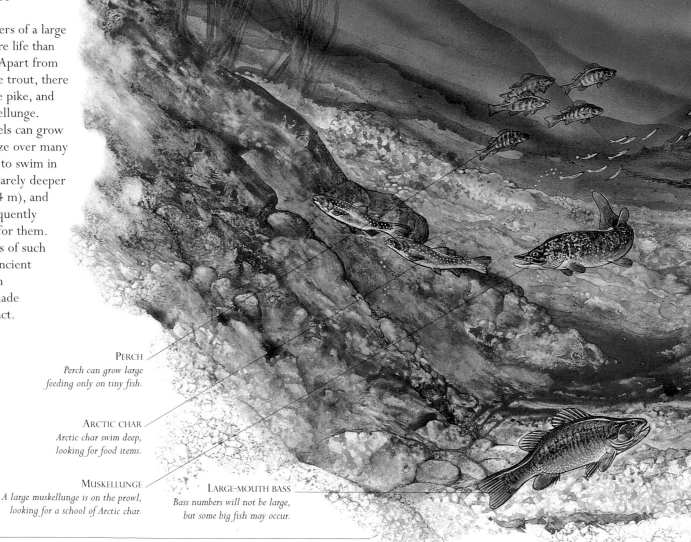

PERCH
Perch can grow large feeding only on tiny fish.

ARCTIC CHAR
Arctic char swim deep, looking for food items.

MUSKELLUNGE
A large muskellunge is on the prowl, looking for a school of Arctic char.

LARGE-MOUTH BASS
Bass numbers will not be large, but some big fish may occur.

Islands and rocky outcrops can often attract both predators and their prey, and drop-offs (sudden changes from shallow to deep water) also provide predators with ambush points. Inflowing streams and rivers act as magnets for fish, especially in autumn, when char schools are starting to move into the quick water to spawn. Where the schools go, the predators — pike, lake trout, and brown trout — are almost bound to follow.

Strong subsurface currents are often found within mountain lakes. The fish — both predators and prey — are moved about in the lake by these currents. Electronic tracking experiments in the Scottish lochs have shown that the big ferox trout are hardly ever at rest; they move continually through the dark realms of water on these currents, always on the lookout for prey.

In these large lakes, the season begins in late spring, when surface waters approach 50° F (10° C). Flies hatch, and rising small trout, char, and whitefish begin to attract predators from the deeps. Spring schools of char number in the hundreds of thousands but soon divide into smaller groups. The char spend summer searching the surface and the shallows for flies before massing again in autumn prior to spawning.

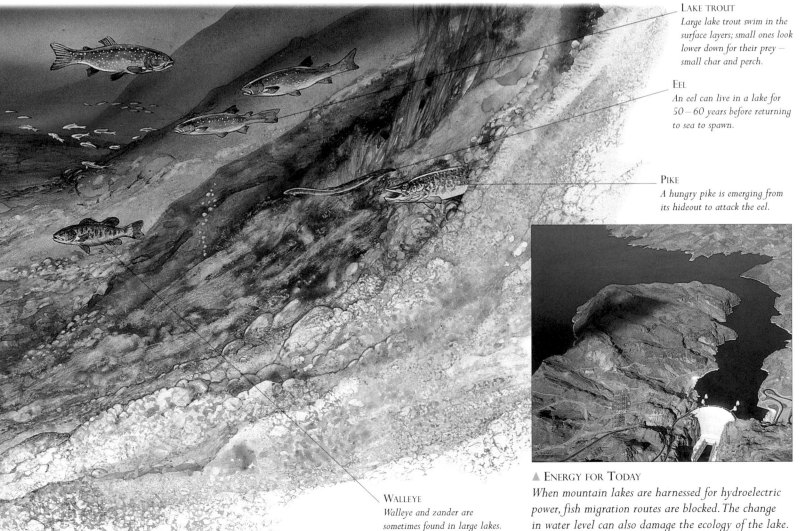

LAKE TROUT
Large lake trout swim in the surface layers; small ones look lower down for their prey — small char and perch.

EEL
An eel can live in a lake for 50–60 years before returning to sea to spawn.

PIKE
A hungry pike is emerging from its hideout to attack the eel.

WALLEYE
Walleye and zander are sometimes found in large lakes.

▲ ENERGY FOR TODAY
When mountain lakes are harnessed for hydroelectric power, fish migration routes are blocked. The change in water level can also damage the ecology of the lake.

LARGE RIVERS

B Y THE TIME A RIVER gets to the sea, it is fully grown – wide, deep, and slow-moving. At its estuary it will also be affected by tidal influences, and the previously pure water will be brackish with a noticeable salt content. This obviously affects all manner of aquatic life. So do humans! Nearly all estuaries are heavily developed places, often in the heart of cities and surrounded by harbors and docklands. Industry will almost certainly utilize the estuary, perhaps using the water to cool machinery or to wash away effluent and discharges. Heavy boat traffic will also have an impact, so it is not surprising that many of the estuarial reaches of rivers around the world are among the most polluted waters.

Nearly always, however, there is some sort of life, and over the past 20 years or so many large cities have tried to come to grips with the problems of pollution, the result being a general upturn in water quality. Salmon even run the lower Thames through London now, if in very limited numbers.

TYPICAL FISH OF A LARGE RIVER

The final reaches of a river see a great intermingling between freshwater and saltwater species, but they cannot be home for the brown trout, the grayling, or any other fish that demands a large amount of dissolved oxygen. Fish that are found around the estuaries are survivors, able to tolerate pollution, scavenging for food in the silt. Many of the fish species are small, but predators can grow very large: if the water is pure enough for pike to survive, they will benefit from resident species and from migratory fish pushing through. This widely varied diet can produce huge fish.

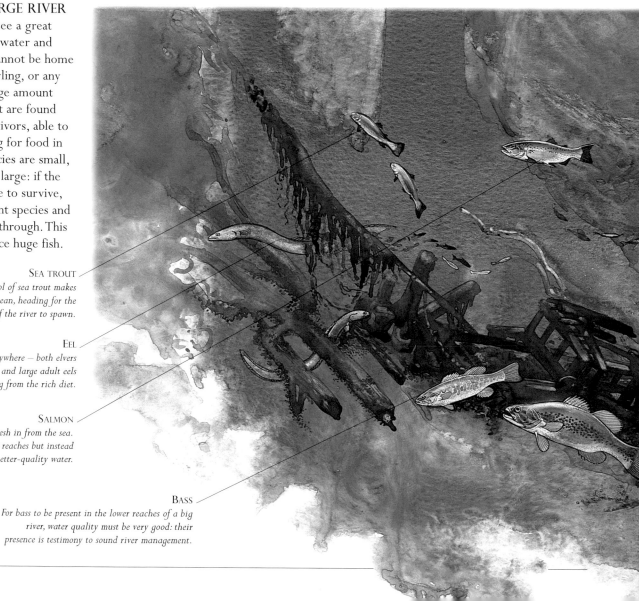

SEA TROUT
*A school of sea trout makes
its way in from the ocean, heading for the
upper reaches of the river to spawn.*

EEL
*Eels will be everywhere – both elvers
moving upstream and large adult eels
benefiting from the rich diet.*

SALMON
*A salmon moves upstream, fresh in from the sea.
It will not stay in the lower reaches but instead
hurries through to reach better-quality water.*

BASS
*For bass to be present in the lower reaches of a big
river, water quality must be very good: their
presence is testimony to sound river management.*

Typical freshwater species are beginning to peter out at this stage in the river's life, but perch and roach may well still be present. Pike, too, are able to cope with slight salinity. There will also be those fish that are happy moving in brackish water, comfortable in both salt and fresh alike. These include eels, mullet, flounder, and sea bass. There will also be the migratory species that breed in fresh water but live and feed in the sea, such as salmon, sea trout, shad, and lamprey. Who knows, there could even be the occasional monstrous sturgeon nosing its way under the boats and the bridges.

FOOD SUPPLIES

Most of the food that the fish are seeking tends to be bottom-dwelling, often found deep in the mud. Ragworms and lugworms are eaten by many of the species, and there could well be clams and other types of shellfish. Shrimp will also be abundant, vast numbers drifting in with every flowing tide. Weed, though, is likely to be very sparse indeed, especially in badly polluted estuaries with severely depleted levels of dissolved oxygen.

MULLET AND SEA BASS
Schools of these fish come into the lower reaches to feed on shrimp, weed, and small fish.

STEELHEAD
Sleek, silvery steelhead push in from the Pacific, nosing their way upriver.

STURGEON
There is always the chance of a surprise in these estuarial reaches; here a great sturgeon looks for a feast.

▲ **WIDE RIVER**
The mighty Brahmaputra nears the sea, hundreds of miles from its source and tributaries on the other side of the Himalayas. A wide variety of fish live in the deep, clouded waters, in sufficient quantities to sustain a population of freshwater dolphins.

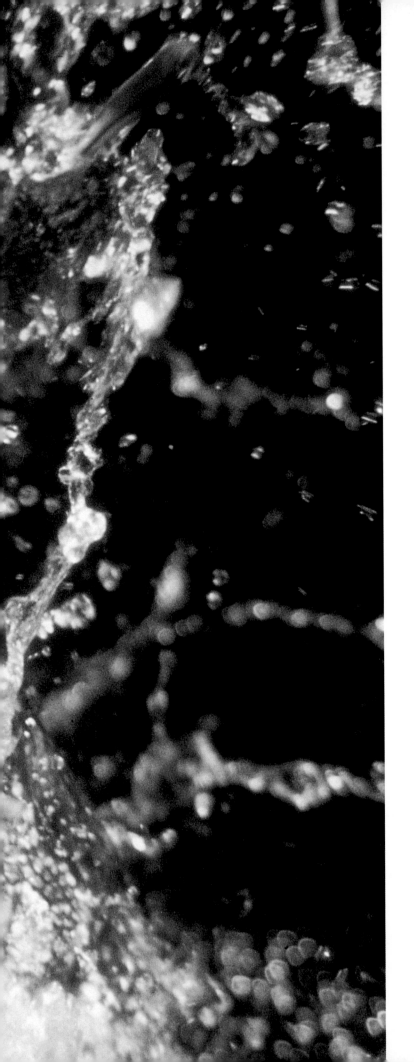

CATCHING PREDATORY FISH

IT IS ALWAYS THE THOUGHT OF THE PREDATORS that sends shivers up the angler's spine! Predators tend to be big, and they are nearly always mean. Let us take the pike. When that plug of yours disappears in a swirl, you know that after one heck of a tussle, a fish will come up toward you, all gnashing teeth and malevolent eyes, a fish that would eat you if it possibly could. Some anglers spend their entire careers in pursuit of predators alone: when you consider the drama and challenge presented by muskies, bass, barramundi, or walleye, you can certainly see why.

PIKE ATTACK

In an eruption of spray, a pike hammers into a school of prey fish. They may be tiny, but the big predator could still use a few of them for breakfast. Get that lure out fast!

PIKE & MUSKELLUNGE

EUROPE HAS ONLY ONE member of the pike family, and that is the pike itself *(Esox lucius)*. North America has five: the pike (known there as the northern pike), the muskellunge *(see p. 45)*, and the chain, grass, and red-fin pickerels. China, Siberia, and Mongolia have the Amur pike, as big as the muskellunge but magnificently colored, with leopardlike dark spots on a tawny skin.

PIKE

NOT ALL WATERS ARE CAPABLE of maintaining very large fish, and, in principle, the bigger the water, the bigger the pike is likely to be. This is simply because prey fish are likely to be more abundant and easier to catch. The inshore waters of the Baltic Sea are a perfect example: considerable numbers of pike spend long periods in the sea and live well there, feasting on schools of herring and codling. But nature loves to surprise, and many is the small pond that has produced the traditional monster of angling history.

▲ GREAT LAKES, BIG FISH
Larger waters have the huge schools of prey fish that pike need if they are to grow large. Juvenile bass, yellow perch, "shiners" (small lake fish in general), and char all fulfill this function.

◄ SMALLER LAKES
Smaller lakes generally mean smaller pike, but if food supplies are particularly prolific, then the occasional surprise giant may lurk unexpectedly. Such fish often go uncaught for life.

PIKE ANATOMY

The pike is the shark of fresh water, and it is a formidable-looking fish. Its muscular frame and streamlined design enable it to lunge forward and capture anything from a frog to a perch. The pike is the ultimate hunter, adapted to eating virtually any living thing that it can find in its environment.

EYES UP
The pike's eyes are set high on the head to scan the water above for any possible prey fish moving near the surface.

SURFACE DISGUISE
The dark, mottled camouflage on the back allows the pike to blend in with the riverbed, providing security from any aerial attack.

STREAMLINED BODY
The torpedo shape of the pike makes it perfectly suited to its role as a fast-swimming hunter-killer.

SKULL OF A PREDATOR

The head of a pike is an awesome creation, adapted perfectly for its job. On the top of the skull, the eyes are perfectly positioned to see any prey fish as soon as they swim past overhead. The jaw's construction allows the mouth to swing open cavernously and engulf prey fish of the maximum possible size. The jaw is equipped with formidable teeth, longer on the lower jaw, but all needle-sharp and designed to rip, pierce, and slash. The teeth will pin the prey down during its slow death, allowing the pike to take its time before the final swallow. The pike's head is exceptionally broad, making it possible to swallow deep-bodied prey fish such as bream.

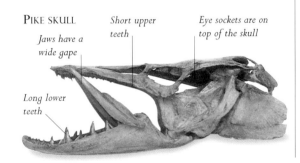

PIKE SKULL

Jaws have a wide gape

Short upper teeth

Eye sockets are on top of the skull

Long lower teeth

YOUNG AND OLD PIKE

Up until around two or three years of age, the young pike hides from its cannibalistic parents in the shallows of the lake. It will be lurking there amid reed stems, and nature has given it vertically barred markings that enable it to blend in perfectly. As the pike matures it will begin to occupy deeper waters and start preying on larger fish. Now the purpose of camouflage is to hide the pike from its prey, and those bars on the flanks become spots that merge with the snags of the deeper, darker water.

▶ AMBUSH!
The spotted flanks of an adult pike provide perfect camouflage. By taking care to move slowly, and by always making full use of any available cover, the pike gradually gets very close to its intended prey. Once the ambush is set up, all that is needed is to move in with a sprint for the final kill.

▲ JUVENILE PIKE
This small pike is well hidden among grass and reeds in dappled sunlight. This near invisibility offers it a degree of safety from its cannibalistic parents.

SIDE MARKINGS
Dappled sides help the pike mount successful ambushes by blending the fish in with boulders, sunken logs, and waterweed.

THRUST FROM THE REAR
Dorsal (upper) and anal (lower), fins are grouped close to the caudal (tail) fin to give powerful acceleration.

PIKE *Esox lucius*
APPROXIMATE GUIDE TO WEIGHTS
US AVERAGE 8–12 lb (3.6–5.4 kg)
EUROPEAN AVERAGE 10–15 lb (4.6–6.9 kg)
WORLD RECORD 55 lb (25 kg)

Dorsal fin

Caudal fin

STRONG WRIST
The tail wrist (the stem of the tail) is broad and strong to give thrust; the tail, too, is powerfully built.

Anal fin

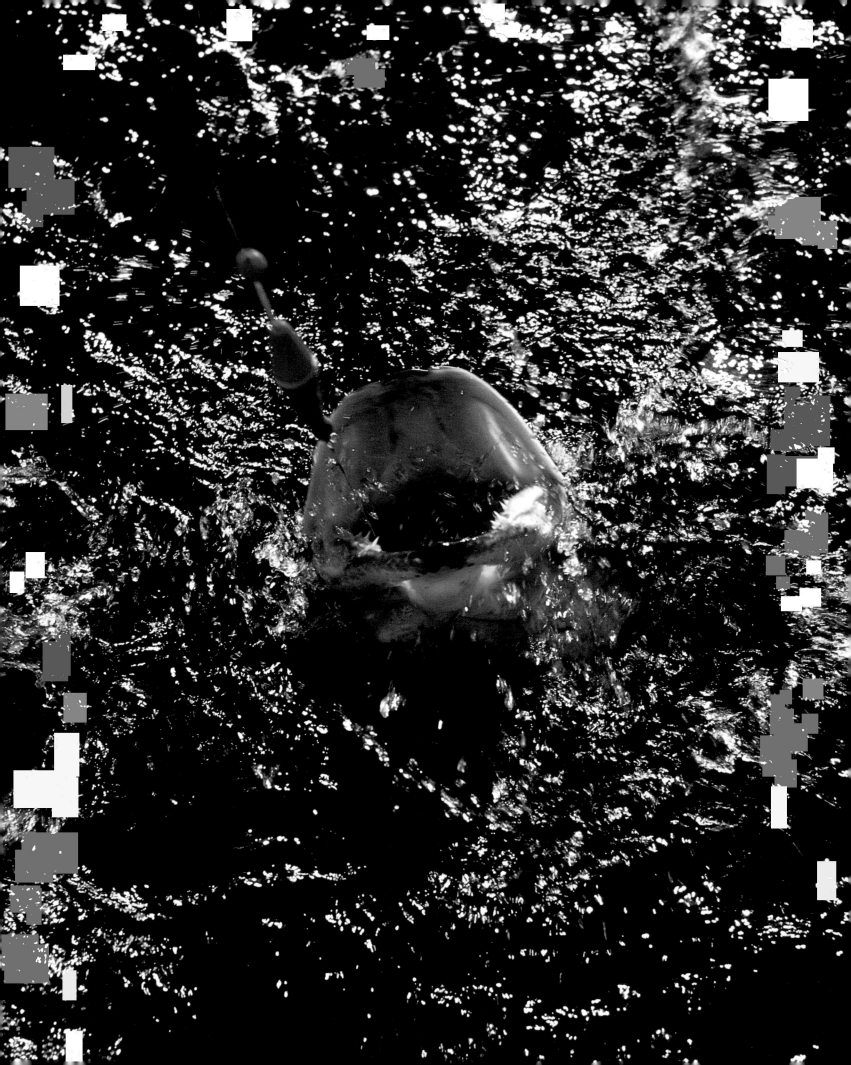

MUSKELLUNGE

THE MAJESTIC MUSKELLUNGE is one of the most highly prized trophy fish in all North America. It inhabits lakes and rivers across that continent, as far south as North Carolina and mid-California, and as far north as the southern edge of Canada.

The muskellunge, or muskie, hunts by sight, and for this reason prefers clear water. It cannot adapt to a habitat that is permanently cloudy. Besides pure water, the muskie needs plenty of oxygen, its requirement being higher than that of a pike. To make another contrast, a muskie tends to stay close to its home area and does not roam as far as a pike.

Muskies are rarer than pike because their eggs do not hatch so successfully as pike eggs, and because pike hatch earlier. The young pike then prey on the younger muskies. Muskies do, however, live longer than pike, and grow larger; the record weight for muskie is some 15 lb (7 kg) heavier than the world record for pike.

▲ LARGE WATERS
Large, coldwater lakes like this one in Canada do not often hold large numbers of muskellunge, but those living in such a water are often enormous and well worth fishing for.

◄ GOING FOR MUSKIE
Since muskies often live in large waters, it is vital for the angler to be mobile. You need a well-maintained boat with a high-speed engine, which cuts down traveling time.

ANATOMY

Books refer to three color "phases" (variants): clear, barred, and spotted. The coloration of muskellunge is infinitely more variable than this. It is true that there are phases, but each appears in many dramatic variations, often stunningly beautiful.

MUSKELLUNGE
Esox masquinongy
APPROXIMATE GUIDE TO WEIGHTS
AVERAGE 10–15 lb (4.5–6.9 kg)
TROPHY 20 lb (9.2 kg)
RECORD 70 lb (32 kg)

◄ HEAD OF A HUNTER
The muskie has several different types of teeth, with distinct shapes. Each is used for a specialized purpose, such as holding prey, piercing, crushing, and chewing food.

HEAD
Head is similar to that of the pike, except that the cheeks and gill covers have scales only on the top half, rather than all over.

COLORATION
Colors are a mixture of green, brown, and silver. Belly is lighter than upper body and can be white or cream.

SPOTS
Muskellunge have dark spots on light background (in pike it is the other way around).

TAIL
Tips of fins are more pointed than those of pike. (Tails of both species are the same color.)

UNDERWATER HABITAT

Muskies are hunters, so they are nearly always found around cover and structure. Lilypads provide cover and also keep the water beneath slightly cooler than the surrounding areas. Rocky points or any exposed rocks on the bottom attract muskies, especially in lakes where there is little weed or woody-stemmed cover.

On rivers, look for muskie in the pools below rapids, where a wide variety of prey fish are bound to gather, especially in low water. In clouded water, the areas around boat bays and docks also prove popular. Remember that clear, open water does not often hold any muskie for long, although they may hang there for a short while, perhaps on their way from one part of their territory to the next.

▲ UNDERWATER BRANCHES
Muskies like to hang in the midst of a cradle of underwater branches. They often use such a place as refuge in which to digest a meal before going out to look for the next one.

◄ WATERWEED
Wherever there are weeds, you are sure to find prey fish, and therefore muskies will not be far away, either. Broadleaved pondweed, cattails, and water milfoil attract muskies in this way.

FOOD OF MUSKELLUNGE

Muskies take prey fish of around a quarter of their own length and up to a fifth of their own weight. Muskies hunt mainly by sight, and they can see well enough to become nocturnal whenever they come under fishing pressure. They prefer to feed in overcast weather, but if there is a long run of sunny days the muskellunge will feed mainly at sunset and sunrise.

► ONE-WAY TUNNEL
In a manner absolutely characteristic of both the pike and the muskie, this pike lay in ambush until it saw a victim. It was photographed in full charge, at a speed of 20 mph (30 km/h) or more.

▲ YOUNG LAKE TROUT
Lake trout and muskies can overlap in part of their distribution — southern Canada and part of New England. Where they do, muskies prey on young lake trout but find the adults too large to attack.

▲ YELLOW PERCH
Folklore once had it that the spiny dorsal fin of the yellow perch saved it from becoming a meal for the muskellunge. Not so — a school of perch can prove an easy target.

▲ BROOK TROUT
Muskies do not often attack a lone brook trout, but they repeatedly harry schools of these fish. When a muskie launches itself at a big school, it is virtually bound to get a meal.

PIKE FISHING STRATEGIES

YOU CANNOT ENCOURAGE a predator like the pike to feed: it will take in food when it is ready, and for the rest of the time it lies uncatchable in a semicomatose, trance-like state. If there are a number of pike in a given habitat, it is likely that almost all of them will behave in exactly the same way, although there will always be an exception. Pike behavior depends on weather conditions: in cold weather, digestion will be slow and the feeding period brief, whereas in warm weather the pike will spend more time feeding and less at rest.

MATCH THE MOOD

It is no use presenting a very slow-moving pike with a fast-moving plug or spinner. Your strategy must agree with the pike's mood of the day. It is never easy to identify this mood, but there are clues. For example, are pike constantly striking into schools of small fish? No surer sign of active predators exists! If, conversely, you can see small fish happily feeding in known pike haunts, you can be confident that the pike are not stirring. Now is the time for a static bait or a very slow-moving one.

THE STIRRING PIKE

After lying inactive in its haunt for many days, a pike will at last begin to stir. The first movement it makes is with its eyes, then the angle of its body tilts up from the horizontal, and its head rises toward the surface. As the pike lifts itself clear of the bottom weed, the pectoral fins start working, and the tail fin beats slowly. Now the angler has a chance.

A stirring pike may well inspect a deadbait placed close in, especially if you have injected this with oil or artificial scent. Color is often important, and a bait that has been dyed red is often taken. Careful presentation counts for a great deal: try twitching the deadbait, for instance, to trigger an attack.

▲ PIKE FLOAT
A stirring pike will not take bait with gusto. To prevent fish from swallowing your hooks and being injured, use a float; this is your best way to know exactly what is happening to your bait.

▼ AWAKE!
Here is a lovely shot of a pike waking from torpor and looking around its world, the pangs of hunger stirring. You can see that the pike has just risen up out of the brushwood as the muscles in its body begin to exert themselves.

▲ SWEDISH LEVIATHAN
This enormous pike was actively roaming, criss-crossing a small bay on the fringe of the Baltic Sea. Johnny Jensen had observed it for most of the day, and it eventually fell to a quickly worked plug.

◄ VANED FLOAT
When you fish at long range, this float gives an instant, easily visible signal of a take.

◄ VERY TASTY
There are several ways to make deadbait attractive. Vary the type of deadbait; eel tails are very good, or you can try herrings or sprats. You can dye the deadbait red, blue, or green. A deadbait can be spiced up by injecting oils with an appetizing scent, which will spread out in the water in an enticing underwater slick.

THE DRIFTING FISH

A pike that is becoming alert starts to drift slowly around its lie (a lie is the position a fish occupies in the water). Now awake, the pike is hungry, and all its body systems are functioning, although it is not yet willing to do a great deal of chasing.

Deadbaits still work on a pike in this state, especially if they are drifted slowly around under a vaned float (*see facing page, bottom left*), which can be seen from a distance.

Now that the pike is stirring, lures begin to come into the equation. Try any kind that is eye-catching. Try lures, for instance, that can be worked slowly and fished quite deep, perhaps even nudging the bottom in such a way as to send up puffs of silt. A big, highly colored plug may work, especially one that makes the pike think that it is going to have a decent meal and is worth a bit of a chase.

▶ ON THE LOOKOUT

A drifting pike is alert and hungry enough to want to make a kill. It moves up toward the surface, where it can hunt small amphibians and fish. It may well be persuaded to take an imitation frog that it sees hovering above its lie (see inset). Move the frog around the lilies in an erratic, twitching fashion. Always work lures in as lifelike a movement as possible.

FLY FISHING FOR ROAMERS

A roaming pike is one that is fully alert and actively hunting. It swims in the upper layers of the water, looking for fish schools, ducklings, voles, or any other prey that is small enough for the pike to attack. The presence of roaming pike is betrayed by bow-waves, especially in shallow water. Alternatively, look for small fish skimming the surface as they flee, or listen for water birds, such as coot, calling in alarm.

This is the perfect moment to get out the fly rod. Choose big flies that can easily be seen and send out vibrations. Takes can be dynamic, so make sure that your trace (the final section of the line) is a wire one, strong enough to take the strain. Surface plugs that make a lot of vibrations as they churn across the water work well, too.

◀ THE PERFECT FLY

Fortunately (otherwise there would be no sport) there is no perfect fly, but this is a good try! It has body and lots of movement – a fly that is very suggestive of real life.

▲ FLY AND LURE IN TANDEM

It is often a good idea to work fly and lure together: the lure attracts pike from a distance, and once in the swim they may snap at the fly out of either aggression or hunger.

LURE FISHING FOR PIKE

FISHING FOR PIKE WITH LURES — spinners, plugs, or spoons — is the most thrilling and efficient way of catching both pike and muskellunge. The technique is attracting a growing number of anglers in both America and Europe who want to hunt their fish in an active fashion.

The lure angler is always thinking, always experimenting, always plotting the downfall of the next fish. The key is to read the water: you must know where those fish are lying. Then you need to choose the right lure. Will the pike respond to something fished slow or fast, deep or shallow? The lure fisher needs to consider color, size, and action, and how best to work the bait back on the retrieve. There is never a dull moment . . . or if there is, you are not doing the job properly.

▲ KNOWING WHERE TO LOOK
The skilled lure angler knows that fallen branches attract pike. They hang beneath them while digesting prey and use them as cover when mounting an ambush.

LAGOON SPINNING SESSION

The illustration and photographs here depict a pike session on a lagoon beside the River Wye in England. Pike sometimes follow prey fish into areas of still water like this, but they are not always in search of food. They may come in to get away from the current and to rest before moving up or down the river to hunt again. Today, I was fortunate. Within minutes, I spotted a bow-wave to the left of a fallen tree.

Submerged branch

Spot from which I fished

4 ft (1.2 m)

2 ft (0.6 m)

6 ft (1.8 m)

2 ft (0.6 m)

Bait cast under trees

Submerged branch

Pike lying under trees

Trees overhang water

LAGOON LAYOUT

The swim consists of a shallow, muddy lagoon connected to the river. It is ringed with large overhanging trees, many of which have shed branches into the water. Trees and fallen branches make the lagoon a perfect sanctuary for both pike and their prey.

Trees overhang water

2 ft (0.6 m)

Reedbed

Open fields

SIGNAL FROM THE LURE
The lure sends out vibrations as it moves in the water. These are sensed by the pike's lateral line (see p. 17) and nerve endings. The alerted pike scans the water visually.

LIKELY SPOT
The angler has read the signs correctly, and a large pike is using this clump of water plants as a hideout.

READY TO GO IN
A good pike stalker must be prepared to go in and search for his fish. Take care in areas of deep, soft mud.

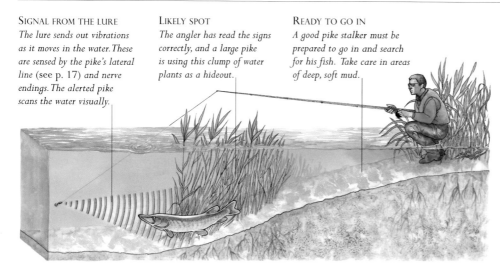

THE PIKE STALKER

This angler really knows his business! He is wearing chest waders so that he can get in there with his fish, where it counts. His polarizing glasses enable him to see through the surface glare and watch both the lure and the pike. As he is crouching down, the reeds conceal his outline. His legs send out no ripples across the water, for he is totally still. He can see the bed of weeds and knows that this is a likely spot for a pike. He casts his lure a rod's length beyond the lie and begins to reel it back in a jerking, erratic fashion.

SEARCHING AND CASTING

1 WATCHING FOR A PIKE
I knew for certain that a sizeable pike had come into the lagoon out of the river's main flow because I had seen its bow-wave. I scanned the water to work out the fish's exact location.

2 PINPOINT PRECISION
I have now seen the pike and am preparing to cast a large spoon. If I am careless with a lure this big I will scare the fish, but I intend to make my first cast count. I cast beyond the fish and reel the spoon back past the pike's nose.

THE FIGHT IS ON

1 THE RUNNING FISH
As I hoped, the first cast proved the pike's downfall. Barely had I begun to reel the spoon back when the pike twisted, grabbed, and was hooked firmly. The first run was like being hooked onto a keg of dynamite.

2 TO THE BANK
For 20 minutes the pike fought on my light rod and 8 lb (3.6 kg) line. It even got out into the main river before I was able to pull it in toward the bank.

3 JUST A BIT PREMATURE
I drew the pike into the shallows, where it burst into life again. I bent my knees to go with the running fish. I had the clutch of the reel correctly set, so it gave line at the critical moment.

4 NOSE-DIVING MADNESS
This really was a furious pike, still possessing the energy to hurl itself from the water. The line could have broken but for a responsive reel and a delicate rod, which was flexible enough to take the strain.

5 THE PRIZE
After that final thrash I was able to lead the pike back to the shallows, slip the hooks out with forceps, and pose with the fish in my hands before making a quick return.

FISHING FOR MUSKELLUNGE

THERE ARE RARELY as many muskellunge in any water as there are pike. It follows that competition for food is frequently less pressing among populations of muskies than it is among those of pike. Muskellunge can therefore be much more selective in what they eat, and this is one reason why they present one of the greatest challenges in freshwater fishing and are called "the fish of 10,000 casts."

Muskies are careful fish, and chances are that they have "seen it all before." It was once said to me that there is not a muskie alive in North America that has not seen what an angler can do, and they all remembered the experience. Whether or not the person who said this was right, you should not consider yourself defeated before you even set out! Muskies, and lots of them, are caught every year. Success is a matter of confidence, careful thought, and doing everything as right as you possibly can.

▶ FIGHTING SPIRIT
Remember that muskies are formidable fighters. If you have invested all the time and effort that it takes to hook one, you should have confidence that your gear really is up to the challenge. Don't take any chances!

A CAUTIOUS CUSTOMER

Muskies are known to be great "followers" – fish that will track a lure or bait again and again without making the mistake of getting themselves hooked. The successful muskie angler must have every single method at his or her fingertips and go equipped with top-water lures, subsurface lures, jigs, natural baits, and even fly tackle. He or she needs to know when, where, and how to fish, and this might include speed trolling *(see p. 116),* fishing in weed, or even night fishing.

The basic requirement is that you never relax, become complacent, or fish routinely. Keep one step ahead! Your mind should be constantly busy thinking up new methods, new approaches, and new ways to trick one of the craftiest fish around.

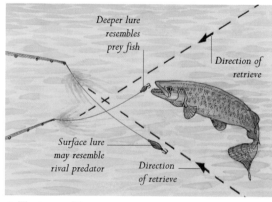

▲ TWO-LURE TRICK
Two anglers in the same boat cross the retrieve paths of their lures. One lure is at or near surface level, the other deeper in the water. A muskie follows the deeper lure toward the boat and then sees the surface lure crossing its field of vision. Perhaps taking the surface lure for a competing predator (we cannot really tell), the muskie strikes quickly at the one it is following and is hooked.

▲ SUCCESS!
This big muskie eventually snapped at a spinner. Notice, however, that the hooks are only just in the fish's mouth. The muskie rarely commits itself fully.

LURES TO USE

Lures of 7–8 in (18–20 cm) are generally used for muskies, but try smaller ones in spring, when the water is cooler, and larger ones in autumn, when fish are feeding hard. Use a selection that covers all depths from the surface down to around 30 ft (10 m).

The traditional approach is to use lures with a subtle action in spring and change to livelier ones as the water warms. One good tactic is to speed up your retrieve, then slow it down or stop. Another is to switch your rod from side to side, so that the angle of the retrieve changes. In short, do anything that will convince a muskie that your plastic, wood, or metal is in fact a tasty fish.

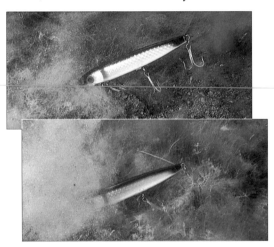

▲ PHANTOM FEEDER
In these two pictures, a lure is retrieved along the bed. It noses its way along (top) until it reaches a patch of loose silt where, because of its shape, it digs in (above) and makes a puff of silt — as do bottom-feeding fish.

▲ MISSION ACCOMPLISHED
Andy Goram, the renowned English fisherman, pledged himself to catch a muskie — and here it is. It is good to see anglers crisscrossing the world, learning new things and passing on their own knowledge to others.

BIG WATERS

Generally, the biggest muskies live in big rivers and big lakes, because this is where they have a chance to hide from their enemies and remain relatively inconspicuous.

You will need a boat if you are going to tackle these large waters. It needs to be some 15–18 ft (5–6 m) in length and have a large, open floor that can take the big tackle boxes and all the gear muskie anglers use. Do not forget that muskies are big fish and you cannot "land" (or "boat") one in a tight space. An elevated casting platform, and a front deck large enough to mount a bow trolling motor, are also essential items.

Once you are afloat, look for clusters of islands, stretches of gravel, outcrops of rock, patches of waterweed, bays full of weed, banks of cattails, lilypads, stream mouths, old river channels, and any sunken timber. Look especially for deep water around any of these features. Make a point of fishing the "drop-offs" from shallow to deep water.

▶ FIGURE EIGHT
This trick is used at the end of a long retrieve on a large water. The idea is to prolong the movement of the retrieve as long as possible and, if a muskie is following, make the lure seem to be trying to escape. Do this at the end of every cast, because large muskies often slide in unseen beneath your boat. Sweep the rod in a wide arc, keeping the tip below the height of the side of the boat.

▲ TRY A DEADBAIT
When muskie become very finicky, deadbaits can be an effective way to catch them. Try deadbaits that are natural to the fish's environment, but sometimes a change to sea fish can work — perhaps because they contain more oil.

▲ BOATING A MUSKIE
When bringing in the catch, any net that you use must be soft and be made of fine mesh that is less likely to split the muskie's fins. A "fish cradle" (made for landing fish) is better. Better still, release any fish below trophy status without taking them from the water.

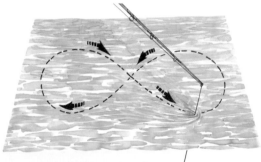

If muskellunge is down deep, lower rod to allow line to reach down to fish.

When fish takes lure, set hook by striking upward into its mouth.

BASS

ANGLERS THE WORLD OVER hunt fish that they know as bass, although these fish are different on every continent. North America has the black bass group, which belongs to the sunfish family, and several members of the "true" bass family *(see p. 159)*. Europe's two species of sea bass, and Australia's Murray cod and Australian bass, belong to other families in turn *(see p. 56)*.

BLACK BASS

TWO OF THE MOST popular species of sport fish in North America are the large-mouth and small-mouth bass. These are the largest members of the black bass group, a collection of closely related species whose smaller members include the Suwannee, Guadalupe, spotted, and redeye bass.

Black bass belong to the sunfish family. Sunfish are small freshwater species that are included among the panfish *(see p. 158)*.

The large-mouth bass is divided into two subspecies. The larger of these is found in Florida, the smaller in the northern United States. Both large- and small-mouth bass have a preference for clear water, but large-mouths adapt more easily to murky water. Black bass feed either by opening their mouths rapidly to draw in water and, with it, tiny food particles, or by seizing larger prey, such as fish, frogs, and crayfish, which they turn in their mouths to swallow headfirst.

Black bass spawn in shallow water over sand or gravel. The fish clear a space to use as a nest, often in a clearing in the weeds. After spawning, the male hovers above the eggs, fanning away silt and debris. Any small fish moving in to take the eggs are chased off. The hatched fry are also guarded for a while before they disperse, then the male bass leaves for a well-deserved feeding spree.

▲ COVERED WATER
Lily pads like these begin to grow toward the surface a little before bass spawning time. The pads offer excellent cover for adult large-mouths and the newly hatched fry. In the weeks prior to spawning time, bass find shelter among the stalks of immature lily pads and under drifting clumps of other weeds.

SEASONAL MIGRATION

In spring, both large- and small-mouth bass are occupied with spawning, and for this they move to the shallows, where the water warms quickly. They take one or two weeks to recover after spawning and then resume feeding, both in the shallows and in deeper water. In summer, strong sunlight and warm surface temperatures tempt the bass into the deep water, where they look for a comfort-able temperature and light level.

In autumn, as the water cools and the sun sinks lower, bass spend more time in the shallows again. From late autumn, however, the surface water becomes colder than the water in the depths. The bass again move down into the deeper parts of the lake or river, where they remain through the winter.

◀ BASS COUNTRY
Bass like pools and ponds where they can spend time looking for dead-end channels, shallow bays, and areas of cattails and brushwood. Look for bass around extensive root systems, where they forage and mount ambushes on prey.

▲ A BASS AT HOME
A bass will often choose a particular structure as its long-term home and will not move away unless water conditions change or fishing pressure grows.

BLACK BASS ANATOMY

The black bass is a tough, muscular customer with a gaping mouth and the keen senses that are needed for successful hunting. Its eyesight and hearing are well developed, and its lateral lines *(see p. 16)* can pick up underwater vibrations very precisely. The black bass also has a strong sense of smell and can detect minute amounts of scent in the water.

LARGE-MOUTH BASS *Micropterus salmoides*

APPROXIMATE GUIDE TO WEIGHTS
TROPHY (NORTHERN US) 6–8 lb (2.7–3.6 kg)
(FLORIDA) 10–12 lb (4.5–5.4 kg)
FLORIDA RECORD 22 lb (10 kg)

▲ SMALL-MOUTH BASS
The jaw of this species does not extend back as far as the eye, the first dorsal fin has a flat profile, and the dorsal fins are joined.

MOUTH
Hindmost point of mouth is slightly to rear of eye.

FIRST DORSAL FIN
Fin has nine spines and is more arched than first dorsal fin of small-mouth.

SECOND DORSAL FIN
Fin has soft rays, not spines, and is almost separated from first dorsal fin.

FLANK COLOR
Flanks vary in color according to water clarity and weed growth (this also applies to small-mouth).

ANAL FIN
Fin is supported mostly by soft rays, but there are three short spines at the front end.

▲ UNDERWATER JUNGLE
Black bass will venture into shallow water as long as there is overhead cover: without it, the fish would be too visible to predators such as herons, let alone anglers. Fallen branches also provide points of ambush from where black bass dart out to capture smaller fish.

▲ DUMPED VEHICLE
Black bass are attracted by dumped motor vehicles, bridge pilings, fallen trees, or rock masses. They also like to hang near underwater cliffs, crevices, caves, or any other feature that will give them shelter.

◀ MAKING USE OF THE COVER
Black bass are masters in the use of cover and are rarely found far away from it. The only exception to this is when they swim out and hang below the surface as a hunting tactic, for example to scan the water for a school of panfish.

UNDERWATER FEATURES

In fishing terms, a "feature" is anything that is "different" in the underwater world. This means any kind of cover, including man-made or natural structures, and some differences that might be less obvious to humans, such as currents or shadows. Black bass need cover from the moment they hatch: the fry force their way into dense beds of weed in the hope of escaping predatory fish.

As they grow larger, black bass make use of weeds and submerged rocks, timber, brush, and logs. They have three main uses for features: shade, shelter, and hiding places from which they can mount ambushes.

The physical makeup of the bottom is also important to black bass. The fish seek out "drop-offs" (any places where the depth changes radically). An outcrop of rock might attract them, or any place where the bottom make-up changes from one type, such as mud or gravel, to another.

BASS SPECIES

MENTION BASS TO ANY freshwater angler and the immediate thought will be of the black bass of North America, and in particular the two sport fish in this group, the large-mouth and small-mouth bass. However, many more fish than this go by the name of bass. They are all feisty customers, and it is no wonder that anglers all over the world find them fascinating.

Here are a few examples: the sea bass, which lives in the eastern North Atlantic and often ventures into the brackish (partly fresh and partly salt) water of European estuaries; the striped bass, which lives in the western North Atlantic and in some North American estuaries, with a few landlocked populations in some rivers; the peacock bass, which thrives in the vast rivers of South America; and the spot-tailed bass, which inhabits some rivers of tropical Australia.

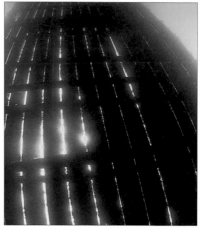

▲ LANDING STAGE
This dock provides exactly the type of cover that all bass need. The fact that they are hunters themselves does not diminish their own need for security.

◄ UNDERWATER STRUCTURE
The supports of the landing stage are covered with weed that harbors millions of insects — food for smaller kinds of bass and juveniles of the bigger species.

AUSTRALIAN SPECIES

There are several kinds of fish known as bass in Australia. To begin with, there is the Australian bass itself. This is an important game fish in the coastal rivers, estuaries, and still waters of southeast Australia. It is not a huge fish, but it fights well and can be caught on both fly and spinner.

The biggest of all the bass in Australia is the Murray cod. This fish does not belong to the true bass family *(see p. 54)*, but it is very basslike in appearance. The record weight for all time (set in the early 20th century) is 250 lb (113.5 kg), and while such sizes are unknown today, the Murray cod is still the largest freshwater fish in Australia. It lurks in deep holes in muddy, slow-flowing rivers. It is native to the Murray-Darling river system of New South Wales and South Australia and has been introduced to various other waters in New South Wales and Victoria.

The Murray cod has a mottled, brownish yellow color that suits it well for its life in the coffee-colored waters of its natural habitat, where it is camouflaged from its prey.

MURRAY COD
Maccullochella peeli
APPROXIMATE GUIDE TO WEIGHTS
AVERAGE 4½–17½ lb (2–8 kg)
TROPHY 44 lb (20 kg)
RECORD 92 lb (41.6 kg)

◄ PORTRAIT OF A MURRAY COD
The Murray cod has large eyes that give it the best chance of vision in water that can be extremely murky. This view shows the massive jaws of the fish, capable of admitting even medium-sized prey fish. This is a fearsome predator indeed.

► TROPICAL RIVER
This river in Queensland contains fine examples of the sport fish of Australia's rainforest zone. The water is brown with mud that has been washed in by recent rains. Barramundi swim up this river, pausing to hang behind snags and rest in reedbeds.

BASS HABITAT

Bass are adaptable creatures, and while we think of them as freshwater fish, many can tolerate a little salinity. Contact with salt water actually stimulates the growth of some forms of bass.

Whether living in brackish or fresh water, what the bass look for most of all is cover. Their normal mode of hunting is to ambush schools of fish from behind a rock or a snag. If the water is clear, they may use deep pools as hiding places. Locating bass of any kind requires an intimate knowledge of both the water and the behavior of the fish, and therefore local guides are indispensable.

▲ ANDRU RIVER, WEST NEW BRITAIN
The magnificent Andru River is found in West New Britain, Papua New Guinea. One of the fish species it contains is the spot-tailed bass, the local form of which is known to anglers as the "black" spot-tailed bass.

▲ WRECK!
This wrecked boat, together with its accumulated driftwood, lies in a river mouth off Queensland. It is a magnet for barramundi and several species of bass. Fishing after dark is particularly successful.

TROPICAL BASS

It has long been known that Australia provides excellent coastal and freshwater fishing, but the fishing of Papua New Guinea has been discovered (by the wider world) only recently. Today, good roads are being built, both on the mainland and on some of the islands, and it is possible to travel about relatively easily.

Pioneering anglers have started exploring some of the rivers of the southern parts of the country. They have found barramundi in large numbers and huge sizes. Bass here grow bigger and fight better than almost anywhere in the world. There are mangrove jacks and spot-tailed bass as well as catfish and eels. However good the fishing, never ignore the tangled foliage above your boat: it is quite possible that a great python will be coiled up in there, waiting for its lunch!

DORSAL FIN
Fin is divided into two sections, as in black bass.

HUMANE GRIP
This accessory is used to grasp the fish firmly without causing any pain or stress.

▲ SPOT-TAILED BASS
This superb spot-tailed bass was taken from one of the southern rivers of Papua New Guinea. These fish can fight like fury, so you will need to equip yourself with sensible tackle.

▼ MANGROVE JACK
This trophy represents its species well. Once hooked, heavy fish like this thrash their way back to cover and it takes strong tackle, a strong arm, and a strong will to keep them out in open water.

◄ RAINFOREST RIVER
This turbulent, shallow stretch of river in West New Britain is used by local people as a ford. The fishing is good in this stretch, especially in areas where interesting pools can be found. Locations like this are no longer difficult to reach by land, thanks to an extensive road-building program in many parts of Papua New Guinea.

BASS FISHING STRATEGIES

A DUMB BASS JUST DOESN'T EXIST, and to fool a bass you need to do everything right . . . and often a bit more besides! The range of bass fishing strategies is pretty well endless. You can fish on the bottom, fly fish, fish through ice, jig, troll, fish with plugs, or fish with soft plastic lures. There are more strategies besides, and you can use each of these in a hundred different ways!

I should add that, as a general principle, the word "bass" in this book (as in most other fishing books) means the large- and small-mouth bass. Any other bass big enough to be sport fish are caught in much the same way.

JIGGING A SPOON

There are many anglers who would select a fast-running plug as the prime rig for bass, and this strategy is given special coverage elsewhere (see pp. 60–61).

However, there are some bass that ignore plugs. These fish will often strike instead at lures that are jigged vertically, very close to the fish's hiding places. The strategy I shall describe is to jig a spoon (see p. 174), but other lures can be jigged. Jigging is a really good start if you are fishing deep water.

Carefully lower a jigging spoon near a structure, stopping to jig for a few seconds at varying depths. It pays to stop occasionally, so that the spoon hangs idle. Bass sometimes prefer a spoon that isn't moving at all.

You can tip your jigs with a whole variety of plastic attractors to lend them just a little bit more movement and attraction.

▲ A GREAT CATCH
This fish was hooked close to a submerged tree on a jigged spoon. Afterward it went storming out into the open water, where it could be played out safely.

◀ HAIRY TAIL
This is an alternative to the tail spinner for working shallowly submerged structures or the fringes of fallen trees.

▲ PLAYING YOUR BASS
Anyone can lose an acrobatic bass, but there are ways to prevent this: use a rod that you can trust, test the strength of your tackle beforehand, and, if you get a bite, make sure your fish is firmly hooked and keep your line tight all through the battle.

▲ CRAB LURE
It is worth trying everything at least once, even a little crab imitation like this. Let it sink to the bottom and then jerk it erratically, stirring up puffs of silt.

▼ TEMPT THEM OUT
The closer you can work your spoon around cover the better. A tail spinner is a good choice in cold, dull conditions. This is a spinner with a heavy, lead body and a tail-mounted blade, and it has proved tempting to many a large bass.

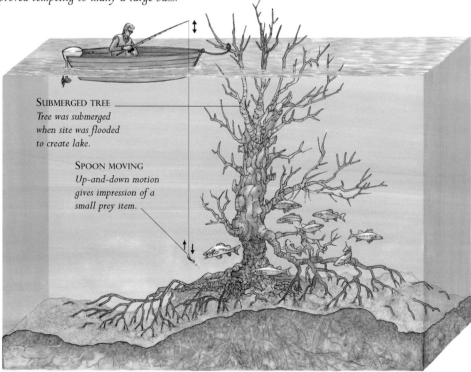

SUBMERGED TREE
Tree was submerged when site was flooded to create lake.

SPOON MOVING
Up-and-down motion gives impression of a small prey item.

SOFT-PLASTIC LURES

The soft-plastic lure (resembling a worm, an eel, a salamander, a lizard, or even a small snake) is probably the most favored bass lure. Soft-plastic lures work best when the water is relatively warm. They have the advantage of being able to retrieve them through thick weed or bushes without snagging.

Plastic lures 6–8 in (15–20 cm) in size are most commonly used, but the real trophy bass might go for something bigger, and it might be wise to change to a smaller lure in very clear water or after a cold front. Purple and black are favorite colors.

▲ GETTING RIGHT IN
Sometimes dignity needs to be sacrificed for success. If you cannot get the bass to come to you, then you must go to it — but always take great care. This angler is tackling the problem of a tangled line.

◄ PLASTIC-LURED BASS
A black worm on a large, long-shanked hook lured this beautiful fish. The angler retrieved the lure (reeled it in across the swim) slowly, with a lifting and dropping motion of the rod. Keep a tight line as you lower the rod — bass often take the lure as it sinks.

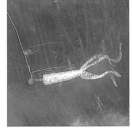

▲ LOOKING LIVELY
The whole allure of the plastic worm lies in its poetic motion! Sometimes a plastic worm works better than anything found in nature, so it pays to give one of the many designs a whirl. Put this one in front of a world-weary bass!

FLY-CAUGHT BASS

Fly fishing for bass really does work. The best flies are known as "streamers," which imitate those bait fish or large nymphs (immature forms of aquatic insects) that bass eat.

Apart from these sinking flies, floating "bass bugs" also inspire some really exciting fishing, especially early in the morning and around dusk, when bass can be found feeding in calm, shallow water. You can even try dry flies on occasion, especially when river fishing. Cast downstream, let the fly drift, then skate it over a likely spot, creating a wake behind it to attract attention.

Think hard about your retrieve, and if a steady, rhythmic one is not working, vary it and make it erratic. Try to impart every bit of life into that fly that you can.

▲ FLY ON THE WATER
Flies work so well because the fur and feather have a lifelike motion in the water, making ripples and catching air bubbles.

► CAUGHT BY A FLY
Fly fishing for bass tends to be best when the water warms. Fish at shallow depths from April to June, but go deeper during the midsummer period from mid-June till mid-July.

PLUG-FISHING FOR BASS

PLUGS ARE LURES *(see pp. 172–176)* whose design turns on how they travel through the water when retrieved from a cast. They enable you to explore large areas of water more quickly than would be possible when fishing with edible bait or plastic worms.

There is an endless list of plug types to try, and each type comes in many variations of size, color, and action. Color can be just as important as size: if you are fishing in murky water, choose brightly colored or fluorescent plugs.

The larger plugs are generally for large-mouth bass: if hooked on a big plug, small-mouths can spit out the plug and get away.

MATCH THE MOOD

Bass experts talk about finding the "pattern": the style of fishing that is right for the time. The main factors involved are the location of the bass and the presentation needed to make them bite. It takes time to learn how to find the pattern, and for beginners the best advice is to keep moving, cover as many areas of the water as possible, and learn as you go.

▲ PLUG-FISHING FROM A BOAT
Today's bass fishing boats have aluminum hulls, high-powered engines, foot-operated controls for steering and acceleration, electric winches for trolling, swivel chairs in which the angler sits to fight the running fish, onboard "wells" for livebait, radio communications, and graph recorders for scanning the underwater scene.

WHERE TO PLUG-FISH

First look in the area of any structures or snags that may be present where you are fishing; look for bass under overhanging cliffs, bridges, and any overhead cover that offers ample shade. Try thick vegetation such as bushes or floating weed, for these can provide refuge in even the clearest waters.

Remember that in crystal-clear water, long casts will help you avoid scaring the bass. To make a greater casting distance possible, cut down on line diameter.

Any murky water created, for example, by in-flowing streams or waves washing against a shoreline will offer a hiding place for bass. Once they have found some murky water, bass continue to be attracted by fallen trees, weed, and brush. Always select lures that remain visible to bass in murky water, especially light-colored, fluorescent ones.

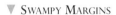

▼ SWAMPY MARGINS
Bass spawn in and around swampy bogs in the spring. They remain in this environment for most of the summer, hunting small fish and taking advantage of the plentiful insect life that is attracted to swampy areas. It is only in the height of the summer's heat that bass will go in search of deeper, cooler water.

▲ LARGE WATERS
Very large bass live in large waters, but locating them is a problem. Solve it by trolling from a boat (see p. 69, 116) and mooring up when you find the fish.

▲ TREE COVER
Cover for bass is essential, especially in hot weather and clear, shallow water. Certainly for most of the day (dawn and dusk excepted), bass will not stray into areas of open sunshine. Tree cover also provides food — insects occasionally fall from overhanging foliage.

SUBSURFACE PLUGS

Plugs that are retrieved underwater are known as crankbaits. There are three types:

(i) Minnow imitations, which stay close to the surface during the retrieve.

(ii) Plugs that float when they are at rest and dive and beat to and fro when retrieved. These plugs have a "lip" (an example is seen on the right) that determines the degree of movement: the larger the lip, the deeper the dive and the more violent the beating action.

(iii) Vibrating plugs, which always sink. After casting, you let the crankbait sink, counting the seconds with a stopwatch while it is sinking. When you estimate that it will have reached the depth you require, you then start to crank it in.

▶ SIGN OF A CAUTIOUS FISH
You would think the mouth of this bass big enough to engulf an elephant, but notice how the hooks have only just caught the outer edge of the fish's upper jaw. If you needed proof that bass are suspicious creatures, this photograph provides clear testimony.

▶ OVERHANG TROLLING
Bass love to lurk around overhangs. To be sure of getting one to bite, practice the technique of making a plug bounce around the contour of the overhang. Try the "stop-go method," in which you reel in slowly to pull your plug over the top shelf, where the water is shallower. As the plug reaches the edge, increase the rate of retrieve so that the plug falls rapidly down the incline — exactly as a small fish would do in nature.

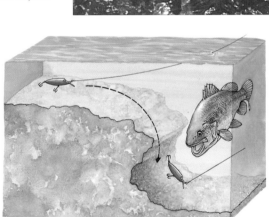

▲ DEEP-RUNNING CRANKBAIT
Troll this kind of crankbait over underwater structures. Reel in the line rapidly to make the lip strike against the structure, kicking up silt like a scurrying crayfish.

SURFACE PLUGS

Surface plugs work best on calm summer mornings and evenings, when bass feed in the shallows. Four types are good for bass fishing: (i) propeller-type plugs, which have long, thin bodies with a propeller at one or both ends; (ii) "poppers" and "chuggers," which have a concave face that makes a gurgling sound while being retrieved; (iii) top-water crawlers, which have a metal lip that causes the lure to wobble (attractive to fish); and (iv) "stickbaits," which look like propeller-type plugs without the propellers!

▲ CAUGHT ON THE SURFACE
If you see a wake behind the lure while you are cranking it in, stop reeling and let the lure rest for several seconds. Then try twitching it . . . the effect could be explosive!

▲ WHAT THE BASS SEES
Bass find food by homing in on a disturbance in the surface layer that shouts out "food." Noise, wake, and bubbles are as meaningful to them as an attractive silhouette.

PERCH

THE PERCH OF THE WORLD are a large and complex family. For convenience, anglers divide them into two groups: northern perch, found in the temperate countries of the Northern Hemisphere; and warm-climate perch, such as the Nile perch and barramundi *(see p. 64).* All perch are characterized by sharp-spined dorsal fins and pugnacious, predatory behavior.

EUROPEAN PERCH
Perca fluviatilis
APPROXIMATE GUIDE TO WEIGHTS
AVERAGE *1–2 lb (0.45–0.9 kg)*
TROPHY *3 lb (1.4 kg)*
RECORD *12 lb (5.4 kg)*

NORTHERN PERCH

TWO SPECIES OF northern perch are important to the angler. One of these is the European perch. This species occurs in both Europe and Asia as far east as Mongolia and eastern Siberia. Its range extends from Finland in the north to Kazakhstan in the south, on the shores of the Caspian Sea. The other species, the yellow perch, is like a European perch apart from the body color. It occurs in Canada and the eastern United States as far south as South Carolina. The usual weight of northern perch is in the range of 1–3 lb (0.5–1 kg), but occasionally it reaches 6 lb (3 kg) in weight.

All northern perch are fierce predators, looking for prey up to a third of their size. They have very large mouths in proportion to body size and tend to hunt in schools.

▲ PERCH IN QUIET WATER
Perch are normally found in quiet water, away from the main flow. They patrol slacks and eddies, where minnows and other small fish gather. Sometimes, however, perch will brave fast currents in pursuit of small prey.

MOUTH
Mouth can open very wide on hinged jaws, allowing perch to swallow large prey for its body size.

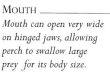

EYE
Perch have big eyes and sharp eyesight, being primarily sight feeders.

HOW PERCH SPAWN

Northern perch spawn in April and May, sometimes continuing into June in cold latitudes. The eggs are joined together in ribbonlike strings 3–6 ft (1–2 m) long and ½–¾ in (1–2 cm) wide. The female lays the strings on stones, submerged branches, roots, or aquatic plants in shallow water, very often at night. The male perch fertilizes them immediately. The eggs generally hatch in around two weeks. The parents will eat the eggs as well as the emerging fry.

▲ GLACIAL LAKE
In both North America and Europe, perch can be found in glacial lakes. In these deep, cold waters, the perch feed on insects and small fish in shallow bays around the shoreline. They also feed on their own young.

▲ LOWLAND RIVER
One of the most typical perch habitats is a slow-moving lowland river with weed-fringed banks. The perch find food and shelter among the weeds.

◀ PERCH SPAWN
The ribbons of spawn are sticky and quickly attach themselves to objects wherever they are laid. Fish managers or park wardens can easily restrict the numbers of perch in a lake or river (for example, to protect the salmon or trout population) by taking out submerged branches with perch spawn attached.

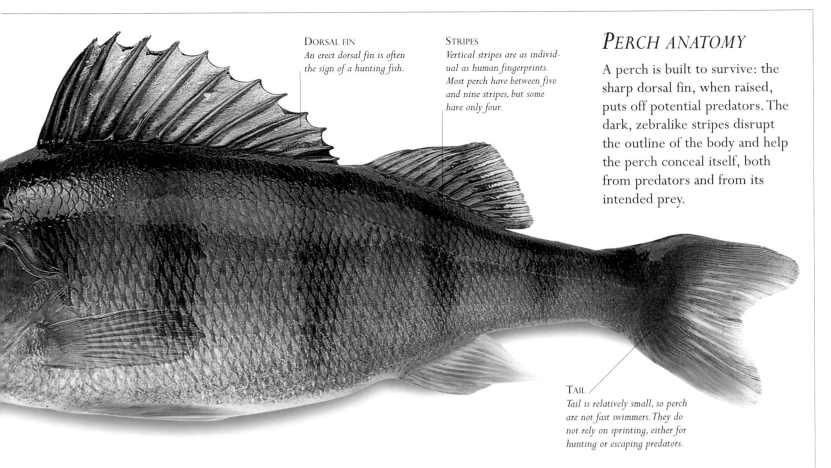

DORSAL FIN
An erect dorsal fin is often the sign of a hunting fish.

STRIPES
Vertical stripes are as individual as human fingerprints. Most perch have between five and nine stripes, but some have only four.

PERCH ANATOMY

A perch is built to survive: the sharp dorsal fin, when raised, puts off potential predators. The dark, zebralike stripes disrupt the outline of the body and help the perch conceal itself, both from predators and from its intended prey.

TAIL
Tail is relatively small, so perch are not fast swimmers. They do not rely on sprinting, either for hunting or escaping predators.

UNDERWATER FEATURES

Perch like to keep close to underwater structures of whatever kind. Open water, to them, is simply something to be crossed during hunting. Whenever they are at rest, perch seek the shelter of weed, branches, a sunken boat, the supports of a pier, or anything that gives them cover. In this they are aided by their camouflage coloration. The pattern of vertical black bars down their flanks allows the fish to merge in with water that is dappled by reeds.

▲ FEEDING GROUND
Younger perch often hunt among soft weed for beetles, water shrimp, water boatmen, and the like. If they see a carp rooting on the bottom, small perch will hover close by to pick up displaced bloodworms.

▲ MANMADE STRUCTURE
Wherever man has left evidence of his presence, there are likely to be perch. Boathouses, docks, piers — perch are found anywhere where the natural contours of bank and bed are broken up, creating plenty of nooks and crannies.

◄ REEDBED – A PERCH'S HAVEN
Notice how the stripes blend in with the reedy background. Perch spawn here, hide here, and feed here. They also seem to like rubbing against reed stems, perhaps to rid themselves of parasites.

PERCH SPECIES

THE PERCH IS EVERY ANGLER'S favorite species, if only because so many of us began with crude tackle, elementary baits, and skill no more than enough to outwit the suicidal "stripeys"! Trout anglers may scoff at a perch that has the temerity to take their wet fly but, deep down, affection is there.

Perch of one kind or another are available to almost every angler in the world: yellow perch in all of North America; the European perch throughout Europe apart from Spain, parts of Scandinavia, and the far north of Scotland. The more dramatic perch, such

SANDSTONE FOSSIL
Features visible include lateral line, eye, mouth, fins, dorsal spines, and anal spines.

▲ EOCENE ANCESTOR
Around 45 million years ago, in the Eocene epoch, this fish was trapped in the sand of what we now call the Green River Formation in the United States. The fish is similar to a northern perch, except that the lower jaw seems to protrude more, and the dorsal spines extend farther back, when compared to the modern fish.

as the Nile perch and barramundi, fill the niche in Africa and Australasia. Large or small, these are all magnificent fish.

Northern perch – European and yellow, among others – are in the Percidae family. Australia's Macquarie, golden, and estuary perch belong to the Percichthyidae. White perch, jungle perch, and silver perch each belong to other families. But why worry? Northern perch and barramundi are similar only in their high, humped back, spiky dorsal fin, and greedy, predatory nature. However, Australians call the barramundi the "great perch," so a perch it is!

CHANGES IN DISTRIBUTION

The distribution of perch species is never quite stable. All through the 1970s, European perch suffered an epidemic of perch disease, which ravaged stocks across the continent. In some areas, the species became temporarily extinct. Now, however, it has recovered all of its old territories and is even gaining new ground in the north of Scotland.

Perch have been advancing in other parts of the world: imported stocks of European perch are doing well in Australia and New Zealand. The barramundi, too, is expanding its range and is being found unexpectedly in rivers in Papua New Guinea.

▶ SPREADING SOUTH
European perch have been introduced to this beautiful lake in New Zealand and are flourishing. These fish are as popular with anglers as the trout stocks that were introduced to New Zealand by earlier generations of anglers.

▼ NEW FISHING LOCATIONS
The angler of today tends to be an explorer by nature, ever restless in the quest for new challenges. This is one of the rivers in Papua New Guinea where intrepid anglers are now catching some fabulous barramundi.

▲ STRONGHOLD IN THE NORTH
Ancient estate lakes, provided they are properly maintained like this one, make perfect waters for northern perch. The water is clear, and there is always a plentiful supply of the small fish on which the perch like to prey. Northern perch do not flourish in cloudy water.

BARRAMUNDI

The barramundi, or great or giant perch, is found in the lower reaches of mainland rivers and rivers on offshore islands across Asia from the Persian Gulf to China and all along the north coast of Australia. It also occurs in Papua New Guinea with its Pacific islands and may also inhabit some islands of Indonesia. The barramundi lives in rivers, creeks, and mangrove swamps; it spawns in estuaries and coastal waters of the sea.

Being a migratory fish that moves through a variety of environments, the barramundi enjoys a varied diet, and this is one of the factors enabling it to grow to its large size. It can achieve a weight of 132 lb (60 kg) as it engulfs fish, crayfish, crabs, and shrimp.

Barramundi hunt in snag-infested waters, from which they ambush passing prey. The scales have an impressive sheen: barramundi caught near the coast are often silver in appearance. Those caught in fresh water often have gold or butter yellow tints. The eye has a startling yellow color that is opaque, like that of the walleye.

DORSAL FINS
Dorsal fin is divided into first and second sections. This specimen is missing a few rays from its second section.

HEAD
Head is large and bony, with large jaws capable of taking in large prey fish.

▲ A FISH FROM THE SWAMP
My colleague, Simon Channing, looks delighted to have caught this lovely, glowing barramundi. This is a silvery example, taken from one of the swampy rivers of Queensland in northern Australia. Barramundi, or "barras," are never the easiest of fish to catch, and a specimen this size can be considered a trophy. As well as the powerful physique of the species, this picture clearly shows the strong eye color.

TIGERFISH

Anglers associate the tigerfish with perch, if for no other reason than that it is found in the same waters as Nile perch. It is possibly the most aggressive predator in the world, and it bears the most ferocious teeth. The mouth is well armored, and it is so difficult to sink a hook into the bony jaws that only one in seven or eight fish hooked are landed.

The tigerfish is a fearsome beast, and it has a large brother, the Goliath tigerfish. The average weight of the tigerfish is 5–10 lb (2.2–4.5 kg); Goliaths can exceed 100 lb (45 kg). The Goliath lives in some of the most inaccessible waters in the world, in the Congo (Zaïre) basin.

▲ CRUISING THE NILE
While the perch in the Nile are not as common as they once were, there are still some prize fish to be found, expecially in the region of Murchison Falls in Upper Egypt. This is not an easy place to reach, but the rewards can be great.

▶ A MIGHTY FISH
If you could imagine the vertical bars of a northern perch painted onto this fish, disregarding size, the appearance of the two species would be strikingly similar. The deep, well-fed body of the Nile perch is evidence of its great hunting ability.

▼ A DELICATE BALANCE
Nile perch and tigerfish live together in a delicate state of harmony: each preys on the young of the other, but never to the point where one fish exterminates the other. The relationship evolved over millions of years and is one of dependency as much as competition.

RAZOR-SHARP TEETH
Teeth are extremely sharp and are capable of tearing open an angler's hand in a moment.

NILE PERCH

This fish is related to the barramundi and is found in the great lakes of central Africa and the whole length of the Nile, including Lake Nasser, where it flourishes. No one is quite sure how big it grows. Weights of 300 lb (135 kg) are believed possible, and there are even rumors of fish weighing more than 500 lb (225 kg).

Nile perch are themselves heavily preyed upon. Many an angler, while playing a Nile perch, has found the fight going heavy, dour, and leaden. The line starts to unwind from the reel uncontrollably. It is only when every inch of line is lost that a crocodile will clear the surface with the hooked Nile perch clamped firmly between its jaws.

DORSAL FIN
Size and shape of dorsal fin is similar in all perch.

FISHING FOR NORTHERN PERCH

PERCH ARE GREAT FAVORITES all through the Northern Hemisphere because you can pursue them with standard gear and use a variety of methods to catch them. The main kinds are the European perch and, in North America, the yellow perch.

Perch have healthy appetites, and they are willing to feed in most conditions, even in deep winter under the ice. All perch are schooling fish, so the action can be fast and furious if you come across a decent-sized school. However, always remember to strike (flick the rod to pull the hook tight in the fish's mouth) at the very first sign of a bite. Leave a bite and the fish will swallow the bait. Once the hook is in the fish's throat, you will not be able to remove it safely.

Location is essential: the perch will not be scattered everywhere around the water but tend to form schools in specific areas. Find snags, and you will find perch.

CONSIDERATIONS OF COVER

Perch will group in the most extraordinary places and are quick to take advantage of any new development. For example, if you are boat fishing, a school of perch will quickly assemble underneath the craft, even following the anchor rope down to the bottom.

If fish cages have been placed on the water (some do this to enhance stocks), perch are almost bound to congregate beneath these. Any man-made structure with its footings in the water will attract perch schools, but so do fallen tree branches. In the winter, look very carefully for perch around died-back lilybeds. I remember one fish that lived for a whole year inside a cookie tin!

▲ UNDERNEATH THE ARCHES
Perch and bridges go together. Perch like the shelter from the light, and there is always rubble underneath in which they can hide. Bridge pools often are deeper than the rest of the river and tend to harbor food supplies for the perch.

▼ ROOT AND BRANCH
Perch schools spend time in spots like this, hanging around fallen branches and submerged tree roots for safety. Then, when they become hungry, they move out and hunt in the open water.

SUBMERGED STRUCTURES

Fishing platforms, piers, and boat jetties all attract great numbers of perch. Boathouses also are long-term favorites, and perch will also investigate sunken and rotting boats. Apart from this, submerged cars and even crashed airplanes have provided homes for perch schools. Apart from feeling protected, perch like to rub and scratch themselves against wood or metal, perhaps dislodging skin parasites in doing so.

▶ UNDER THE PLATFORM
These pictures were taken under a fishing platform — a structure built for anglers to fish from. The bait (inset) was a soft-plastic worm (see p. 174). A perch came along (main picture) and, although this fish was not actively hunting, the soft plastic aroused its curiosity.

▲ FISHING THROUGH ICE FOR YELLOW PERCH
The weather just cannot be too cold for perch fishing, and all across the Northern Hemisphere, wherever the winters are cold, anglers will set out to fish for perch through the ice. First take an auger to drill through the ice, then fish by jigging (hoisting up and down) either natural or plastic baits.

BOTTOM FISHING

Bottom fishing with livebait for perch is a thrilling method. Particularly effective are large worms, the fresher and more lively the better. Fish these on the bottom or drifting around in midwater under a float. Small deadbaits are especially favored by big perch. Use whole fish of around 3–4 in (8–10 cm) or cut larger ones in pieces this size, and strike quickly at any sign of a bite.

For groundbait, a good, strong-smelling mixture of different baits (a "rubby-dubby") can draw perch schools into the swim. Use a combination of chopped worms, maggots, pieces of luncheon meat, even a few strips of bacon – anything that will give off a good scent and look attractive to passing fish.

▲ LOOSE FOOD
Loose maggots and casters (the chrysalises, or pupae, into which the maggots develop) fed by hand will often be successful in attracting perch to your swim. The fish will take the bait readily, either in midwater while it is still sinking or off the bottom when it has arrived there.

◄ A TASTE FOR NATURALS
Being an assiduous hunter, the perch will accept almost any natural food. Minnows, slugs, leeches, and tadpoles are just some of the most common items on the perch's extensive menu of natural foodstuffs.

▲ BAIT DROPPER
This device gets maggots to the bottom quickly, even in deep water. Load in the maggots, cast out the bait dropper, and, as it hits bottom, the lid is triggered open and the maggots are released.

TWISTER FISHING

One of the most exciting ways of catching perch is to use soft plastic or rubber baits *(see p. 174)*. These are known as "twisters," and there are designs resembling worms, frogs, and even baby squid. Any twister that gives the impression of life will attract perch.

Perch will often toy with a twister before taking it firmly, so always wait for a good pull before striking. It pays to fish twisters close to a snag – either in deep or in comparatively shallow water. Move your twister energetically, letting it rise and fall in a natural-looking way. Many of the bites will come "on the drop" (as the bait sinks), so make sure you have a tight line at all times.

► A LIKING FOR RUBBER
This perch is attacking a rubber worm with gusto. Sometimes a change of color brings a fierce response. Yellow is excellent, but red and green also work well. A long, wriggling tail that creates a sinuous action is an essential part of any twister.

FISHING FOR SOUTHERN PERCH

WHEN WE LEAVE the temperate latitudes and look at the African and Australian members of that loose family of fish known to anglers as perch, we find some monsters! Nile perch and barramundi are the sort of fish to get the adrenaline pumping overtime. They are magnificent to look at, difficult to fool, and capable of fighting like maniacs.

Mystery surrounds both species: how big do the barramundi of Papua New Guinea grow? And what is the ultimate size for Nile perch in the great lakes of Africa?

BARRAMUNDI

The barramundi is often called the giant or great perch, and one look at the fish shown at right and below, bright with the gleam of their massive silver sides, explains why.

Look for big barramundi close to cover. Submerged trees, beds of weed, and any kind of structures on the bottom provide the sort hiding places in which they wait to mount an attack any passing prey fish (or lure).

You can't be too careful with barras: do not get your boat too close to their stronghold or they will "spook" and refuse to come out. Sometimes they will shy away from one kind of lure, so you will need to try a different size, color, or action to provoke a strike.

▲ BARRA BEAUTY
No wonder Simon Channing looks so delighted with this barra, taken on one of his history-making trips to Papua New Guinea. This fish fought like an absolute demon, even on heavy gear.

▼ GRADUAL RECOVERY
Hold the fish like this in the shallows so that plenty of water can flow through its gills. You will find that during hot weather the barras will take time to recover before slapping those mighty tails and disappearing into the depths.

▲ NILE PERCH BROWSING
This remarkable shot shows several colossal Nile perch feeding among marginal rocks and boulders in Lake Nasser in Upper Egypt. They are hunting out small fish and can be caught by the stealthy angler.

MANGROVE JACK

This fish, placed in the snapper family by zoologists, has the look of a black bass, but to an angler it is a perch, being highly aggressive and with a mouth large enough to take a lure meant for the biggest barra. It occurs in estuaries and mangrove swamps in Papua New Guinea and northern Australia. It will shoot out of its hiding place, seize the lure, and rocket back in: you can't give it an inch if you want any chance of success.

◄ A REAL HANDFUL
Sally Channing is tremendously proud of this great, bulldog-headed fish. The colors of the mangrove jack tend to vary with age, size, and habitat, but very often they have this silvery sheen.

TROLLING FOR NILE PERCH

These illustrations show my colleague, Simon Channing, fishing for Nile perch on Lake Nasser in Egypt. The right way to do this is to troll big lures behind a boat. On a water this size you cannot know where the schools are, and you need to cover large areas to find them. This may not seem the most exciting way to fish, but when the rod buckles in its support, and the reel spins so fast that it screams, you might think again.

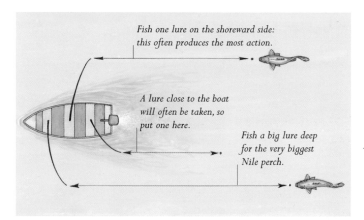

Fish one lure on the shoreward side: this often produces the most action.

A lure close to the boat will often be taken, so put one here.

Fish a big lure deep for the very biggest Nile perch.

◀ TROLLING TACTICS
It is not uncommon to troll with three or four rods at a time: some use even more. Place lures at a variety of depths and distances, and they will be less likely to tangle. If you vary the speed of the boat and sometimes take a zigzag course, this may provoke an angry Nile perch into striking.

PLAYING A NILE PERCH

1 THE TAKE
Simon trolls one of his lures at a depth of 1 ft 6 in (0.5 m) and a big Nile perch comes to the surface and prepares to seize the lure. The fish shows like a great silver plate in the Egyptian sunshine, and suddenly it hammers the rod down, the line zinging tight at the strike.

2 THE LEAP
Alarmed and angry, the hooked fish throws its huge body out into the hot air, struggling and gyrating wildly, the spray cascading from its body. If the hook-hold is the least bit loose it will be easily shaken free at this moment.

3 THE HEADSHAKE
This is the most dangerous maneuver any big Nile perch can try on you. Head-shaking is an absolute nightmare, and even deeply set hooks can be thrown free. All you can do is try to give line fast enough.

LANDING AND HANDLING

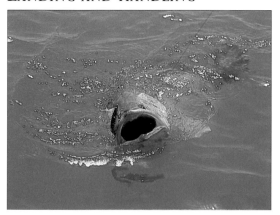

3 A PROUD MOMENT
Simon is one satisfied angler: this fish is in magnificent condition, its silver scales gleaming in the sun.

1 BEATEN
The fight of the Nile perch is short and furious. It does not last too long because the intense African heat saps the fish's strength. The big perch soon knows that it is no match for Simon's gear and comes exhausted to the boat. Simon reels it in carefully and patiently.

2 AT THE BOAT
Look at the size of that monstrous mouth, dwarfing the lure at its lips. Take the lure out at this stage if possible.

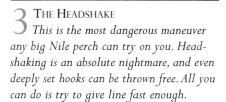

HUGE FINS
This photograph gives a good view of the pelvic fins, which are huge and act like paddles, providing massive swimming power.

STURGEON

STURGEON EVOLVED 135 million years ago, early in the Cretaceous period. They do not have bones, as the majority of fish do, but their skeletons consist mostly of a gristly substance called cartilage. They have this and other features – such as their unevenly divided tails – in common with sharks, which belong to an even more ancient and primitive category of fish.

STURGEON INCLUDE the largest fish in fresh water, although the very biggest species are anadromous *(see p. 88)*, breeding in rivers and migrating to the sea to feed. They occur in rivers of northern continents, in coastal waters of the Atlantic and Pacific oceans, and in inland seas. Sturgeon are bottom-feeders, and the position of the mouth, on the underside of the body, reflects this.

Sturgeon have survived partly because of their ability to produce eggs prolifically, but this ability has turned into something of a disadvantage by today's demand for caviar. Until recently, sturgeon were also important as the source of isinglass, a substance used in making glues and printer's inks.

A MIGRATORY FISH

The principal migration of sturgeon is the spawning run of the large species. Some of these fish travel several hundred miles up rivers to their spawning grounds. Sturgeon feed only rarely on the spawning run but feed plentifully after spawning, when they return to the estuaries. Large sturgeon will take carp, asp, bream, and pike; the largest will even attack catfish.

During the time they spend in the oceans, sturgeon feed on mollusks, crustaceans, and bottom-living fish. They may undertake feeding migrations during this period if they need to find better food supplies.

▲ FROM THE CASPIAN . . .
When the urge to spawn comes on them, beluga sturgeon move from the Caspian Sea into the mouths of the great rivers: this is the delta of the Ural River.

▲ . . . TO THE URALS
Beluga sturgeon migrate through this section of the Ural River to its upper reaches in the Ural Mountains, where the flow is rapid and the bed stony.

STURGEON ANATOMY

All sturgeon have skeletons made of cartilage, not bone. Apart from this, their two most unusual features are the long snout and the heterocercal tail (one in which the upper lobe is much longer than the lower lobe). The mouth extends to open in "telescopic" fashion and is equipped with four barbels. Sturgeon lack scales, apart from the scutes (hard plates) on their sides and back *(see right)*.

PROBOSCIS
Snout is long and is supported by the skeleton; it is used for digging out bottom-living fish and invertebrates.

SMALL EYE
Eye is comparatively small for the sturgeon's size, indicating that the fish hunts more by its sense of touch than by vision.

KNOBBLY BACK
Scutes along the backbone are not flat but conical in shape, creating a "saw-edge" profile.

SLENDER BODY
Most sturgeon species are slender and lithe; an exception is the beluga, with its bulky body.

◄ DORSAL VIEW
Large pectoral fins enable the fish to dig in and hold its position in strong tides. This view shows that the head and the front end of the body are wide, enabling sturgeon to swallow large prey.

PECTORAL FINS
Pectoral fins are broad and long, reaching far down the flanks of the sturgeon.

SETBACKS FOR STURGEON

After living on earth for at least as long as the entire class of mammals, large sturgeon are today threatened with extinction. River pollution, hydroelectric programs, and over-fishing are all affecting sturgeon numbers.

The most lethal of threats is probably the international demand for caviar: as long as wealthy consumers will pay hundreds of dollars for a single helping of the small black eggs, these fish will always be overfished. It will be a sad reflection on modern society if unbridled market forces prove to be the cause of the loss of a sturgeon species.

▲ SHRINKING WATERS
Some sturgeon strongholds are already lost: the Aral Sea, shown here in a satellite photograph, has shrunk as a result of drainage and no longer contains sturgeon.

▲ IMPASSABLE OBSTACLE
Great dams like this placed across major rivers are impossible for sturgeon to negotiate in their efforts to reach their spawning grounds. A single hydroelectric plant can block a river totally and destroy an entire population of these threatened fish.

EXTENDING MOUTH

To open its mouth, a sturgeon extends its lips forward, acting like a vacuum cleaner to create an inward rush of water. This sucking force is capable of dragging a large carp or even a pike between the sturgeon's lips.

A sturgeon has no teeth in its mouth. It does, however, have teeth in its throat. These are called pharyngeal teeth, and they have a powerful crushing action. The lips are tough and can exert a powerful grip on the prey, preventing it from escaping.

▲ CLOSED MOUTH
At rest, the mouth of the sturgeon looks small; the lips fold together neatly under the head. Four large barbels are located at the front of the mouth, under the snout. The sturgeon uses the barbels to detect worms, crabs, or any other small creatures that may be lying in the mud.

▲ OPEN MOUTH
When a sturgeon wishes to feed, it opens its mouth with gusto. The very powerful lips extend forward to form a tunnel. This action creates a partial vacuum in the mouth, and this sucks in prey to be grasped by the lips.

DORSAL FIN
Dorsal fin is comparatively small and is placed unusually close to the tail.

◄ STURGEON SCUTES
A sturgeon has four rows of scutes (hard, armor-like plates) on its side, and a fifth line along its back. A scute from a large sturgeon can be as much as 4 in (10 cm) across.

UNEVEN TAIL
Upper lobe of tail fin is much longer than the lower one. The backbone continues along the top edge of the upper lobe, almost to the tip.

PELVIC FINS
These are located much nearer to the tail than in most kinds of fish.

ANAL FIN
Anal fin is small in relation to size of body.

EUROPEAN STURGEON *Acipenser sturio*
APPROXIMATE GUIDE TO WEIGHTS
AVERAGE 90—160 kg (200—350 lb)
(BELUGA AVERAGE 300—800 lb/140—360 kg)
(BELUGA RECORD 3,000 lb/1,400 kg)

STURGEON SPECIES

STURGEON MAY BE REGARDED as living fossils, and the two dozen or so species existing today represent a group that was much more abundant 60 million years ago and more. Sturgeon are widely distributed in the cool waters of the Northern Hemisphere, and among them are the largest fish that live in fresh water. Some species spend much of their time in the sea or in brackish (mixed salt and fresh) water, moving into rivers to spawn in the spring. Others live in lakes and travel up feeder-streams at spawning time.

Sturgeon are very long-lived, and some are estimated to exceed 150 years of age. The skeleton of the sturgeon is mainly cartilage rather than bone, and several rows of bony plates extend along the body. The sturgeon's snout is long and generally shovel-shaped, and underneath it there are four sensory barbels that detect morsels of food on the bottom. The tubelike mouth then stretches out to suck in its prey. Sturgeon have always been prized as food fish, but it is the eggs – the caviar – that command the highest price.

▲ SPECIES UNDER THREAT
Many sturgeon species are threatened by industrial pollution. Harmful discharges can kill the fish that the sturgeon prey on and can decimate the young sturgeon, too. Hydroelectric plants prevent sturgeon from climbing rivers to their spawning sites, and whole river systems have lost their stocks as a result.

SEVRUGA STURGEON

Compared to the large sturgeon, some species are relatively small. The sevruga, a fish found in the Caspian and Black Seas and in rivers flowing into them, is one of these. It rarely exceeds 5 ft (1.5 m) in length and is very slim in body. The skin in tinged with red, and it has a particularly long snout.

The sevruga is especially valued for the high quality of its eggs and also for its flesh. Commercial netting by licensed companies and unchecked poaching have decimated its numbers throughout its range, which extends from eastern Europe into southern Russia.

▲ GLEAMING SPECIMEN
This Russian angler took a fine sevruga on a night-line baited with a very large frog. The flesh from this fish kept his family in meat for over a week, a welcome addition to their diet in a remote area.

ATLANTIC STURGEON

This sturgeon lives in the waters along the Atlantic coast of North America and runs up many Canadian and American rivers in spring to spawn. Exceptionally large specimens can weigh around 800 lb (360 kg). Most of those caught today weigh less than 200 lb (90 kg), but there are occasional reports of larger fish. The back of the Atlantic sturgeon is olive brown, sometimes tinged with red; its belly is white.

The Atlantic sturgeon feeds on both plants and animals, picking items from the bottom with its great vacuuming mouth. The species has a counterpart in the eastern Atlantic – the European sturgeon (see p. 71).

▶ MASSIVE RANGE
All sturgeon migrate, both to spawn and in search of food. Sturgeon will travel hundreds of miles up rivers and almost endlessly across the oceans, looking for rich feeding on herring, mackerel, or sand eels.

WHITE STURGEON

The white sturgeon is the largest freshwater fish in North America. Among those that were taken during the 19th century, three were reported to weigh more than 1,500 lb (700 kg). Even today, a weight of 1,000 lb (450 kg) is relatively common.

The full range of the species extends from Alaska to middle California. All the giant-sized specimens come from Oregon and Washington and from British Columbia in Canada. They are caught in the Columbia and Fraser Rivers.

The white sturgeon is today prized as a sport fish and has become one of the most sought-after trophies; this is a good development from the point of view of the sturgeon because local fishermen have come to realize that the sturgeon are worth more to them alive than dead.

▲ VAST NUMBER OF EGGS
A large white sturgeon can shed over 3 million eggs in a year, her total weight of roe amounting up to 250 lb (115 kg). The beluga holds the record: a large female can carry 8 million eggs, making up a third of her body weight.

LAKE STURGEON

There are several types of sturgeon around the world that live exclusively in fresh water and do not travel to the sea. In North America, the red sturgeon lives in lakes and rivers from the St. Lawrence westward. Its range extends through the Great Lakes and into the Mississippi River.

Another important species of lake sturgeon is found in Lake Baikal, a very deep, high-altitude lake of southern Siberia.

Lake sturgeon spawn in spring or early summer, migrating out of their lakes into tributary streams to lay their eggs. Generally, they do not grow as large as their seagoing cousins, and fish of more than 100 lb (45 kg) are comparatively rare.

BELUGA STURGEON

The beluga is the largest of all the sturgeon and grows to well over 3,000 lb (1,400 kg). Beluga are also reputed to live for more than 150 years, attaining sexual maturity only when they are between 18 and 20. Their spawning run takes them into the heart of Russia, into the Ural Mountains hundreds of miles from the Caspian Sea. The Caspian is their home for three-quarters of the year.

The caviar from beluga sturgeon is the most highly prized of all, and this has led to great pressure on the species in the Black and Caspian Seas, where organized crime is now involved in poaching operations. There is, however, a beluga sanctuary in the delta of the Ural River, patrolled by armed guards working from boats and helicopters.

The beluga can eat very large prey fish, and carp and pike of 20 lb (9 kg) or even more are not safe from very large beluga.

▲ HUGE LAKES
Many of the world's great lakes – this is Lake Baikal – contain enough prey fish to support sturgeon. Lakes need to have large inflowing rivers for the sturgeon to use at spawning time. The eggs will hatch only in fast-flowing water.

◀ A MOST SENSITIVE SNOUT
Sturgeon of all kinds depend on their long whiskers to search out food in the mud. These are highly sensitive organs: a sturgeon can detect the tiniest vibration from any eel or flatfish that may be trying to hide in the mud.

▲ FACE OF A BELUGA
The head of a beluga sturgeon is ivory in color, and the snout consists of the toughest gristle. The eyes are small but need be no larger: in the murky waters in which it lives, the fish depends more on touch and smell than on sight.

FISHING FOR STURGEON

CATCHING A STURGEON is probably the most serious job in freshwater fishing anywhere around the world. So vast is the fish that an enormous strain is put on tackle and angler alike, and absolutely nothing can be left to chance. Check and recheck every single knot. If in any doubt whatsoever, then retie. Are the hooks absolutely perfect? If there is any question over the strength of the wire or sharpness of the point, then choose another. Line checks are necessary – essential after the capture of a fish.

Now let's consider the angler. Are you fit enough for the battle? This could prove to be anything up to an hour, possibly even more, of grueling physical labor! And are you prepared mentally for the pressure that the battle could put upon you?

▲ DEADBAIT IS BEST
A dead fish is the most successful sturgeon bait. If it is a very large fish, cut it in half; otherwise, you can leave the fish whole. In the US, anglers swear by rainbow trout, whereas for Russian anglers nothing can beat a roach or a bream.

▲ STURGEON FLY
A successful sturgeon fly will be around 6 in (15 cm) in length and be tied very bushy because it needs to make a wake on the surface when retrieved. Deadbait hooks are the best to use when making sturgeon flies.

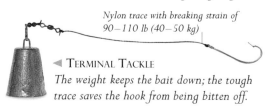

Nylon trace with breaking strain of 90–110 lb (40–50 kg)

◀ TERMINAL TACKLE
The weight keeps the bait down; the tough trace saves the hook from being bitten off.

THE ROD AND REEL

The ideal rod is probably an uptider, the sort of powerful tool that you would use for large conger in deep water. The rod will be quite short – just over 6 ft (2 m) – to give you maximum leverage.

There is not a fixed-spool (spinning) reel in the world that can take this type of pressure, and all sturgeon anglers use multipliers (baitcasters). Make sure that the reel holds 600 ft (200 m) or more of 66 lb (30 kg) line.

Choose only the best brands, because the gearing will come under severe examination. Check that the clutch is correctly set, because the first run of a sturgeon is unstoppable and line must be allowed to run out in a controlled, steady fashion.

▲ BUTT PAD
The sort of butt pad that is used by deep-sea anglers can help a great deal in a sturgeon battle. It supports the rod-butt, giving extra leverage.

▼ EQUIPPED FOR THE JOB
My Danish colleague Niels Ortoft, fishing the Ural River in Kazakhstan, is in the last stages of an hour-long battle with a very big fish. He has caught many large sturgeon and knows the demands they impose on tackle and angler. Niels pays great attention to detail.

TOP RING ROLLER
Pressure of line can cut a groove in the top rod-ring. Niels fits a roller to spread the pressure and avoid the worst damage.

MASSIVE POWER
Niels' rod is bending right down to the butt, giving him the leverage that he needs in the final stages of the battle.

STURDY REEL
The reel has worked overtime during this fight, but it can still give line instantly if the fish powers off.

CHEST WADERS
Niels will need to get into the water to wrestle the fish to the bank, and without chest waders he would be soaked.

MONSTROUS FISH

The fish that run up the Ural and Volga Rivers can be vast, and it is quite possible that an angler will find himself hooked to a fish of 1,100 lb (500 kg) or more! Gigantic fish like this are hardly ever landed nowadays, but even a 220 lb (100 kg) fish is likely to test an angler to the limit. Most commonly, anglers that are hooked up to a sturgeon will take to a boat so that they can follow it through the reedy channels of the river delta. Sometimes a sturgeon will even take its captors out to the sea itself.

On one particular occasion, the Danish fisherman Johnny Jensen and I were towed by a monster sturgeon down one of the arms of the delta of the Ural River and over the sandbars into the Caspian. Eventually, our boatman decided to cut the line after we had been pulled southward a further 5 miles (8 km), by which time we thought we were headed for Iran!

In all, including the journey downriver, that fish, estimated at 1,750 lb (800 kg), had pulled the three of us and our boat more than 8 miles (12 km) in just under six hours!

▶ ONE THAT DIDN'T GET AWAY
The size of this 330 lb (150 kg) sturgeon gives a rough idea of the enormity of our Caspian monster. Sturgeon can live for hours out of water, so this quick photograph of fish and captor did not place the fish at risk.

▶ FINAL SURGE
The final moments of battle with a sturgeon are often the most risky. When the sturgeon first feels the reeds on its stomach it turns to bolt back into deep water. The angler then needs to be prepared to give line or even run alongside the fish. He must do whatever he can to avoid pressure building up to the critical point of a breakage.

ILLEGAL STURGEON FISHING

In Russia and other countries passed through by the migrating sturgeon, wages are low and the temptation to poach a sturgeon is a hard one to resist. Sturgeon are protected by law throughout most of this region, but the proceeds from the meat of one fish can exceed a man's average annual income.

Then there is the caviar. If the fish caught is a ripe female, the result for the captor can be untold wealth. The risk of imprisonment is considered well worth taking.

Past generations of poachers once worked on their own or in small groups, but today organized crime is in the trade and is turning it into a sinister affair.

▲ THE MARKET
As long as people in the rich economies are willing to pay vast prices for tiny tins of caviar, there will always be a market. But would people dine on the eggs of sturgeon so happily if they knew of the killing that was involved?

◀ HOOKS OF DEATH
This line of evil hooks, tied to a length of thick rope, was found stretched across the Volga River and seized by police in southern Russia. The rig had been set up by a gang of poachers. They hoped a sturgeon would snag itself on one of the hooks, then panic and become fully entangled in the rig so that the poachers could take it on board their boat the next morning.

CHUB & ASP

CHUB AND ASP ARE BOTH middle-range, rather than big, predators, but lack of size is not a problem for they are bold, dashing, free-biting fish, capable of much cunning. It is no wonder that anglers across Europe choose to specialize in one or the other of these species. Chub are found throughout most of Europe, asp from the eastern Netherlands across to the Caspian Sea.

CHUB AND ASP are school fish and prefer to hunt and rest together. Both species will choose to rest under submerged trees or in weedbeds before setting out to look for food. Dusk and dawn are prime feeding times for both species. Chub and asp have very catholic diets that include many insects. It is, however, small fish that most interest the larger specimens of both species.

Of the two, asp are the more predatory and will travel long distances to track down schools of smaller fish. Both asp and chub are long and lean fish, capable of violent acceleration in order to secure their prey. Both possess tunnel-like mouths and fierce throat teeth that are capable of crushing the shells of crayfish with ease.

▲ WOODED LANDSCAPE
Find trees, and you are bound to find chub or asp! They love the shelter that trees give them. Roots may be exposed underwater, providing hiding places. Overhead, a steady supply of terrestrial insects, such as lacewings, bugs, and flies, is blown by the wind from the foliage onto the water surface.

CHUB AND ASP HABITAT

Chub and asp are usually regarded as river fish, but both make the transition to still waters with great success. Both species are adept at using all the "features" of a piece of water, lying in pools, behind boulders, under logs, or in the vicinity of a drop-off (change in depth). And yet they will also hunt in shallow, fast-flowing water where small fry can be caught.

Both species are territorial fish – much of their behavior is based on occupying and defending an individual territory – but they will also travel many miles both to spawn and in search of food.

CHUB

Chub have appetites as large as their mouths! I remember once feeding 1 lb (0.45 kg) of cheese to a single 4 lb (1.8 kg) chub! It ate the lot and came back for a few slices of bread! I often wonder if that chub weighed 5 lb (2.25 kg) as a result of its gluttony! It does not matter how cloudy the water is either – the chub just keep feeding.

CHUB *Leuciscus cephalus*
APPROXIMATE GUIDE TO WEIGHTS
AVERAGE 4 – 6 lb (1.8 – 2.7 kg)
TROPHY 5 – 6 lb (2.3 – 2.7 kg)
RECORD 8 lb (3.6 kg)

▲ SMALL RIVERS
This stretch of a small lowland river contains a perfect chub hole, shown in the foreground. There is deep water under the tree, and the current is just a little slacker there. Ideal!

▲ UNDER BRIDGES
Chub and asp love to lie under bridges: as the river squeezes itself between the supports, the current speeds up, gouging out a deep pool beneath. The pool is an ideal ambush point for catching the many small fish that pass by, swimming both upstream and downstream.

BIG MOUTH
Mouth is shaped like a tunnel and opens up to a vast width to take in slugs, caterpillars, crayfish, and small fish.

LARGE EYE
Large, brassy eye is an important aid to hunting and makes it possible for the chub to hunt at night and in murky water.

Pectoral fin

ASP

Asp look like chub but grow bigger and are even more savage in their attacks on small fish. The mouth opens just as wide as a chub's, but the lower jaw has a grooved tip that fits into a notch in the upper one. The distribution of asp extends north into Scandinavia and south through central and eastern Europe to the Caspian Sea. In the Volga Delta, asp grow huge, feasting on the abundant food supplies. There, in the maze of drains and canals, very large asp harry small pike and catfish. Asp, like chub, spawn in the spring in clean, fast-running water. Lake populations will not succeed without rivers flowing into or out of the lake.

INJURED TAIL
This very large asp from the Volga Delta has been attacked by a large fish — a pike, catfish, or sturgeon, resulting in injuries to the tail.

ANAL FIN
Anal fin is particularly large. The underside of the body is protected by a sharp ridge known as a keel.

ASP
Aspius aspius
APPROXIMATE GUIDE TO WEIGHTS
AVERAGE 4 – 6 lb (1.8 – 2.7 kg)
TROPHY 8 lb (3.6 kg)
RECORD 25 lb (11.3 kg) OR MORE

◀ **HUGE MOUTH**
This really is the head of a hunter: look at the big, staring eye and that great, hinged mouth — capable of taking prey of at least a fifth the asp's own weight.

ASP HABITAT

Asp are found in all water types, but some of the biggest fish almost certainly live in the huge European rivers, in reaches where food stocks are at their highest. Asp and small fish go inexorably together, and the asp cannot grow big without ready stocks of school fish to feast upon. Clear water is an advantage to them in their hunting.

◀ **EASTERN ASP**
Big rivers like the Volga, pictured here downstream from Astrakhan, provide the perfect environment for large asp. The rivers are rich in nutrients and hold limitless stocks of 3–5 in (8–12 cm) prey fish, ideal fodder for the roving asp schools.

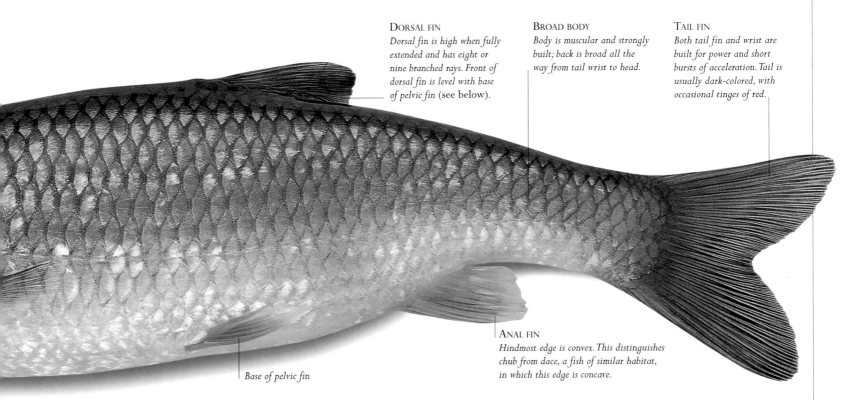

DORSAL FIN
Dorsal fin is high when fully extended and has eight or nine branched rays. Front of dorsal fin is level with base of pelvic fin (see below).

BROAD BODY
Body is muscular and strongly built; back is broad all the way from tail wrist to head.

TAIL FIN
Both tail fin and wrist are built for power and short bursts of acceleration. Tail is usually dark-colored, with occasional tinges of red.

ANAL FIN
Hindmost edge is convex. This distinguishes chub from dace, a fish of similar habitat, in which this edge is concave.

Base of pelvic fin

FISHING FOR CHUB

CHUB WILL FEED HAPPILY on any type of bait anywhere in the water. Big baits or small baits, fast water or slow, surface or bottom – none of it matters to a school of hungry chub. These are fish with large eyes, big mouths, and appetites to match. Despite this, chub can show great wariness of any bait that does not behave naturally. Here, together with an illustration of the site, are photographs of how I caught a chub in the River Wye in Herefordshire, England. It was a fine summer's day, and I fished from just before dawn.

▲ SIGHT OF THE FISH
A careful approach into the wooded area reveals a huge school of chub milling around beneath the fallen branches. The day is warm, the chub are near the surface, and a floating bait is called for.

CONFLUENCE ZONE
I decided to fish on the confluence of the main river and a small side stream. I like this area because small prey fish drift from the stream into the main flow, attracting chub. The trees downstream from the confluence also attract chub because a supply of insects, such as moths and caterpillars, drops from the foliage.

6–7 ft
(1.8–2.1 m)

I place my loose bread here to drift downstream

Open meadow

4–5 ft
(1.2–1.5 m)

Sloping bank

BREAD ON THE WATER

I aim my cast toward drifting bread

4–5 ft
(1.2–1.5 m)

6–7 ft
(1.8–2.1 m)

Line falls straight
to desired spot

Chub swimming against flow
and near to shelter of trees

1 THROWING OUT THE GROUNDBAIT
I have decided to use a large white unsliced loaf as bait for this job. Pieces about the size of a matchbox are broken off, and you see me throwing them out into the main current with the intention that they will be carried downstream toward the fish that are sheltering under the trees.

2 THANK YOU VERY MUCH
The first of the pieces of bread are taken by a good fish of a couple of pounds or so, and it won't be long before the rest follow suit. Chub are always alert to a welcome food source, and soon the pieces of fluffy bread and crust are being attacked with vigor.

3 SCANNING THE SURFACE
All the chub have now emerged from the shelter of the trees and are swimming close to the surface of the water, looking out for more tidbits. This is now the perfect time to drift

HOOKING THE CHUB

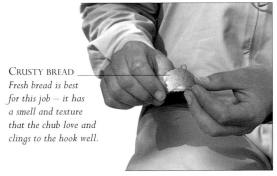

CRUSTY BREAD
*Fresh bread is best
for this job — it has
a smell and texture
that the chub love and
clings to the hook well.*

1 PREPARING THE BAIT
*Push the hook through the crust so that the point
and bend emerge. Wrap a piece of your line around the
crust and under the bend. Then pull the bread back
over the point of the hook so it is buried in the bread.*

MENDING THE LINE
*I cast my bait near the trees, then "mend"
the line (straighten loops so that the line
lies direct from rod tip to hook).*

2 CASTING FOR MY FISH
*A gentle underhand swing is needed to lob the
crusts of bread toward the bank of the main river where
the chub hang. I use my rod to straighten loops in the
line, because the current can catch loops and move line
and bait suspiciously — anything unnatural will be
noticed immediately by the fish.*

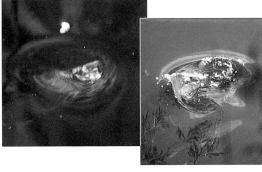

3 A CHUB FOOLED
*A good-sized chub moves in and noses the bread
momentarily (left). A second fish approaches, and this
competition prompts the first to suck in the bait and
drop down (right) to chew and swallow it — hooked!*

A QUICK, CLEAN STRIKE
*The line moves as a fish bites: I
jerk the rod briskly, fixing the
hook in the fish's mouth.*

4 PLAYING MY FISH
*As soon as the line draws tight, I strike firmly
and far back to pick up any loose line. The next job
is to draw the fish quickly upstream away from the
rest of the school to avoid scaring them. This is done
by leaning the rod outward to guide the fish away
from the bank.*

LANDING AND RELEASE

1 SLID TO THE SHORE
*This is a very nice fish but not
one that I need to take from the water,
either for a photograph or to weigh it.
Therefore, I simply slide the chub into
the shallows next to the spot where I
am kneeling, and the captured fish
rests quite still.*

2 CAREFULLY UNHOOKING
*With a barbless hook and forceps,
it is an easy job to put down the rod,
bend over the fish, and slip the point
out of the mouth. Make sure your hands
are wet for this job so that there is no
possibility of any damage to the fish.*

3 AND A QUICK "GOOD-BYE"
*I lift the chub to look for any
distinguishing marks that I might
recognize if I were to catch it again in
the future. The wound of a heron's beak,
for example, can help you identify a
fish. Then back into the water it goes.*

FISHING FOR ASP

IT IS NOT AT ALL SURPRISING that asp are such a popular quarry throughout so much of Europe. They fight well, can be caught by a wide variety of methods, and you will not need specialized tackle.

Good specimens of asp are found in still water as well as in rivers, so learn to hunt the schools on large and small lakes alike.

Asp fishing is always exciting. The angler becomes very much the hunter, looking for the heavy swirls and splashes that indicate an asp school harrying smaller fish. Once these have been sighted, everything is pell-mell haste to cast in a lure or other bait before the highly mobile school is on its way again.

▲ THE WILD WATER
Asp work all types of water, from the slow to the quick. More so than any other predatory fish, asp seem to be prepared to move into very rapid water indeed in their ruthless search for prey.

▲ WORKING THE FEATURES
Search for asp — individuals or schools — behind rocks, around fallen trees, or deep in reedbeds. They are attracted to these spots, where the water is a little more serene and allows them some respite from the current.

PLAY ON AGGRESSION

A school of hunting asp cannot be mistaken for one of any other predator. Above all they attack in numbers, as do perch, but they are much more aggressive than perch and attack with such fury that smaller fish will beach themselves in their efforts to escape.

Naturally, when the feeding frenzy is on, everything is in the angler's favor, providing that he or she can get the right lure or other bait into the killing zone at the right time. If there is a problem with asp fishing, it is that everything needs to come right at once, and apart from those isolated opportunities you may find yourself fishing barren water for most of the day. So, the moral is to keep your eyes open, scan the surface, and watch out for the volcanic eruptions that spell asp feeding time.

CHUBLIKE
Chub and asp seem similar, but the asp is a heavier, bigger-headed fish.

▲ SURFACE LURES
When asp are feeding on the surface, nothing can beat a surface-popping lure skittered in among the school. Work the lure energetically, sending out splashes and vibrations all around.

▲ MIDWATER ATTACK
There are times, however, when the asp feed more circumspectly lower down in the water, especially in deep pools. It is on occasions like this that a bigger lure, worked close to weed or snags, produces unmissable takes.

▲ A BOTTOM BAIT
The very biggest asp often choose not to hunt too energetically but cruise the depths of pools looking for easy prey. A natural bottom bait of dead minnows, slugs, or worms attracts massive fish.

◄ HEAD OF A HUNTER
When fully open, the mouth is extraordinarily wide. The jaws are vise-like — perfect for both grabbing and holding smaller fish. The big eye enables the asp to pick out the movements of prey fish clearly.

ASP FISHING ON LAKES

When you are fishing on a lake, the key to successful asp hunting is mobility, so your first consideration is to arrange to have the use of a reliable boat. A rowboat will do, but many anglers prefer an outboard motor.

Asp schools spend most of their lives on the move, so the asp hunter needs to recognize this and follow them. The thrashing of an asp school at the surface is the best sign to look for, and binoculars will help you spot this.

◀ A LIVELY CATCH
This fine asp weighed 8 lb 12 oz (4 kg), and it fought for 10 minutes on moderately heavy gear. A big asp just bristles with vitality and aggression. Once returned, a fish like this will simply explode into life and rejoin its school.

▲ COVERING THE WATER
These asp anglers make it their practice to search all areas of the water, sometimes letting their boat drift and sometimes driving under power from one spot to another. Any sight of asp feeding on the surface, then the engine will be gunned into life and the pursuit will be on!

ASP FISHING ON RIVERS

Most asp rivers shout out the vital features. You are looking for anywhere that is going to harbor prey fish, and that is why slacks, eddies, and the still water under trees and among reed stems are favored.

THE MARGIN
Asp will often be found hunting close to the bank if there is weed or an overhanging tree to attract prey.

EXTENSIVE SHALLOWS
Asp will prowl the shallows, especially at dawn, hunting for small fish.

MIDRIVER WEED
Asp often make use of weedbeds in midriver: these provide hiding places and shelter from the current.

ALONGSIDE LILIES
Lilybeds often harbor the schools of small fish that asp depend on for food.

GAP IN THE LILIES
Look for holes in the lilybeds, and cast your lure or bait in these. Be prepared to play the fish hard to stop it from tangling in the stems.

TRAILING BRANCHES
Asp will often hang around submerged branches waiting for prey fish to pass.

▶ ASP HOT SPOTS
This picture shows a small river with a slow-to-medium speed current, well suited to asp. The current flows from left to right, with deeper water close to the river's right bank. Dotted lines show casts aimed at the hot spots, each marked with an x. If you have no luck at the hot spot, a well-chosen plug may attract asp at any point along the line of your retrieve.

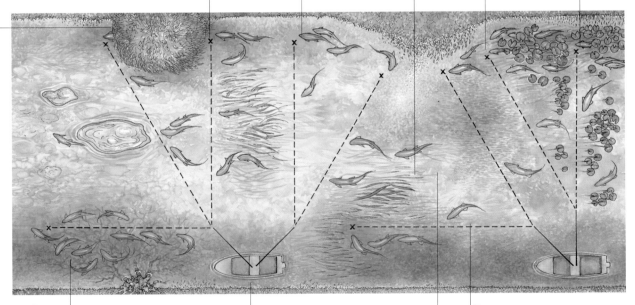

CURRENT

WIND DIRECTION

DEEP WATER
Deep holes will attract the biggest asp, especially with the overhead cover provided here by a tangle of roots.

DROP-OFF
The boat is placed over a "drop-off" — a sudden drop from shallow to deep water, which will attract the asp.

WIND-RUFFLED WATER
A slight chop on the water can stir sediment in the shallows and create ideal hunting conditions.

EDGE OF THE WEEDS
Try working your lure along the edge of weedbeds where hungry asp may be hunting.

ZANDER & WALLEYE

THE ZANDER, WHICH IS NATIVE to Europe, and its North American relative the walleye are typical medium-sized predatory fish. Both species normally attain weights of 2–10 lb (1–5 kg). The zander, however, will grow much bigger when conditions are favorable, and in large waters with plenty of prey and little pollution, examples of up to 20 lb (9 kg) can be found.

ARGUMENT HAS RAGED for years as to the wisdom of introducing zander to waters where they are not naturally present. Sharp declines in prey fish, such as roach, bream, or perch, have occurred in waters newly stocked with zander. This has been taken as proof that zander destroy prey fish schools. Anglers have argued that since the schools are the food of sport fish, introducing zander must be permanently harmful to sport fishing.

Certainly, when initially stocked in a water, zander do multiply quickly and make large inroads into the stock of prey fish. Soon, however, scarcity of prey causes the zander themselves to decline. This gives the prey fish a chance to grow in numbers. The cycle is repeated until a balance is achieved between predators and prey.

▲ REEDY BAY
Zander choose shallow, warm, reedy bays in which to lay their eggs. The fish use stems of standing reeds as part of the structure of their nests. Bays like this are also a magnet for prey fish, providing easy food after the stress of spawning.

◀ LARGE LAKES
Both zander and walleye prefer cooler water, so they frequent large, deep lakes that contain cool water during the heat of summer. They also favor northerly latitudes: walleye are found as far north as Labrador in Canada; zander are common in Scandinavia.

ZANDER

Zander (also known as pike-perch) occur in slowly flowing rivers and canals and food-rich lakes across Europe, from England to the Baltic Sea and far into Scandinavia.

Local forms (subspecies) of the zander include the sea pike-perch, which can spawn in both fresh and salt water, and the Volga pike-perch.

When spawning, the male zander courts the female by circling around her for 20 minutes before they join together and lay the eggs over a period of 10–15 minutes. The parent fish stay together as a pair and cooperate in rearing the young.

ZANDER
Stizostedion lucioperca
APPROXIMATE GUIDE TO WEIGHTS
AVERAGE 6–8 lb (2.7–3.6 kg)
TROPHY 10 lb (4.5 kg)
RECORD 25 lb (11.3 kg)

EYE
Large eyes enable zander to hunt at night. Eye position allows good view above and in front.

IRIDESCENT SCALES
Scales of zander living in clear water reflect a range of different colors depending on the angle of view.

TEETH
Teeth are sharp enough to grip prey fish firmly. Two particularly strong teeth are located at the front of each jaw.

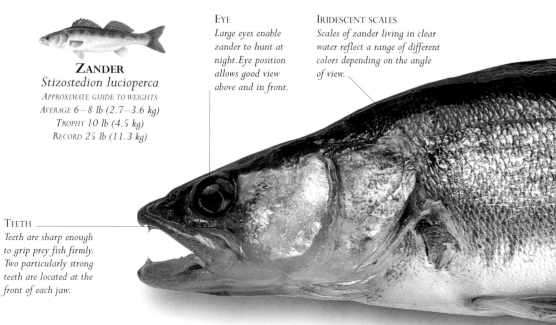

WALLEYE

The walleye's strikingly large eyes have a milky, almost opaque appearance. When a light is shined on a walleye at night, its eyes glow like those of a cat – hence the fish's American nickname, "old nobble-eye."

The large eyes are a clue to the walleye's way of feeding: it hunts by twilight and at night, avoiding bright sunlight.

In past times, the walleye occurred only in Canada and the northern United States, but the practice of stocking fishing waters with walleye has extended its range to Tennessee, Mississippi, and even New Mexico.

WALLEYE
Stizostedion vitreum
APPROXIMATE GUIDE TO WEIGHTS
AVERAGE 2–5 lb (0.9–2.3 kg)
TROPHY 8 lb (3.6 kg)
RECORD 20 lb (9 kg)

FIRST DORSAL FIN
Fin is supported by hard, sharp spines and is only faintly spotted.

SECOND DORSAL FIN
Fin is supported by soft rays, not spines; length is variable; second dorsal is not connected to first dorsal.

TAIL
Walleye derives its power and speed from the thrust of its large tail.

FAVORITE FOODS

Very young zander and walleye feed on tiny crustaceans, such as copepods or freshwater shrimp. Larger young feed on midge larvae and mayfly nymphs. As they grow to adult size, the young predators start to live on a fish diet, first taking fry, then adult fish. Both species are cannibalistic, though to a lesser extent than perch and pike.

Both zander and walleye hunt by active pursuit. They feed at all times of night but most intensively at dawn and dusk, aided by their large eyes, which have a special light-reflecting layer behind the retina.

▲ INJURED FISH
When attacking a school of prey fish, the predators pick off the weak ones first. Some of these are fish that have been injured in an earlier attack.

▲ SCHOOL FISH
Zander always hunt schooling fish. Unlike most of their prey, perch are swallowed headfirst, perhaps to avoid injury from the dorsal spines (see p. 63).

▲ NUTRITIOUS FRY
Young zander and walleye are fry-feeders. They often form groups that cooperate to drive fry into the shallows, where there is less chance of escape.

FIRST DORSAL FIN
Fin is supported by hard, sharp spines (lowered in this picture).

SECOND DORSAL FIN
Fin is supported by soft rays, not spines, and is not connected to first dorsal.

TAIL WRIST
Tail wrist (this can also be called the tail stock or tail stem) is long and slender.

TAIL
Thrust from large and powerful tail gives zander speed when chasing prey.

FISHING FOR ZANDER & WALLEYE

WHOEVER THINKS that zander and walleye are easy won't catch many of them! It is true that big schools of small fish can behave in suicidal fashion, getting themselves caught in a moment; but larger specimens of both species are very difficult indeed and learn to escape the angler amazingly quickly.

Adult fish soon learn to pick at baits very gingerly. They might even begin to change their feeding times. If there is a lot of angling pressure on a lake or river during the day, then nighttime feeding soon becomes the norm. The successful zander and walleye angler just cannot afford to relax but instead must keep changing tactics as soon as results begin to look a bit sparse.

The zander or walleye angler needs to know the water as well as the fish. It is essential to look for boulders, humps of mud, sandbars, hollows in the bed, weed beds, mouths of streams, or sluice gates – anything that gives "character" to a particular place in the water could be a hideout for a predatory fish.

SHARP TEETH
The sharp teeth of the zander can cut nylon, so use a trace (final section of line) made of light wire.

▲ **SINK AND DRAW**
Deadbait is tremendously effective for zander and walleye. Most commonly it is fished on the bottom, but here it is being twitched a yard or so upward and then allowed to fall back – it usually works.

◄ **CAUGHT ON A HAND LINE**
Zander are a favorite sport fish all around the Northern Hemisphere. This particular fish was caught by a Russian fisherman who was fishing with a hand line. His bait was a very small silver spoon, which he jigged up and down just off the bottom (see below).

BOTTOM TROLLING

Zander and walleye do not always hug the bottom, but the serious angler will "troll" (drag) a lure across the bed to look for the bigger specimens – they tend to lie on or close to the bed. A good way to do this is by "jigging" your lure up and down as you troll.

This should be done slowly. Advance your lure over the bed in short hops of approximately 6 in (15 cm). The up-and-down motion of the lure is irresistible to the fish, especially if the lure kicks up puffs of silt now and then as it lands on the bottom. The fish will see these puffs from a distance and be attracted to the area you are trolling.

▲ **A DEEP DIVER**
This deep-diving lure is ideal for bottom trolling. The beauty of trolling is that it often makes light work of locating the fish.

▼ **TYPICAL HABITAT**
This profile of a zander or walleye location shows where the fish lie. It is imperative that your lure passes close by the fish, following every contour of the bottom.

SURFACE ATTACK
A zander that is hunting for prey will sometimes chase a lure to the surface.

ROD POSITION
Work the rod close to the surface of the water and twitch it to give the lure a lifelike appearance.

OVERHANG
Both zander and walleye like to hang beneath overhead cover. Here they watch for prey and wait for the best moment to pounce.

ROCK FACE
A "drop-off" or sudden change in depth is a good place to find fish. Suspicious fish often follow a lure some distance before attacking it.

PERFECT LIE
This is a perfect big fish lie, deep below the surface and under plenty of root cover. Be sure to bring your lure past this spot!

LONG-DISTANCE TROLLING

Often zander or walleye can be scattered all around a lake or stretch of river. If so, a quick way to locate them is to troll a plug *(see p. 172)* across wide areas of the water. Favorite plugs are Wiggle Warts, Fat Wraps, Mann's Hot-n-tots, Long A's, and Shad Rap. Use any plug that goes down deep, disturbs the water, and looks like a meal!

Do not expect strong tugs when fish take the plug; it pays to hold the rod when trolling so that you can feel any slight movement. If you feel anything, strike quickly and firmly. Both species are notorious for ejecting plugs the instant their suspicions are aroused.

Try trolling with a dead fish: deadbait seems to tempt zander and walleye to hang on longer, giving you time to strike.

▲ HARVEST THE SHALLOWS
Both zander and walleye will occasionally come into the shallows, hunting for small fish. When they do, using a small surface plug such as this would almost certainly reap a harvest.

TREE COVER
Both zander and walleye will investigate areas beneath dead branches and other overhead cover.

SURFACE LURES
A surface popper or chugger (see p. 61) will work effectively over the shallows.

BOAT FISHING
A boat gives you mobility and enables you to get close to snags where fish might be lying.

▲ FISH THE SURFACE
Always scan shallow areas for any sign of fish activity. Do not bring the boat too close up to the fish, for both zander and walleye are sensitive species and your boat could easily disturb them.

◄ SURFACE-CAUGHT ZANDER
This fish was caught in bright daylight, in midmorning when it was hunting minnows among brushwood. A plug that made a splash proved irresistible.

BEST AT NIGHT

Night fishing is particularly productive if a lot of angling pressure has affected the lake or river, or if the water is so clear that the fish can see daytime anglers.

You will find that the fish change the times at which they feed. Sometimes, especially in autumn and spring, the first and last hours of darkness are the best. However, there will be other occasions, often in winter, when the midnight hour is the most rewarding. There are no rules about this – you must learn how the fish are behaving locally.

Deadbaiting is the simplest night method, but make sure that your rig will be sensitive enough to indicate very gentle bites. Even at night, zander or walleye will pick up a bait, reject it, and be gone before you even suspect that they were there.

▲ A NOCTURNAL FEEDER
This chunky Scandinavian zander was caught two hours after darkness on a particularly hard-fished water where daylight fishing had proved useless.

◄ DEADBAIT SUCCESS
This fish was caught as dusk was falling. The angler used deadbait, which he presented just above the bottom. Notice the float: nothing gives a swifter indication of a zander bite. Strike quickly at the first sign of a bite, or the fish may either swallow the bait or spit it out.

CATCHING GAME FISH

THE WORLD OF THE FLY FISHERMAN IS A varied one. Salmon, trout, grayling, and char inhabit the most blissful waters of the world – singing rivers and lakes that mirror forests, snow-clad mountains, and, at times, blue skies. Fish that live in crystal waters demand the very highest of angling standards. You will not hook that steelhead unless your approach is as quiet as a heron. That brown trout will be down among the weeds in a second, unless your presentation is pretty well perfect. Even when not fishing, the angler can be tying flies for the next season, sitting perhaps by the fireplace, lost in dreams of springtime.

EMERGENCY IN ALASKA
A humpback salmon races home in a stream near Glacier Bay. Its eye seems to express awareness of the danger it is passing through: most of its body is out of the water, and bears could be watching!

SALMON

NEARLY ALL SALMON ARE ANADROMOUS – they exploit the safety of mountain streams for breeding sites and the rich food supplies of the sea for growth. To live like this, they must make sacrifices: they eat little or nothing on their spawning run up the rivers; after spawning, nearly all of them die. Six species of salmon live in the Pacific *(see p. 90)*, just one in the Atlantic.

ATLANTIC SALMON

THE SPIRIT OF THE ATLANTIC salmon is truly unquenchable, and if any fish deserved the epithet "Brave Heart," then this is it. Nothing will stop the salmon on its run from the sea: it endures droughts, fights floods, and, in a triumphant arc of silver, jumps waterfalls that seem completely unscalable.

Where has a salmon been in the Atlantic? How did it find its way back? Why are prize specimens so often male, when with most species of fish they are female? For anglers, biologists, and nature watchers alike, mystery surrounds this majestic traveler.

▲ THE RIVER TAY
One of the world's premier salmon runs is the River Tay in Scotland. This river is home to huge salmon that forge their way upstream to the headwaters. There, 3,300 feet above sea level, spawning takes place in late autumn and winter.

◄ SPAWNING WATERS
Salmon redds are found in the tiniest of tributaries, often in water barely deep enough to cover the backs of big fish. This environment is freer than most from egg predators, which include trout and waterside birds such as dippers.

ANATOMY

Straight from the sea, a mature Atlantic salmon is a combination of beauty and power. Its silver sides ripple with strong muscles. Its fins are large and capable of propelling the salmon's stream-lined body over almost any obstacle. The fish has fat reserves sufficient to keep it alive in fresh water for many months, still fit and able to perform the final rites of spawning.

TEETH
Sharp teeth are used for hunting at sea, where the salmon feeds on herring, mackerel, and even small codling (young cod).

GILL COVER
Four or fewer spots on gill cover identify Atlantic salmon. Sea trout, which can be confused with salmon, usually have more spots on gill cover.

COLORATION
Salmon that are freshly run from the sea have silver sides. These become redder after a period in fresh water.

ATLANTIC SALMON *Salmo salar*
APPROXIMATE GUIDE TO WEIGHTS
AVERAGE 8–12 lb (3.6–5.4 kg)
TROPHY 20 lb (9 kg)
RECORD 70 lb (32 kg)

Pectoral fin

LIFE CYCLE

The eggs hatch, releasing alevins (salmon larvae), which become parr (juvenile fish) within a few months. At around two years old, parr become smolts, which are silvery young fish, 6–8 in (15–20 cm) in length. Thse migrate to sea, where they grow into salmon and live for up to four years. The salmon then return to the redds *(see right)* and spawn. Spawned salmon, known as kelts, live for no more than a few weeks, except for a tiny proportion. These fish resume their migration and may survive to spawn again.

▲ SALMON KYPE
The great kype (jaw) of the adult cock (male) salmon is an awe-inspiring weapon. The cock needs to defend his redd against all comers, and the huge kype, even if not very effective in a fight, looks terrifying.

▲ PREPARING THE REDD
Females arrive first on the spawning grounds and use their strong tails to cut troughs in the gravel. They lay their eggs in the troughs while the male fish fertilize them. The fish sweep gravel back over the vulnerable, fertilized eggs to provide some protection.

◄ THE SPAWN HATCHES
The fertilized eggs lie in the gravel for the rest of the winter. The time at which they hatch depends largely on the temperature. Very often two to three months will elapse before the alevins begin to appear in the water.

DORSAL FIN
To conserve wild stocks, a salmon from a farm was used for this photograph; a wild fish would have a larger fin (see illustration, far left).

ADIPOSE FIN
Only fish of the salmon family have an adipose fin. Little is known about any evolutionary advantage it may bring to the fish.

TAIL
Tail fin produces thrust for long-distance swimming. Specimen shown here is a farmed salmon and has lost parts of its tail fin, probably because of living in confined quarters.

ANAL FIN
Anal, dorsal, tail, and adipose fins are single fins, as opposed to the paired pectoral and pelvic fins on the underside of body.

Pelvic fin

PACIFIC SALMON

SIX SPECIES OF SALMON live in the northern Pacific Ocean, spawning in rivers in Asia and North America. Five species – chinook, humpback, coho, chum, and sockeye *(shown in detail on p. 92)* – occur on both sides of the Pacific. They are found on the west coast of North America, from California to northern Alaska, and on eastern coasts of Asia, from northern Japan to the Arctic.

The sixth species is the masu or cherry salmon. This is a dashing sport fish, though smaller than the others and with a stockier body. It occurs on the Asian side of the ocean, spawning in the rivers of northeast Asia.

The six species are more closely related to one another, and to the rainbow trout and steelhead, than to the Atlantic salmon.

▲ SPECTACULAR HABITATS
Pacific salmon run up rivers into some of the most magnificent countryside in the world. An ideal salmon fishing trip is weeks long: you need time to acclimatize if you are not normally in this exciting environment.

▲ SPAWNING REACHES
Like Atlantic salmon, Pacific salmon seek out shallow, fast-flowing, well-oxygenated water in which to spawn. Riverbed gravels and running water make a relatively safe, healthy environment for the eggs until hatching.

CHINOOK SALMON

The largest of all salmon, let alone those of the Pacific, this species is also known as the king salmon. The rod-caught record is over 80 lb (36 kg), and the net-caught record is held by a mighty specimen of 126 lb (57 kg). The chinook is a great traveler, and although its spawning runs can be modest, there are some that cover vast distances.

Chinook spawn in water up to 9 ft (3 m) deep. The female is the nest-builder, and she will drive off competing females that invade the area of her redd. Once satisfied with her redd, she moves into it with at least one and sometimes several males. She lays 9–26 lb (4–12 kg) of eggs, which the males fertilize immediately. As the old fish die, the eggs begin their life and hatch in 7–12 weeks. The alevins *(see p. 89)* become parr within a few months and, at two years, smolts, which migrate to sea. There they grow into salmon and can double their weight in a summer.

HUMPBACK SALMON

The humpback (humpy) or pink salmon is the smallest of the Pacific salmon. The males develop a hump just behind their head as spawning time approaches . . . hence the obvious nickname *(see also pp. 86–87)*.

The distribution of humpback salmon in North America extends from California to Alaska, and the species is abundant farther south than other salmon. Humpbacks become mature at two years of age, when they average 3 lb (1.4 kg). Very occasionally, individuals attain weights in the region of 10 lb (4.5 kg).

Humpbacks are not long-distance migrants, for spawning takes place relatively low in the rivers, just above the level of the highest tide. They are the most numerous Pacific salmon and are therefore important commercially. As sport fish, however, they are unparalleled, and their small size is no disqualification to the angler who appreciates a fish capable of wholehearted and defiant resistance.

CHINOOK SALMON
Oncorhynchus tschawytscha
APPROXIMATE GUIDE TO WEIGHTS
AVERAGE 15 lb (6.8 kg); TROPHY 25–40 lb (11.3–18 kg); RECORD 126 lb (57 kg)

▲ A MAJESTIC HEAD
There are few more impressive sights in fresh water than the sight of a huge chinook pushing upriver on the way to its spawning grounds.

HUMPBACK SALMON
Oncorhynchus gorbuscha
APPROXIMATE GUIDE TO WEIGHTS
AVERAGE 3–5 lb (1.4–2.3 kg); TROPHY 8 lb (3.6 kg); RECORD 14 lb (6.4 kg)

▲ AT THE REDDS
Humpback salmon swarm up a river from the sea in vast numbers, jostling for space in the shallow headwaters where they make their redds (spawning sites).

COHO SALMON

Also known as the silver salmon, this is an aggressive and hard-fighting fish that is loved by all serious game anglers. It is the second largest of the Pacific salmon and can be distinguished from the largest, the chinook, by two features. First, the coho's gums are white, whereas the chinook's gums are black. Second, the coho has black spots on only the upper lobe of its tail, while the chinook has spots on both lobes.

Coho return from the sea to spawn during late summer and autumn, between July and November. The eggs are laid in winter and hatch out in spring or early summer. Coho salmon are relatively small when they arrive in the sea but grow rapidly once they have completed their downward migration, for they then indulge in a feast of herring, small fish known as needlefish, and crustaceans.

▶ COHO ON MIGRATION
Although not as numerous as humpback, coho run in large numbers at certain stages of their autumn run: a thrilling time for the angler in search of good sport.

COHO SALMON *Oncorhynchus kisutch*
APPROXIMATE GUIDE TO WEIGHTS
AVERAGE 8 lb (3.6 kg)
TROPHY 12–15 lb (5.4–6.8 kg)
RECORD 26 lb (11.8 kg)

CHUM SALMON

The chum salmon is also known as the "dog salmon," a reference to its flesh, which is not considered as palatable as that of other species. Indeed, in past times, trappers and native Americans once fed their dogs on chum. This nickname also refers to the large teeth the fish grow before spawning.

One reason why anglers value chum less highly is that it will not attack a lure or bait in as dramatic a fashion as a coho. That having been said, chum show great stamina and fight. Most weigh 7–10 lb (3–4.5 kg) but larger fish are caught, especially in nets.

Chum are capable of migrating very long distances, although most will travel less than 100 miles (160 km) to their spawning areas.

▶ FEARSOME WEAPONS
A mature chum displays its jaws as it passes: the teeth inside have grown large and strong in the last few weeks up to spawning time. Males like this can inflict vicious wounds on competitors for space on the redds.

CHUM SALMON *Oncorhynchus keta*
APPROXIMATE GUIDE TO WEIGHTS
AVERAGE 7–10 lb (3.2–4.5 kg)
TROPHY 12–15 lb (5.4–6.8 kg)
RECORD 27 lb (12.2 kg)

SALMON MIGRATION

THE FISH THAT HAVE FEASTED in the sea, some for a winter, some for as long as five years, now return to the rivers where they were born. Some salmon, including the sockeye (see right), die after spawning, making their ascent to the spawning grounds once and once only. Others, for example the Atlantic salmon (see p. 88), do not necessarily die at the spawning grounds but may live to migrate three or four times in their life.

For centuries mankind has marveled at how, after journeying far across the ocean, a salmon can find the river in which it hatched. Does this remarkable power of orientation have something to do with magnetic fields, the sense of smell, an instinct, or something else at which we cannot possibly guess?

For those interested in statistics, in the Yukon River of Alaska and Canada, king salmon that were tagged and tracked traveled 2,000 miles (3,200 km) in 60 days. A leap performed by Atlantics at Orrin Falls, Scotland, measured 12 ft (4 m).

On entering the rivers, salmon cease to feed. From now on they live on the fat built up when feeding in the ocean. Others benefit from this stored energy: bears, eagles, mink, otters, martens, wolves, and many more hunters await the salmon migration with all the eagerness of human anglers.

▲ A HAZARD AT EVERY TURN
The ascending salmon are a vital food source for many creatures in the river valley. For bears, approaching their time of hibernation at the time of the run, the protein-rich salmon are an essential food, and the big mammals have become adept at catching them.

JOURNEY OF THE SOCKEYE

Native Americans of the Pacific Northwest considered one salmon species so important for food and barter that they named it *Saukie,* meaning "Chief of Fishes." The spelling has changed, but the sense is still real. The sockeye remains a miracle of nature: its spawning runs provide us with one of the most spectacular aquatic sights in the world.

▲ NONBREEDING SOCKEYE
The salmon in the sea is a living bar of silver, streamlined and swift, profiting from a plentiful diet. The brown and red coloration begins to appear after a period in fresh water.

1 RUNNING HARD
Seemingly impassable waterfalls can be leapt by the schools of ascending salmon. The large, muscular fins, the powerful, pulsing body, and above all the indomitable spirit carries a salmon over virtually anything that nature can place in front of it. Only the barriers that man imposes can obstruct the run.

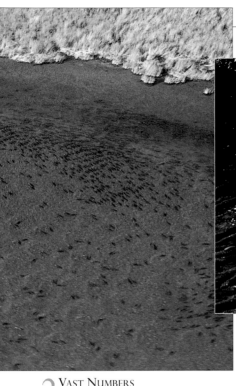

2 VAST NUMBERS
Sockeye swarm into the river system in huge schools. In 1980 the number of salmon entering the rivers at Bristol Bay, Alaska, was calculated at over 60 million!

3 THE RIVER RUNS RED
Sockeye generally return to spawn between June and October. They simply jam the rivers. Males are vividly colored, with a crimson body and a parrot green head.

4 AT THE SPAWNING GROUNDS
The female lays 2,500–4,000 eggs in a series of nests. The male fertilizes the eggs as they fall into the crevices between the stones.

6 THEIR WORK DONE
Sockeye die a few days after spawning, exhausted by what they have undergone. Their bodies flake apart and are eaten, or they decompose to enrich the river system.

5 THE MALE DEFENDS HIS REDD
Males compete for redds (spawning sites); a successful male chases away others. His hooked, toothed jaws make formidable weapons.

SALMON FISHING STRATEGIES

ONE OF THE many marvelous things about salmon is the number of ways in which you can catch them, despite the fact that they are not supposed to eat anything once they have left the sea!

True, there is little to beat the excitement of seeing a salmon turning in the water as it takes a fly fished in the surface layers; and the quick tightening of lightweight line is an electrifying sensation. On the other hand, a great deal of drama occurs in other modes of fishing, too. Have you ever watched an angler who is skilled in the use of spinners, bouncing, say, a Devon Minnow (see p. 175) off the river bottom, in raging water?

Bait fishers, too, bring amazing skills to bear in catching salmon. Shrimp anglers need to read the water like a book and must have fingers as sensitive as a catfish's whiskers. So, yes, let us agree that salmon fishing with the fly represents the art in its purest form; but never let us lose sight of the other strategies for catching this magnificent fish.

LURE FISHING

In early-season floods, use a big, silvery spoon (see p. 174). A spoon that is 3 in (8 cm) or 5–6 in (13–15 cm) long will fly like a bullet when cast. Work the spoon slow and deep in the water, barely reeling, letting the current do all the work. As the spoon thuds its way around the pool, its kicking action makes the tip of the rod nod steadily up and down.

If you decide on a spinner (also on p. 174), you will do well to fish a Devon Minnow in the same way – slow and deep, searching the riverbed. Devons of green, yellow, brown, and gold are the usual favorites, but if the water becomes very cold and clear try blue and silver. In cold, deep water in spring, use minnows about 3 in (8 cm) long, but as soon as the water begins to warm up, minnows of ¾–1 in (2–2.5 cm) are more common.

▲ QUICK WATER
In summer, especially, you are more likely to find a salmon in the shallower, faster-flowing water, where there is plenty of oxygen, than in the deep, slow-moving pools. Cast your lure across the current and barely retrieve it at all, merely letting it flutter in the flow.

▼ JUMPING SALMON
Playing a salmon is a thrill never to be forgotten. Be prepared for long, scorching runs and a high leap as the fish tries to throw the hooks clear. It is exciting with a fish of 10 lb (4.5 kg) or so like this one, but just imagine playing a 50 lb (22 kg) fish in a Norwegian torrent!

▲ THE KING
This must be one of the greatest photographs in the book: just look at this extraordinary testimony to the splendor of nature! We salute the accomplishments of the angler, too: well done indeed, Adela Batin, for landing such a magnificent creature.

BAIT FISHING

In my own experience, the most successful worm fishing has almost always been at dawn and dusk, possibly because the light hides me from what are always "spooky" fish.

It pays to vary the size and the number of worms on the hook, and my first approach would be to try two medium lobworms. Bounce these along through the water, just off the bottom and as close as possible in front of the fish, as skillfully as you can.

▲ WORMING FOR SALMON
Here I am inching my worm around the tail end of a pool where I have seen two handsome fish hanging. I can see the worm and I can see the mouth of the salmon, and the two are getting closer and closer.

SALMON LIES

Salmon look for good places to lie, just like other fish. As soon as they are in fresh water they begin to search out places in which to lie up and wait for floodwater to refresh and invigorate them for the journey upriver.

Salmon often lie in deep pools that contain boulders or snags, or under bridge buttresses. My favorite place for salmon is where a bridge collapsed years ago. Undercut banks attract salmon, as well as any water that is well sheltered by overhanging trees. Don't make the mistake of thinking that the salmon will always be out in midriver: they often press themselves hard to the bankside.

▲ UNDERCUT RIVER BANK
Here the current has undercut the bank and left an overhang of 6 ft (2 m) or so. When the water is low, as in this picture, salmon will ease themselves into dark crevices, often not moving for days. Then rain hits the highlands, and a fresh flow of water beckons the fish upriver.

◄ FALLEN TREE
Here is a hiding place, as well as shelter from the current, for a salmon. Often a salmon will spend time among other fish in such a lie, perhaps consorting with perch or barbel for a while before moving on to fulfill its destiny.

THE ANGLER'S CHESSBOARD

Bait fishing for salmon is like a chess game in that it matters how wisely you take myriad features of the water into account. You must know where your worm is at every moment, so that you can guide it around rocks, avoid snags, and ease it toward the fish.

A long rod can be useful for this, but don't expect to fish in a static way. You have to be mobile, moving up and down the bank, sometimes wading out into the river. Hold the line between the fingers of your non-casting hand and try to learn the difference between the nudge of a rock and the suck of a taking salmon. If in doubt, lick your fingertips: wet fingers are more sensitive than dry ones.

If you are wading, remember that fish often lie in very shallow water indeed, and you can frighten them if you are not careful. The best course is to scan the shallows very attentively through polarizing sunglasses *(see p. 181)* before you step into the water.

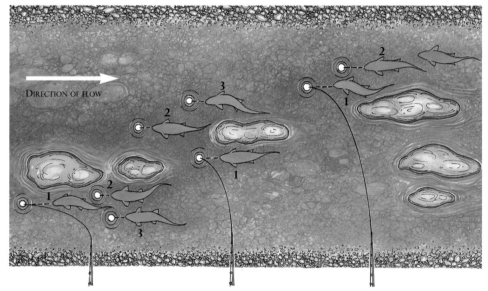

DIRECTION OF FLOW

▲ NEAR ZONE
The favorite lie is the one in the front position in the channel between the rock and the bank: big fish compete for lies like this, where the water is freshest. Lies farther back in the channel are still promising.

▲ MIDDLE ZONE
From the fish's point of view, the best lie is in the shelter of the rocks upriver. Big fish will take this spot, forcing others to move over into faster-flowing water. Lies 2 and 3 do have the advantage of deeper water.

▲ FAR ZONE
Two lies are worth considering: the one at the front, where the water is at its freshest, is the fish's favorite. The lie in the channel is hopeful, but fish any farther away than this are uncatchable at this distance.

FLY FISHING FOR SALMON

CASTING THE FLY is generally agreed to be the most important single factor in successful fly fishing for salmon. Start by teaching yourself if you wish, but you are unlikely to become proficient without professional instruction. There are advanced casts – the spey, half-spey, and roll casts, for example – but on these pages, for beginners, I demonstrate a simple overhead cast.

Next, you need to select the size, dressing, and color of fly *(see p. 176)*. Then the line . . . should it be floating or sinking? Finally, you must learn where to place the fly and how to handle it once it has reached the water.

HOW TO CAST

1 PREPARING TO CAST
Before I begin casting, notice how I hold the line slack in case of a sudden take. Especially when the water is low, any fish that bites must be given plenty of line. On a tight line, the shock will pull the hook out of the fish's mouth.

CASTING ON THE IRFON
The illustration and photographs below show how I cast my line for salmon on a stretch of the Irfon in Wales. It was on a warm day in August, when the river flow was low and water was being funneled into midstream by large boulders to either side.

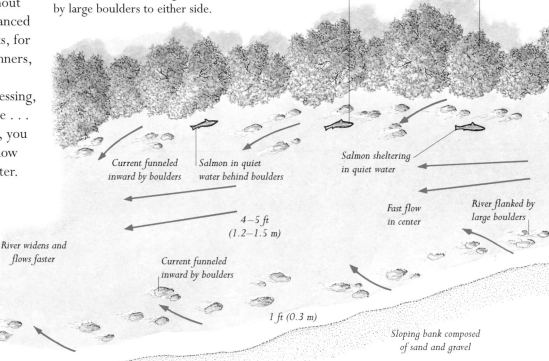

With low water in river, salmon keep to outer side of curve

Line of oak and ash trees overhangs bank

Current funneled inward by boulders

Salmon in quiet water behind boulders

Salmon sheltering in quiet water

River widens and flows faster

4–5 ft (1.2–1.5 m)

Fast flow in center

River flanked by large boulders

Current funneled inward by boulders

1 ft (0.3 m)

Sloping bank composed of sand and gravel

SMOOTHLY DOES IT
Never hurry your cast. Do everything as smoothly as possible so that you do not alert the fish.

TIMING
Timing is everything in fly casting, and with sufficient practice you will find your own rhythm.

2 LIFTING OFF
I lift the rod slowly at first to overcome the resistance that the line meets from the water's surface. Once the line is clear of the surface, I lift it with increasing momentum into the air.

3 SWEEPING BACK
Now the rod moves quickly toward the vertical, and the line flies upward and backward. Just watch out for that flying fly, especially in a high wind that might blow it dangerously close to you. Glasses with polarizing lenses will enable you to see both line and hook.

4 THE BACK CAST
The rod has now moved back to the "one o'clock" position, and the line is flying straight behind me. I pause briefly to make certain that the line is fully extended before bringing the rod forward again.

◄ SCHOOL ON THE MOVE
It can be a good sign if the salmon are moving, or at least swimming in the surface layers. This may mean that the fish are alert and ready to take a fly.

SALMON FLIES: A WIDE CHOICE

Salmon flies have been tied for over 250 years in many countries by many highly skilled fishermen, resulting in a bewildering variety of designs. The size, color, and weight of the fly are what matters. As a broad guideline, you need to use a big fly when the river is full, and a light one in clear, low water. If in doubt, local guides (gillies in Scotland) will advise.

▲ A COLDWATER FLY
This is a tube fly known as the Willie Gunn. Its yellow, red, and black bucktail hairs are tied around a piece of metal tubing. The tubing is designed to sink the fly.

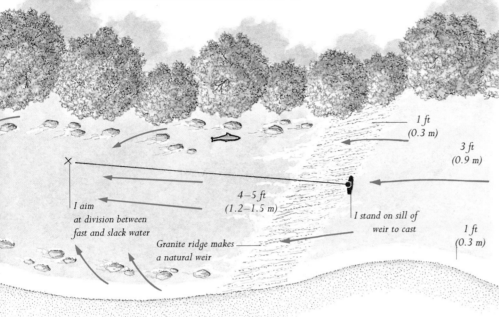

1 ft
(0.3 m)

3 ft
(0.9 m)

I aim
at division between
fast and slack water

4–5 ft
(1.2–1.5 m)

I stand on sill of
weir to cast

Granite ridge makes
a natural weir

1 ft
(0.3 m)

▲ A WET FLY
A wet fly is any type of fly that sinks. Wet flies are often drawn across the current, and in this maneuver they have enticed many a salmon.

▲ A SUMMER FLY
This floating fly was first used for steelhead. With its vivid colors it stays visible to fish even if the river suddenly colors, as after a summer downpour.

POWER
Generally, providing there is no headwind, you should not need to strain your arms or body to cast.

THE LOOP
Ideally, your line should make a well-formed loop in the air directly overhead.

5 POWERING FORWARD
My back cast has loaded the rod with energy like a spring. Now I release that stored energy and force the line to fly back downstream. I am aiming my cast at a point about 3 ft (1m) above the water. If I do this accurately, this will allow the line to fall gently down to the surface.

6 LETTING THE LINE GO
After the cast, I follow the action through with my arms, shoulders, and upper body. By doing this I avoid spoiling a nice, smooth cast with a sharp jerk at the end. It works: the line settles gently onto the water with a minimum of splashing, and within seconds I'm fishing.

SPINNING FOR TAIMEN

THE TAIMEN, IN TIMES PAST, was the king of freshwater fish throughout northeastern Eurasia. Like other types of salmon it is a migrant, but it performs its run only within the rivers – it does not migrate to the sea. The taimen is one of the biggest salmon and is avidly hunted wherever it occurs, which has led to a serious decline in numbers.

Whole populations of taimen in Siberia and China have disappeared, and the last stronghold of this rare fish is in the rivers of northern Mongolia. The key to its survival is peace and quiet, for Mongolia has hardly changed for thousands of years. Taimen flourish in this forgotten land, and no one knows for sure how big they can grow in rivers that are still virgin.

LANDLOCKED SALMON

The taimen possesses great mystique in that it is one of Eurasia's two landlocked salmon species. The other is the huchen, a fish of the Danube basin, which lies between Germany and the Black Sea. During the 20th century, the huchen has suffered from overfishing and pollution and is now almost extinct. This is a shame, because the huchen, when able to feed freely in unspoiled conditions, attains weights in excess of 110 lb (50 kg).

▲ RIVER MIGRANTS
River migrants among the salmonids are the taimen, the huchen, a very few populations of Atlantic salmon (shown here), and some sockeye salmon. The taimen migrates up and down the rivers using shallow rapids to spawn and deep pools for overwintering. Its journey can cover hundreds of miles.

THE TAIMEN TRAIL

In the autumn of 1997 I led a group to Mongolia to fish the remote rivers in the northwest of that country. We arrived there after the rains of August and left before the onset of winter. The illustration and photographs here set the scene for one of several taimen sessions that took place in that time. This location is truly remote, in a mountainous landscape with fast-flowing rivers and valleys alternately barren and wooded. There is virtually no transportation infrastructure, and the local herdsmen move about by horse or camel. Visiting anglers need to think in terms of jeeps and small planes for their transportation needs and remember to take plenty of provisions with them in case unexpected snowfalls block their retreat.

THE TAIMEN POOL
My fellow angler Dave Wilson stood opposite a deep pool in which some very big taimen were waiting to see if a grayling would be washed toward them.

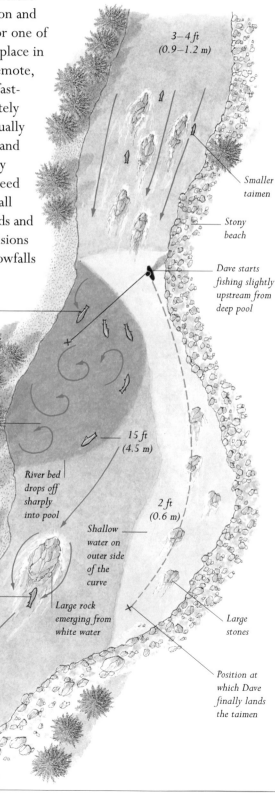

3–4 ft
(0.9–1.2 m)

Smaller taimen

Stony beach

Dave starts fishing slightly upstream from deep pool

Large taimen lurking in deep pool

Water spins rapidly around pool

15 ft
(4.5 m)

River bed drops off sharply into pool

Grassy clearing in between larch trees

2 ft
(0.6 m)

Shallow water on outer side of the curve

Large fish lying in shelter of rock

Large rock emerging from white water

Large stones

Larch trees

Position at which Dave finally lands the taimen

5 ft
(1.5 m)

THE ADVENTURE AHEAD

▲ MONGOLIA BECKONS

Mongolia is nearly as big as the whole of western Europe and most of it is arid land, with desert in the south. In the north, the landscape is greener, and the valleys that cut through the mountains are partly forested. Here the rivers are swift and full of fish.

▲ OUTDOOR LIFE

Anyone hoping to pursue taimen in the Mongolian wilderness must be prepared to lead a backpacker's existence. It is vital to take food, medicine, warm clothing, and everything else needed for survival. On this simple fire we prepared our meals and cooked bait in preparation for our pursuit of the taimen.

◀ TAIMEN LURES

We took dozens of different lures to try on the fish. Taimen will take any big spoon or plug that is fished slowly and enticingly. Silver is a good color for attracting taimen; green and blue lures also work well.

A BATTLE BEGINS

1 THE STRIKE

Dave started fishing from a point on the opposite bank from the taimen pool. When a taimen "hits" a lure, the angler certainly knows about it. Here, Dave was cranking his lure away from the deep water toward the shallows when this big fish hit in an explosion of water.

2 DRAGGED FROM THE DEPTHS

The fish immediately realized its mistake and powered off through the shallow water back to the deep pool from whence it had come. In there, down among the rocks, it held on tenaciously for nearly half an hour. During this time Dave waded downstream in the hope of finding a favorable angle from which to extricate the fish.

THE END GAME

1 WORTH IT ALL

Dave persevered until at last the big taimen lost its grip and surrendered to the tension of the line. Dave reeled in his catch across the expanse of shallow water and took hold of it with both arms. He had got what he came for. His grin tells the story.

2 CAREFUL RELEASE

The catch is a good specimen at 22 lb (10 kg), but nowhere near the maximum size. Dave holds it facing the current until it has regained its strength. It deserves care after so dramatic a battle.

RAINBOW TROUT & STEELHEAD

ON A WORLD SCALE, the rainbow trout is the most popular game fish. It is always athletic and elegant in appearance, its scales a veritable rainbow of colors. Steelhead is the seagoing form of the North American rainbow. Both fish are pugnacious in spirit, willing to attack anything that looks like food.

YOU CAN CERTAINLY call the rainbow trout an international fish. Settlers were impressed by the species when they discovered it in the American West, in such waters as the McCloud River of California. Stocks were taken to Britain and continental Europe, and thence to the rest of the world. By the year 1900, rainbows could be found in northern India and the Himalayas, South America, New Zealand, Australia, and in mountainous parts of Africa. Wherever it travels, the rainbow proves to be a good colonist, adapting itself to hostile conditions and alien food stocks. This explains its success on the world stage.

▲ A STILLWATER CLASSIC
Rainbows rejoice in clear, cool water that offers a variety of foodstuffs. This water is in South Island, New Zealand, home to many big fish. There could be no better place for a day's trolling.

◀ THE MIGHTY TONGARIRO
The Tongariro River runs into Lake Taupo in New Zealand's North Island. Its fame as a river for rainbow trout dates from the 1920s, when the celebrated angler Zane Gray made huge catches in its waters.

RAINBOW TROUT

Rainbows can utilize most food sources. Salmon eggs are one of their favorite foods, and rainbows also feed on the flesh of the dead adult salmon. Rainbows eat every type of aquatic insect but also harry fry and small fish. They attack mice and voles that venture into the water, and in Alaska they have even been known to feed on lemmings!

RED STRIPE
Rainbow trout can be recognized by the splash of vibrant red on their gill covers. The color extends down the flanks as far as the tail root.

BODY SHAPE
Farmed fish like this are generally more portly than those found in the wild.

RAINBOW TROUT *Oncorhynchus mykiss*
APPROXIMATE GUIDE TO WEIGHTS
AVERAGE: EUROPE 1–2 lb (0.45–0.9 kg); US 2–4 lb (0.9–1.8 kg); NEW ZEALAND 6 lb (2.7 kg)
RECORD: EUROPE 30 lb (14 kg); US 50 lb (23 kg)

STEELHEAD

Steelhead are rainbow trout that migrate out to sea to feed and then return to fresh water to spawn. The steelhead gets its name from the steely blue tinge along its head and back. Another noticeable color difference is that the steelhead develops an iridescent pink stripe along both sides of its body before spawning time.

The steelhead is one of the most sought-after game fish, both for its cunning and for its extraordinary fighting ability, gained during its life in the sea.

STEELHEAD *Oncorhynchus mykiss*
APPROXIMATE GUIDE TO WEIGHTS
AVERAGE 6–10 lb (2.7–4.5 kg)
TROPHY 12–15 lb (5.4–6.8 kg)
RECORD 40 lb (18 kg)

▼ METALLIC COLORATION
A steelhead that has come straight from the sea is a living bar of silver, and it is only after a prolonged stay in fresh water that the metallic coloration gives way to the crimsons that are characteristic of the rainbow family.

STEELHEAD MIGRATION

The native range of the steelhead stretches from the Alaska Peninsula in the north down to the Malibu Creek in California. In very many of the rivers that feed this huge area, spawning runs from the sea occur during every month of the year.

After the eggs have hatched, steelhead spend the first two or three years feeding in their native rivers before undergoing what biologists call smoltification. This is a process that prepares them for a life in salt water and allows them to descend to the sea. After spending one to three years feeding in the oceans, the steelhead swarm the rivers on their way back to spawn.

Unlike Pacific salmon, steelhead often survive spawning; some repeat the whole migration and spawning cycle several times. Before dams were built on the Columbia River, steelhead migrated more than 1,400 miles (2,200 km) along its course, searching for exactly the right locations for their redds (*see p.93*).

LATERAL COLORS
Rainbow colors often extend along lateral line.

ADIPOSE FIN
This fin is found only on fish of the salmon family.

SPOTTED TAIL
Tail is heavily spotted, immediately distinguishing the rainbow trout from the brown trout.

▲ MAGIC IN BRITISH COLUMBIA
Some of the most magical and unspoiled steelhead rivers of the present day can be found in British Columbia. Where the logging, mining, and hydroelectric industries have not made their presence felt, the rivers still flow clean and cold and perfectly suited to the steelhead. These are glorious fish that can grow to weights of over 20 lb (9 kg).

FISHING FOR RAINBOW TROUT

IN THE HOT DAYS OF SUMMER, rainbow trout are often the fish that offer the best chance of sport to the fly fisherman, both in deep, cold lakes and in shallower, artificial pools. Even though you might expect the fish to be put off their food by the warm temperature and the staleness of the water, some of the trout will always be willing to have a go at a carefully presented fly.

Mind you, success under these conditions is all about observation. It is important to target a fish that is feeding, not lying lifeless in the heat. Then you need to select the right fly and present it in the right place, in the right way, and at the right time, without scaring the fish away. Quite an art!

▲ FEEDING AT THE SURFACE ...
Rainbows are gloriously catholic in their diet. Any insect on the surface attracts their attention, and they will hunt anything from midges to large crane flies. Rainbows are fond of a kind of small fly known as a buzzer, which often gets lodged in the surface film.

▲ ... AND ON THE STREAM BED
Rainbows will also dig among gravel, silt, or bottom weed to flush out prey. They take shrimp, caddis flies, water boatmen — just about any-thing that thinks it has found cover. Rainbows also eat eggs of other fish. They are notorious for eating salmon eggs but will also mop up the eggs and fry of any freshwater fish.

STILLWATER TROUT SESSION

The illustration and photographs here depict a day's fishing on a lake in Sussex, England. This lake is not large but it holds good fish, which are visible in the bright light. Several are moving in the surface layers, mouths opening as they suck in insects. My approach is that of a hunter, creeping and crawling, using bankside cover. The plot is to get close to a feeding fish and then present it with an artificial bait, using all the skill I can muster.

▲ VITAL RECONNAISSANCE
Polarizing glasses are essential because you must select your fish, follow it around its beat, and observe exactly at what depth it is feeding. There is no room for error.

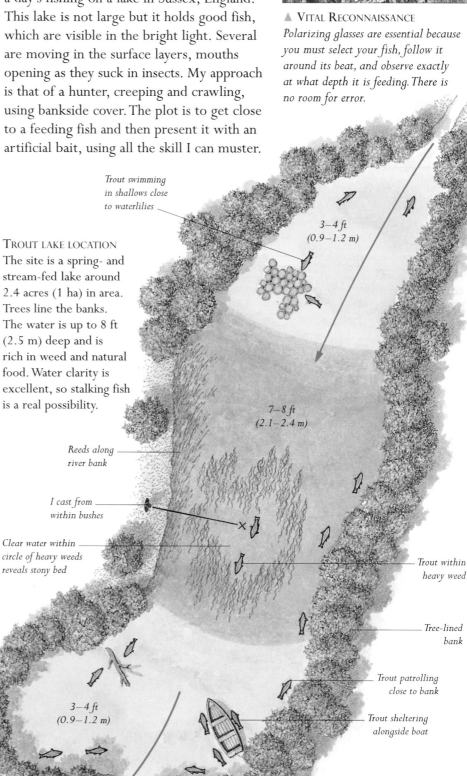

TROUT LAKE LOCATION
The site is a spring- and stream-fed lake around 2.4 acres (1 ha) in area. Trees line the banks. The water is up to 8 ft (2.5 m) deep and is rich in weed and natural food. Water clarity is excellent, so stalking fish is a real possibility.

Trout swimming in shallows close to waterlilies

3–4 ft (0.9–1.2 m)

7–8 ft (2.1–2.4 m)

Reeds along river bank

I cast from within bushes

Clear water within circle of heavy weeds reveals stony bed

Trout within heavy weed

Tree-lined bank

Trout patrolling close to bank

Trout sheltering alongside boat

3–4 ft (0.9–1.2 m)

CASTING TO THE FISH

1 PLOTTING THE CAST
I have selected the fish I want, and I know that I will have only one or two casts before the fish will be alerted. This is all tight, close-in action, so I am very precise about what I do.

2 THE TAKE
The fish saw the fly, turned toward it, and then paused for a second — suspense! Fortunately, the wide mouth opened and took in the bait. I was able to strike quickly and hook the fish securely.

A FINE FISH
This is the trout that I had been watching . . . it is rewarding to hook your target fish.

LANDING THE CATCH

1 THE DIVE
Rainbows will either leap from the water or dive deep, and this one had its eye on the jungle of weed on the lake bottom. My job was to control the fish with my line so that I could turn its head before it buried itself deep in potentially line-breaking vegetation.

2 SURRENDER
In very warm water, the fight of the rainbow trout remains brisk but is comparatively short. After two deep dives and three spirited runs, the fish was on the surface, taking in oxygen, and I knew that it was mine. Now it was just a case of directing the catch in toward the bank.

3 READY FOR RELEASE
Once you have the fish with its head out of the water, you can pull it into the vegetation, where it is within arm's reach. Providing you have used a barbless hook, it is simplicity itself to shake the hook free and guide the fish back to open water.

FISHING FOR STEELHEAD

FROM ALASKA TO CALIFORNIA, the steelhead makes its freshwater home in the rivers that flow into the Pacific Ocean from western North America. Over this huge range, the timing of the steelhead season varies with the latitude. On the Babine Lake rivers in British Columbia, the season is in autumn, but in southern rivers, it is in spring.

Take care when approaching any likely steelhead lie (a lie is a position in the water likely to be occupied by a fish). The water is clear, and steelhead are wary fish. Use sound tackle, since steelhead straight from the sea fight hard. Fish at dawn and dusk: these are the times when big steelies are likely to be most active.

◀ IDEAL LURE
Vary lure size until you get it right, but do try out silver or copper spoons and big bunches of garish red wool. A lure that stirs up the water is also favored.

FLY FISHING

Choose a rod around 9 ft (3 m) long. You are likely to need floating lines with sinking tips. Start with a fly that drifts in the water some way above the bottom. Such designs as the Polar Shrimp, the Meteor, and the Glo-bug are likely to succeed. The fly will not need a sinker except in the deepest, coldest pools.

Stay on the bank: steelhead will detect your boots on the river gravel. Aim your first cast at a point upstream from the likely location of a fish. The fish may be on spawning redds *(see p. 93)* or in their customary lies. As the current sweeps the fly toward the fish, try to trigger a bite by twitching the fly to make it attract the attention of the steelhead.

Surface flies can work well in warmer weather. These are tied in the pattern of a Muddler Minnow, often with big bristles to create the maximum bow-wave. You will see the steelhead powering toward the fly as your line drags it across the current.

▲ FISH OF THE FAST WATER
Your angling guides will point out the regular steelhead lies. Besides these, you should explore every kind of water: "fish and move" is the best policy.

▲ FINE SPINNING WATER
This angler is fishing in a glide (see p.124), where the current is steady over a gravel bottom. A glide can be an ideal place for spinning for steelhead. Explore the edges of the main and side currents. Snags and deep holes in the pool will also be prime locations.

▲ A PERFECT POOL
This pool has it all. There are good steelhead lies beneath the deeply undercut bank and on the bottom, which is peppered with snags. Although the pool is a mass of twisting water currents, there are also quiet areas where the fish like to hide.

DEEP WATER
A prime pool will have plenty of depth as well as underwater features.

CHEST WADERS
Chest waders allow you to get just a bit farther in to make the crucial cast.

◀ GAUDY IS BEST
In the usual turbulent conditions, a big, bright fly can lure a steelhead. If the water is warm and clear, a smaller fly could do the trick.

BAIT FISHING

The favorite of all edible baits for steelhead is fish spawn. Getting the eggs to stay on the hook is difficult and messy work, however, especially in cold weather.

There is another problem with this bait: spawn is easy to swallow, and the steelhead will take it deep into its throat. During the steelhead's ferocious and acrobatic fight, a deeply swallowed hook can wreak havoc inside the fish's throat, even causing severe trauma. Because all steelhead should go back to the water alive and kicking, this makes bait fishing a controversial subject.

Instead, try using a "corky," a colored bead made in imitation of a salmon egg. Two of these are placed on the line, one above the other. Sometimes the upper one carries small propeller blades to make it spin and dance. The hook is set below the bottom bead, often with wool wound around its shank to catch in the steelhead's teeth and make early rejection more difficult.

Corkies can be fished just like worms, with a small weight attached to the line close by. As an alternative, you can even drift them downriver under a float.

THE RIGHT REEL
Steelhead will put up a fight, so you need a reel with good line capacity.

MAINTAINING PRESSURE
Keep up the pressure on the fish as it comes to the shallows.

COLORED FLOAT
A clearly visible float is important at long range.

▲ TO THE SHORE
Gently work the fish toward the water margins, where it can be unhooked in shallows and released. Steelhead are declining, and in order to preserve the species it is preferable not to remove them from the water.

STEELHEAD LIE
This is a typical steelhead pool. It is wide and deep and has a good, fast flow of water.

ADMIRE AND RELEASE

With more and more steelhead habitats being destroyed by humans, the species is declining in numbers. As a result, it is imperative for all steelhead anglers to "admire and release."

When lure fishing, use relatively small and preferably barbless hooks. Is there any need to take any steelhead from the water at all? Strongly colored fish deserve special care, because they are completing their migration up the river and could be about to spawn.

Unhook your catch in the water margin and allow it to swim away. Steelhead are the sport fish of superlatives . . . let's all give them a chance to fight another day.

▶ MALE STEELHEAD
A big male steelhead is an absolute joy to behold, with its huge jaws and its whole body going bronze. This fish was approaching the spawning redds when caught and doubtless arrived soon after this brief interruption.

BAR OF SILVER
The stunning silver of the flanks begins to color after time in the river.

SAVAGE JAWS
As the male approaches the redds, the jaws become more pronounced and serve as a warning to competitors.

◀ FEMALE STEELHEAD
This beautiful fish is bright silver, being fresh from the sea where it has been feeding and growing, possibly for years. Now it has the urge to spawn, and the lucky angler has intercepted it a few miles from the coastline.

▲ HOW TO RELEASE
Hold the fish in the current for as many minutes as are needed for it to regain its strength. As the steelhead revives, you will feel it flexing the muscles along its body. Then watch the tail slowly start to beat, and it is time to say "Good-bye."

BROWN & SEA TROUT

THE BROWN TROUT is becoming one of the most revered game fish species in the world. It is a beautiful fish but, beyond that, it can be very difficult to tempt, and therein lies the challenge and the achievement. Sea trout, the seagoing variety of brown trout, are even more exciting and vie with their landlocked relatives in both beauty and caution.

THE NATIVE RANGE of brown and sea trout is enormous, stretching from Ireland in the west to the drainage area of the White Sea (in effect, as far as the Urals) in Russia. To the north it extends to Iceland, and in the south to Greece and the Atlas Mountains of North Africa.

Adding to the native range, brown trout from England have been introduced in New Zealand, Australia, the Falkland Islands, eastern Canada, South America, and South Africa. Stocks from streams in the Black Forest in Germany were shipped to the United States in 1883. The 80,000 eggs and the 1,300 fish that survived the crossing started a whole new fishing culture in North America.

▲ LOUGH MASK
One of Europe's best brown-trout fish-eries is Lough Mask in County Mayo in the west of Ireland. This limestone water is rich in weed and food items — mayflies are particularly plentiful.

◀ THE FABULOUS RIVER MÖRRUM
The River Mörrum in Sweden is one of Europe's leading sea-trout rivers. Huge fish swarm up from the Baltic to spawn in the deep, clear, turbulent water. Every year, anglers take fish weighing nearly 22 lb (10 kg) from this river.

BROWN TROUT

One of the most unusual features of the brown trout is the way in which it varies with its environment. In Europe, over 50 forms of brown trout are known, each with its own habits and distinctive appearance.

At one extreme is the ferox trout *(see p. 114)*, which takes to a fish diet at an early age, grows long and large, and becomes a fearsome predator.

In contrast, brown trout in a barren mountain stream may grow to only a hand's length. Unlike many other brown trout forms, these tiny fish may be liberally splashed with red spots.

JAW AND EYE
Jaw hinge extends farther back than eye.

GILL COVER
Five or six well-formed spots usually present on each gill cover.

SPOTS
Pattern of spots varies from water to water.

SEA TROUT

Anatomically, sea trout are almost identical to brown trout, any variations in appearance resulting from differences in diet and habitat. If sea trout are unable to escape from fresh water to the sea, they will live as brown trout. Conversely, young brown trout washed down to the ocean become typical sea trout.

▼ SEA-TROUT ANATOMY

The sea trout has a gray back, light pewter sides, and a silver belly. The body is covered with numerous black spots. Compared with the Atlantic salmon (see p. 88), the sea trout has a larger head in relation to its body, and the rear edge of its tail fin is less concave.

UPPER TEETH
These are well developed by a diet of sand eels and crabs.

SILVER FLANKS
Flanks are silver when fish arrive from the sea but become brown in fresh water.

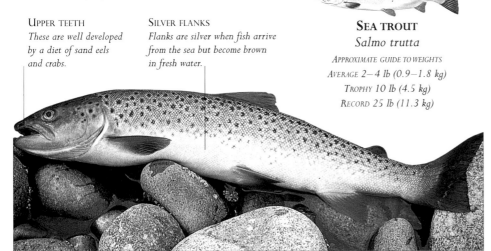

▲ ON MIGRATION

Sea trout generally leave the oceans for the rivers in June or July, but there are many exceptions. A good number of fish wait until autumn to start their run.

SEA TROUT
Salmo trutta
APPROXIMATE GUIDE TO WEIGHTS
AVERAGE 2–4 lb (0.9–1.8 kg)
TROPHY 10 lb (4.5 kg)
RECORD 25 lb (11.3 kg)

A VARIED DIET

For the first two or three years, sea trout live in fresh water and feed on insects and other invertebrates, both aquatic and land-dwelling. Once in the sea, the fish have a more catholic diet and grow rapidly. Their food includes young mackerel and herring along with juvenile bass, mullet, and peeler crabs. In normal conditions, schools of sand eels are a major food source, as are elvers *(see p. 138)* progressing back to fresh water from their birthplace in the Sargasso Sea.

▲ YOUNG HERRING

Young herring are nutritious, and, living in large schools, they are easy to catch. Fish of 4–6 in (10–15 cm) are particularly vulnerable to sea trout.

◄ MAYFLY NYMPH

Young sea trout in their freshwater habitat feed on snails, nymphs, caddis flies, and both aquatic and terrestrial flies. On their return to fresh water, the adult fish will once again take the occasional insect.

TAIL WRIST
Brown trout has a shorter tail wrist than a salmon.

ADIPOSE FIN
Adipose fin is usually well developed in brown trout.

BROWN TROUT *Salmo trutta*
APPROXIMATE GUIDE TO WEIGHTS
AVERAGE: EUROPE 11 lb (5 kg); US 2–3 lb
(0.9–1.4 kg); NEW ZEALAND 6–10 lb (2.8–4.5 kg)
TROPHY: NORTHERN HEMISPHERE 5 lb (2.3 kg);
SOUTHERN HEMISPHERE
10 lb (4.5 kg)

TAIL
Absence of tail spots in brown trout distinguishes it from rainbow trout.

FISHING FOR BROWN TROUT

HE BROWN TROUT is suspicious of any thing unnatural; it is the most discriminating of all trout species, so when you fish for it you must scan the water and establish exactly which kinds of insect or other prey it is feeding on. When you know the answer, the art is to imitate that food precisely.

Brown trout often become preoccupied with a particular kind of insect, even if several kinds are present, so work out exactly which insects are on the water, and which are being taken. Select a fly or lure that imitates the right kind – and if you are in any doubt, a small one rather than a large one.

When you fish for brown trout, three rules apply: if you have no luck, change to a lighter tippet (terminal section of the line) because the fish may be able to see a heavier one; always cast with extra care and control; and keep your shadow away from the water.

USING NYMPHS

Nymphs of different kinds make up the bulk of any brown trout's diet. To catch a trout on an artificial nymph, however, still needs guile, and there are exacting conditions. You need to use the right nymph; you must put that nymph in the right place and work it in the correct way; and you must know reliably when the bite, or take, comes along.

Most brown trout respond to such fly designs as the Pheasant Tail, as long as you twitch them to make them look natural. Watch closely for the take: the trout will normally betray itself by opening its mouth, revealing a flash of white. That is the moment to tighten your line and ensure that the fish is hooked.

▲ KEEP IT SIMPLE
The very best nymphs imitate the natural insect, and that almost always means that the nymph should be tied in simple style. Barely dressed, drab-colored nymphs work best for brown trout in all waters of the world.

▼ THE INDUCED TAKE
Imagine it: a brown trout is lying still but tense, observing your nymph just a hand's breadth away from its nose. It cannot decide what to do. Now is the time to twitch the rod and raise the nymph in the water, as though it is about to escape. Aggression is triggered, and the trout is hooked!

▲ A DAY IN KASHMIR
This photograph is from a brown trout session I was lucky enough to run in Kashmir. The whole trip was a wild experience in the shadow of towering mountains. It was not unusual for water temperatures to be close to freezing while air temperatures soared to over 86° F (30° C). Not that the trout ate any less avidly.

USING LURES

Lure fishing is important in large, still, and featureless waters in the spring, when there is little food or weed. Accurate placing of the lure is the important skill in these conditions, since you have little chance of sighting the fish. You will need to go deep, and for this you need to use a variety of sinking lines.

Work the depths systematically: estimate the length of line you release at each cast so that if and when the lure is taken, you will know its exact depth, and keep on trying a variety of depths until you locate brown trout.

The speed at which you retrieve your line is important, too. Alter this with every cast to make any following brown trout believe that the lure is an escaping fish. Remember that minnows do not swim rhythmically but tend to dart forward in quick, random bursts.

Change lures until you find success. Sometimes color is all-important – whereas white might work one day, only black will succeed the next. Size, too, can play a major part: as a general rule, as the season progresses and the "brownie" becomes wiser, go for smaller rather than larger lures.

▲ A CLOSE INSPECTION
It was a summer's day, and I was fishing on a reservoir. The sun came out, allowing me to gaze into the depths. Though so far fishless, I was quite amazed to see one brown trout after another follow my lure almost to the boat. Hundreds of these shimmering fish followed my lures that day, but I caught only five!

BODY LANGUAGE
There is caution written all over this fish, with its lowered fins and ponderous movement.

▶ THE MUDDLER
This imitation of a small fish nearly always proves irresistible, especially in late spring and summer when fry swim in the water margins.

▲ DRY FLY SESSIONS
A perfect day! A brisk wind slows the rate at which mayflies emerge as their adult, winged forms, but they hatch steadily nonetheless, then grow old and consistently fall to the water surface. The result is that the trout are not satiated but are continually teased into feeding. This young angler takes full advantage!

USING DRY FLIES

Brown trout can be both easy to scare and difficult to deceive with a dry fly. The closer to the surface the "brown" rises, the more wary it becomes, and the splash of a fly line is enough to give the whole game away, so always cast short rather than long.

Successful dry-fly fishing depends on a careful study of insects in the air and on the water. In this branch of brown trout fishing, more than any other, you must match the insects that are hatching as closely as you can. This holds true even during the mayfly season, when even large browns will look at anything that floats past them.

◀ WHAT DOES THE TROUT SEE?
The way a trout perceives a dry fly has been a question that has intrigued anglers for years. Does the trout really take this for a fly, or might a fish actually be tempted by an ungainly concoction of fur and feather?

FISHING FOR SEA TROUT

THE VERY BEST SEA-TROUT anglers are people who are totally obsessed with their sport. They need to be. To catch big sea trout on a regular basis demands total dedication, huge experience, and, above all, an instinctive feel for the species.

Believe me, there is no more exciting fish to catch: sea trout come and go like gray and silver ghosts. They follow the tides and they run at times of the moon. The angler needs to become as nocturnal as a badger if he or she is to fulfill the dream of catching this coveted species.

FISHING AT SEA

The subject of this book is freshwater fishing, but it must be mentioned that sea trout are also to be caught at sea! The main problem at sea is locating the fish, because sea trout are highly nomadic. You need to be very mobile, and this calls for trolling (see p. 117).

There are anglers who decry trolling as a mindless, mechanical method, but, if you troll in the proper manner, this is far from being the case. A good deal of fine judgment is needed in selecting the best types of lure to use and in calculating trolling speeds and depths. When you have a take, the fish is often huge!

▲ HUNTING OUT SEA TROUT
Here, on the inshore waters of the Baltic Sea, two boats are busy trolling for big sea trout. The fish have just arrived from the sea and are now feeding hard on schools of roach and perch.

FISHING FROM THE SHORE

During their time in the sea, sea trout sometimes swim close in to the shore to feed on peeler crabs, sand eels, lugworms, tiny fish, and any other creatures they can find in the crevices among rocks, close to the sandy beaches. At these times, they can be caught from the shore. It pays to be mobile, looking for fish swirling on the surface, chasing small prey. Check out coves, inflows of fresh water, harbors, beds of seaweed, and anything else that offers the sea trout food and shelter.

Spoon fishing is a good strategy: use small silver and gold spoons. Plug-fishing is effective: retrieve a surface plug through calm water, at night or in the twilight hours. You can also try bait fishing, using deadbait: twitch a small fish across the surface, or allow it to sink to the bottom, then draw it up from there. Always aim to be inventive.

▼ TRIUMPH
This stunning sea trout was caught on the Baltic shore by an angler who clearly knows the behavior and movements of the fish. He caught it on a small spinner, fished in the surf, close to the shore where the fish was rooting for crabs and baby flatfish.

▲ SAND EELS
Sand eels are among the most important food items on the sea trout's menu — some sea trout eat very little else.

▲ A PERFECT IMITATION
Rubber eels imitate the sand eel. They can be cast a long way and drawn quickly back through shallow water. Takes are violent.

▲ RAINBOW OF COLORS
Sand eels are silvery, but this does not mean their imitations need to be. Red, blue, green, and yellow are equally alluring.

THE LOWER REACHES

Sea trout that have just come in from the sea are very wary by day, so while they are still in the lower reaches of the river it is best to fish for them at night.

Anglers divide the night's fishing into four periods, named as follows: the "first half" is from dusk to midnight; "half time" is around 12:30 – 1:30 am; the "second half" is until first light; and when daylight is long, there is even "extra time" around sunrise. Try using big, dynamic flies in the first half and slow-moving, deep lures in the second half. At sunrise, try a large, floating fly, skating across the surface; it is just possible that this will attract a fish and tempt it into a slashing take!

▶ SEA POOL
Every sea trout angler dreams of a pool like this, where fresh water cascades down on its way into the estuary. Sea trout gather here in numbers.

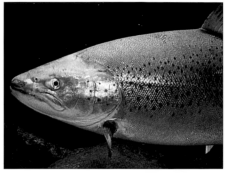

▲ IN FROM THE SEA
A big sea trout, fresh from the sea, noses its way into fresh water. Although the trout is on migration and has ceased feeding in the usual sense, it is still very likely to take a fly if your presentation is sufficiently sensitive.

◀ FIRST-HALF FLY
In the evening, try slimly dressed flies on large hooks, designed to simulate a small, escaping fish. Takes are quite dynamic.

BLUE AND SILVER TEAL

UPRIVER

Once the sea trout has been in the river a few days or weeks it will have pushed its way into shallow, clear water and will have become more difficult to catch. Its cunning will have grown with each hour and with every foot it has swum. Great caution is called for, and fly size needs to be scaled down.

While night fishing remains important, there is a new mood abroad: increasingly anglers are realizing that sea trout can be caught in the day, when it is quite possible to see the silvery schools waiting in pools before moving upstream. Alternatively, they like to find fast-running stretches of water, where they are able to hold their position easily against the current.

For fish in a pool, try casting a dark, fast-sinking fly right into the middle of the school. Some fish will be alarmed, but there could be an immediate take.

▶ A PERFECT LIE
A deep, slow pool surrounded by trees is the perfect pool for a big sea trout in the daytime hours. Fish cautiously, and you may well get one!

▲ FISH THE RIFFLE
Sea trout migrate mostly at night and will pass through riffles (rapid shallows); they choose to hang there by day, too. To catch them, cast small, wet flies down and across the current.

◀ THINK SMALLER
The farther upstream you pursue sea trout, the smaller the flies you are likely to use. The two examples shown here are both tiny, dry flies, and the hooks they are tied to are No. 16s.

KATE MCLAREN

MULLARD AND CLARET

SPECIALTY TROUT

THERE ARE A GREAT MANY FISH that we know as trout, and to most anglers it is enough to know that they are divided into species, which in turn split up into local forms or subspecies. Rainbow, steelhead, brown, and sea trout have already been described. Now it is the turn of less common but equally exciting forms, which for convenience I am calling "specialty trout."

TROUT IN THEIR great diversity are a baffling group of fish for the scientist but a wonderful one for the fisherman. In certain Irish loughs, you can catch three or four quite different trout varieties in a day. This natural tendency of trout to vary is found the world over, giving us such fabulous fish as the Loch Leven trout of Scotland, the golden trout of North America, and the marble trout of the Balkan countries of Europe.

In many places, angling waters have been stocked with introduced, nonnative fish, and these tend to interbreed with native ones, adding man-made hybrids to nature's variety.

Local forms of trout vary hugely in size: there are brown trout that weigh as little as 4 oz (100 g), or as much as 40 lb (18 kg).

▲ SCHOOLING BEHAVIOR
All trout tend to school at certain times of the year. This happens most characteristically when spawning time is approaching, but hunting schools also occur. Certain trout types, like browns, will hunt in solitary fashion, while others (like these lake trout) maraud in packs.

▲ GLACIAL STREAM
Most trout types are able to tolerate changes in temperature. Himalayan trout, for example, can exist in water where glacial ice actually flows along the stream, even though the air temperature can be 86°F (30°C) or more. Most trout have a tendency in hot summer weather to seek out the coolest water available to them, such as a cold spring.

BROOK TROUT

The brook trout is not really a trout at all but a char — except that every angler in the world knows it as a trout! It is native to North America but has been introduced to Europe. Fine brook trout are found in parts of Labrador, the Nipigon River in Ontario, the lakes of Colorado — and even some rivers in Patagonia.

WHITE THROAT
The male brook trout's white throat is a helpful recognition aid — more noticeable when you see the fish in the water.

SPOTS ON THE FLANK
A distinctive feature of brook trout is the series of pinkish spots along the flank.

BROOK TROUT *Salvelinus fontinalis*
APPROXIMATE GUIDE TO WEIGHTS
AVERAGE 2 – 3 lb (0.9–1.4 kg)
TROPHY 5 lb (2.3 kg)
RECORD 14 lb (6.4 kg)

LENOK AND CUTTHROAT

The lenok is an Asiatic trout, inhabiting parts of Siberia, China, Mongolia, and Korea. It displays great variety in color, spotting, and size. At its largest, the lenok can grow to 10 lb (4.5 kg), though 3–4 lb (1.4–1.8 kg) is more normal.

The cutthroat is one of the most beloved of American trout for its wild colors and sporting behavior. It also shows great variety; Robert Smith, in his book *Native Trout of North America,* conservatively identifies 14 types. The cutthroat can grow to 40 lb (18 kg) in deep-water habitats such as Nevada's Pyramid Lake. The species is widespread, and some populations in British Columbia and California are even seagoing.

CUTTHROAT TROUT

▲ LENOK TROUT
The lenok is very much a trout, with its distinctive spotting and the adipose fin that is typical of the salmon and trout family. It has an unusually small, underslung mouth, enabling it to utilize all food sources, even by scraping algae off rocks, in waters that can be barren of food for much of the year.

Adipose fin

◀ CUTTHROAT TROUT
Cutthroats are identified by, and named after, the orange-red slash beside their jaw. This continues down the lateral line (see p. 17) in certain strains. Particularly famous subspecies include those of the Snake River, Yellowstone River, Rio Grande, and Upper Colorado River.

WHITE-TIPPED FINS
Like all char, the brook trout has white tips on all the fins on the underside of its body.

SQUARISH TAIL
The tail of the brook trout is either square or very slightly forked.

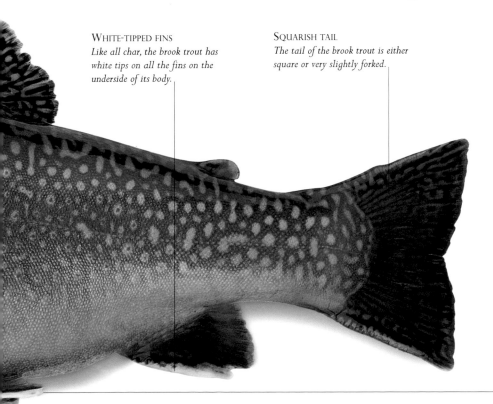

FEROX AND LAKE TROUT

As with lenok and cutthroat trout, here are two trout that come from East and West. The ferox is a subspecies of brown trout and is found in the glacial waters of Ireland, Scotland, and alpine Europe. The ferox has adapted itself to living in these waters by feeding on char. The harsh environment and nutritious diet combine to produce an extraordinary brown trout, capable of long life and growing to an enormous size.

Like the brook trout, the lake trout is not a trout at all! It is a species of char that inhabits large waters across almost all of Canada and parts of the United States, including northern New England and upstate New York in the region of the Great Lakes.

This is what the ferox and lake trout have in common: they are both big fish, and the two are found in equally awesome waters.

▲ FEROX TROUT
The huge ferox trout is, in its prime, a powerful, beautifully shaped and colored fish. Although it is rarely seen or caught, the ferox is one of the dream catches for anglers all across Europe.

▲ LAKE TROUT
Lake trout must have cold, clean water, and they generally inhabit deep, well-oxygenated lakes with good populations of smelt (a small prey fish). They are the premier game fish of huge lakes of the Canadian wilderness, where they grow to 50 lb (22 kg) or more.

FISHING FOR SPECIALTY TROUT

I**F YOU ARE FISHING** for ferox or lake trout and plan to catch a big one, you are going to need to adjust your thinking. The usual strategy for catching trout is to use a fly, but that is simply too small-scale for these very big fish. When fishing the vast lakes they inhabit, you must use big baits and choose a mobile strategy that enables you to explore the water in your quest to locate the fish.

Ferox and lake trout need space: a lake 9 miles (14 km) long, 1 mile (2.4 km) wide, and perhaps 1,000 ft (300 m) deep may well hold only 20–50 fish in all! You will need to search the entire water by trolling (see right and facing page) with lures that are large enough to be seen and vibrate hard enough for fish to sense them from far off.

▲ THE ELUSIVE FEROX TROUT
Ferox and lake trout are often thinly spread over wide distances, but specialized equipment is available for scanning large areas of water to find them. A graph recorder is an electronic scanner that displays images on a screen. Images show either the bed or any sizable object in the water — such as this ferox trout.

FEROX AND LAKE TROUT

A ferox or lake trout will grow big only if it has a plentiful diet of prey fish. The bait — live, dead, or artificial — that you present to one of these trout must resemble whatever prey the trout is accustomed to taking.

Big ferox and lake trout can be lazy fish that forage on the shoreline at night. Use a 6 in (15 cm) prey fish as deadbait, and hook it onto strong tackle to catch either species.

But your main approach must be trolling. You do not always need to troll deep. Some fish are happy to feed in the first 10 ft (3 m) of water. If you do go deep, a downrigger gets results. This is a sophisticated trolling rig, which is refined year by year.

STABLE BOAT
Successful trolling depends on a boat capable of dealing with high winds.

▲ FEROX AND LAKE TROUT LURE
Choose a design that has plenty of flash and movement and looks like the fish that the trout are feeding on. The length should be 4–7 in (10–18 cm). Silver or gold are good colors.

▲ LAKE TROUT
The angler who caught this laker used a spoon (see p.174) that he trolled over a long distance early in the morning at a shallow depth. Early or late, there is a chance that you will see both ferox and lakers harrying prey fish on the surface.

◀ DOWNRIGGER TROLLING
Downriggers are useful tools for getting your lures down deep during the hot summer daylight hours. Downrigging has become a real science. Experts use several downriggers, each operating at different depths, until fish are located.

▼ HOW A DOWNRIGGER WORKS
The downrigger is trailed from a moving boat. A weight is lowered overboard on a cable. The cable is marked so that the angler can know the depth to which the weight is lowered. A quick-release clip holds the line and lure down with the weight.

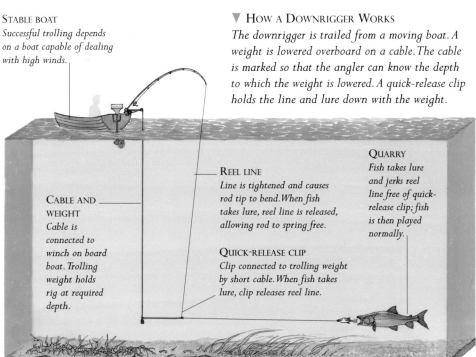

CABLE AND WEIGHT
Cable is connected to winch on board boat. Trolling weight holds rig at required depth.

REEL LINE
Line is tightened and causes rod tip to bend. When fish takes lure, reel line is released, allowing rod to spring free.

QUICK-RELEASE CLIP
Clip connected to trolling weight by short cable. When fish takes lure, clip releases reel line.

QUARRY
Fish takes lure and jerks reel line free of quick-release clip; fish is then played normally.

MULTILEVEL TROLLING

Trolling, which simply means dragging a lure through the water, can be done from the shore *(see p. 81)*, but to catch ferox or lake trout you must do it from a moving boat. As well as searching over a large surface area, you need to look for fish at a variety of depths, so troll three (or more) lures, each designed to operate at its own specific depth.

You need to decide on the speed at which you troll. Go too slowly, and you will give the fish time to inspect the bait and become suspicious; troll too fast, and you will leave even the most enthusiastic fish behind.

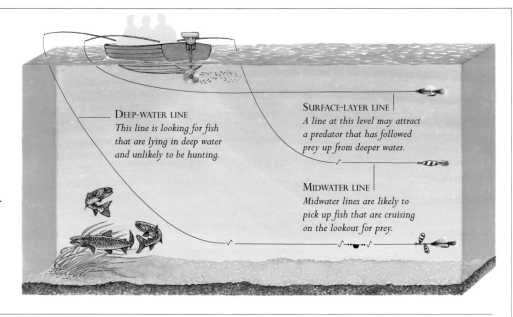

DEEP-WATER LINE
This line is looking for fish that are lying in deep water and unlikely to be hunting.

SURFACE-LAYER LINE
A line at this level may attract a predator that has followed prey up from deeper water.

MIDWATER LINE
Midwater lines are likely to pick up fish that are cruising on the lookout for prey.

CATCHING BROOK TROUT

Many brook-trout lakes have been so overfished that you are obliged to travel far into the wilderness to visit barely fished habitats. Trolling is a popular strategy, using smallish lures. Jigging *(see p. 59)* is effective, particularly for schooling fish; use a spoon, but attach a strip of fish or pork rind to the hook. Bait fishing can also pick up good brook trout, since they are minnow-devourers.

The best fishing for brookies is at "ice-out," the time in spring when melting ice fills the streams that flow into the lakes. Fly fishing now comes into its own; use a sinking line and a decent-sized fly that imitates shrimp or whatever the brook trout are taking. Fish fairly deep and slow, and give the fly an occasional twitch, as erratically as you like!

▶ **BROOK TROUT LURE**
This lure imitates a freshwater shrimp, food of many brook trout. The use of lurex makes it particularly enticing to the fish.

▲ **"ICE-OUT" FISHING FOR BROOK TROUT**
Fish the meltwater-swollen streams and lakes, and start early in the day. Big brook trout are wary of shallow water, so it pays to take your fly rod out at dawn, when the fish are just that little bit more bold. Tread carefully, and search out the places where brook trout love to forage. These include river mouths, any "drop-offs" or steep falls in the bottom, and any rocky, weedy peninsulas leading out into deep water.

◀ **SPAWNING TIME**
In autumn, brook trout gather in the shallows to prepare for spawning. Fortunately, in most of its habitats the brook trout is protected by law in the spawning season, when it is at its most vulnerable.

ARCTIC CHAR

THE ARCTIC CHAR IS A FISH OF MAGICAL BEAUTY: its range of colors includes gray or blue on its back, and anything from silvery white to a glowing red on its belly. The species is divided into two populations. Lake-dwelling Arctic char are found in glacial lakes across the northern continents, while the migratory form feeds in the Arctic Ocean and spawns in rivers.

▲ STEELY BLUE
This fantastic Arctic char, held by the Danish explorer Johnny Jensen, was a summer fish caught just a few miles from the fiord, only hours from the sea.

THE TWO POPULATIONS of Arctic char were separated in prehistoric times, but we know little about how this happened. We know more about the lakes than about the lake-dwelling Arctic char. About 11,500 years ago, as the ice age ended, the glaciers in the mountains melted, laid down barriers of earth and rock, and dammed up water in the valleys behind them. You might expect that the Arctic char, too, were trapped behind the barriers and so ceased to be migratory. It is more likely, however, that char from the ocean overshot their usual destination, found their way into the lakes, and stayed there.

RANGE OF COLORS

The range of colors exhibited by both kinds of Arctic char is truly breathtaking. Sea-run fish have the more dramatic coloration. In late autumn and early spring, the two main spawning times, belly colors include orange *(see opposite, top right)* or vivid red *(see right)*. In summer, when the fish are fresh from the sea, they are bluish above and silvery white underneath *(see main picture, opposite)*.

Lake-dwelling Arctic char show almost as vivid a range of colors, which again are seen at spawning times.

▲ VIVID RED
Never will you see a more beautiful fish! At the time when this picture was taken, summer was wearing on and this stunning fish was preparing to spawn.

MIGRATORY ARCTIC CHAR

Migratory Arctic char are found in rivers all around the Northern Hemisphere between the latitudes of 45° N and 82° N, but mainly in those of Alaska, Canada, Greenland, Iceland, and Siberia. The fish are hatched in the rivers, spend the first two years or so of their lives there, and then migrate to the sea to enjoy the rich food supply there.

At sea, the Arctic char feed on sand eels, shrimp, young herring, smelt, and any other food that they can capture with their power-ful jaws. Once mature, the Arctic char revisit the freshwater rivers to spawn. Just like their landlocked brothers, the migratory char are school fish, moving upriver in great numbers.

For migratory char, 10 lb (4.5 kg) is not an uncommon weight, and fish of 20 lb (9 kg), even 25 lb (11.3 kg), have been recorded. By contrast, an average weight for lake-dwelling char might be 1 lb 5 oz (0.6 kg).

▲ FEEDING AT SEA
This is the marine habitat of the migratory char. It is a cold and seemingly hostile environment, but in fact it teems with life, and the feeding here is fabulously rich.

▲ INTO THE ESTUARY
As the rivers of the North begin to thaw out in spring, Arctic char gather at the estuary mouths, ready to ascend to their spawning beds. Bays like this can look black with fish waiting to move up.

ARCTIC CHAR ANATOMY

The Arctic char is a long, streamlined fish in nearly all its environments. The only exceptions are fish living in lakes where the food supply has been artificially enriched. This is usually the result of fish farming and the fattening effect of food pellets!

Arctic char have a rounder cross-section than the oval one typical of most fish. Another noticeable feature is that, like other char species *(see p. 114)*, the Arctic char has white fringes on its underside fins.

ARCTIC CHAR *Salvelinus alpinus*
APPROXIMATE GUIDE TO WEIGHTS
EUROPEAN LANDLOCKED AVERAGE 1–2 lb (0.45–0.9 kg)
US & GREENLAND SEA-RUN AVERAGE 4–8 lb (1.8–3.6 kg)
RECORD 25 lb (11.3 kg)

▲ GLOWING ORANGE
The name char is taken from the Gaelic word ceara, *"blood-red." This is true of some specimens* (see opposite), *while others, like this one, are orange in color.*

PALE SPOTS
Char have pale spots on dark body colors – salmon and trout have dark spots on lighter body colors (see pp. 88, 100).

FORKED TAIL
The tail of the Arctic char is typically deeply forked, unlike the squarer tail of its relative, the brook trout.

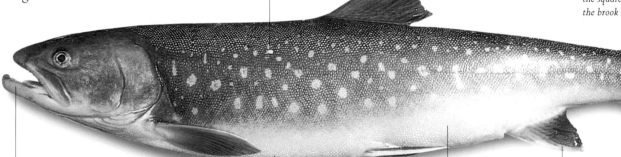

JAWS AND TEETH
Jaws and teeth of migratory form have evolved for feeding on crustaceans at sea.

SLENDER BUILD
Body is long and streamlined, perfectly adapted for migration.

WHITE-EDGED FIN
Tips are edged in white on all fins on underside of body.

▲ TRAVELING UPRIVER
A school of Arctic char moves upriver toward the spawning redds. The fish have stopped feeding now and live on the food reserves they have built up in their bodies. The school travels primarily at night, resting in deeper pools during the day.

▲ GREENLAND LANDSCAPE
A torrent of glacial meltwater in the background joins a clear river in the foreground, but the two do not mix. The Arctic char remain in the clear water.

▲ ARRIVAL AT THE SPAWNING REDDS
The Arctic char arrive at their spawning redds (see p. 93) in growing numbers and wait until breeding activity begins. Very frequently, the biggest fish move farthest upriver, often seeking out the source itself.

FISHING FOR ARCTIC CHAR

ONE WAY TO CATCH Arctic char is to fish in one of the vast, glacial lakes where the species has a stronghold. This can, at times, be exciting fishing, especially when the char come into the shallows to feed on surface flies. For the most part, however, you need to troll deep *(see p. 117)*.

Lake trolling has its attractions, but it must be said that there are more glamorous ways of pursuing the species! In fact, there is nothing more exciting than fishing for char in rivers. Here the quarry are normally seagoing char on their migration into fresh water to spawn, but sometimes you catch lake-dwelling char in the rivers, for these fish migrate, too, and their spawning redds are in the rivers that flow into the lakes.

Whatever the circumstance, char in moving water are dynamite, the "real thing," and I personally can't get enough of them!

▲ DIVING DEEP
Arctic char fight well anywhere, but it is in rivers that you really begin to appreciate them, especially those fish freshly arrived from the sea, which are always bursting with strength and vitality.

▲ SIMPLY THE BEST
A char like this really should be the highlight of any freshwater angler's life. Its colors are simply stunning, and look at those glorious white-edged fins, the hallmark of the char family.

ADVENTURE FISHING

The illustration and photographs here show Johnny Jensen and me fishing for Arctic char in the course of a summer trip to a river in Greenland. The search for Arctic char invariably takes anglers to the remoter parts of the northern hemisphere. Wild Arctic char and civilization rarely mix, and you need to go to the outer limits if you want to catch big fish. Greenland is, of course, nearly all icecap, but the short rivers that run into the Arctic Ocean from the ice can offer some of the most thrilling char fishing in the world.

A MAGNET FOR CHAR
I do not know what it is about this particular pool, nestled in behind a midriver island, but, year after year, char flock to it. It is possible that they actually spawn there; or they may be using the pool as a resting ground on their journey upriver.

*2 ft
(0.6 m)*

*4 ft
(1.2 m)*

*6 ft
(1.8 m)*

Johnny takes prime fishing position, just upstream of deeper water.

Far bank studded with bushes — unusual for Greenland.

*2 ft
(0.6 m)*

*8 ft
(2.4 m)*

Fish tend to string out in shelter of island.

Island 150–180 ft (50–60 m) in length.

*2 ft
(0.6 m)*

*6 ft
(1.8 m)*

I fish lower down glide (see p. 124), where some of the biggest char are caught.

*4 ft
(2.4 m)*

*2 ft
(0.6 m)*

Water is shallower here; few char are found this far down.

Big char occasionally shelter behind small outcrops of rock.

INTO THE WILDS

▲ VAST LANDSCAPE

Greenland is the largest island in the world, but most of its area is covered by an enormous wilderness of ice. This makes traveling from one side of the country to another very difficult indeed. There are next to no roads in Greenland, and most travel is done by sea. To travel on land, horses or donkeys are used in summer, sleds and dogs in winter. The air is startlingly clear, and you can see for extraordinary distances.

▲ RIVERSCAPE

When you are fishing in Greenland, it is really you and nature and very little else! The enormous scale of the mountains and valleys dwarfs the angler. The only sounds are natural ones — the tinkling of the river, the songs of birds, and the occasional roar from a musk ox.

UP TO THE HEADWATERS

1 FISHING THE RIFFLES
Arctic char group up in the "riffles" — places where the water is shallow, rapid, and well oxygenated. They hang at the tail of the riffle, where the water slows down marginally and begins to deepen. Make your approach very carefully, and cast as delicately as you can.

2 FISH ON THE HOOK (BELOW)
Johnny fished a tiny nymph that floated just under the surface, and before long he hooked a hard-fighting char of around 4 lb (1.9 kg). The take was electrifying, and the first run took out all the line and some of the backing (the strong, coarse line attached to the reel).

3 WATCHING YOUR FISH
The clarity of Greenland's rivers is breathtaking. Even when the fish are at depths of 6–7 ft (1.8–2 m) you can see them drifting around or nosing their way through the vegetation. Playing a fish in water like this is exciting because you see so much of what is going on.

4 HELD FOR A SECOND
These beautiful fish are so fragile that overexposure to the air can prove fatal. Kill one, perhaps, for your food for the evening, but return the others as quickly as possible. Always respect nature.

GRAYLING

WHILE THERE IS NO DOUBT that grayling are game fish, recent work on fish classification suggests that they do not belong to the salmon family but to a family of their own, the Thymallidae. This contains several species, all similar fish from an angling point of view. They include the Arctic and European grayling and various Asiatic species, notably the Mongolian grayling.

GRAYLING ARE FOUND in crystal-clear rivers that are cool, clean, and well oxygenated. They also occur in lakes where temperatures remain sufficiently low for the fish to be comfortable in summer.

A good-sized grayling the world over is around 2 lb (1 kg), but bigger specimens can be found in North America, in the rivers of central Europe (including Austria), and in the wildernesses of Siberia and Mongolia.

All grayling species are very similar, color being the only readily noticeable difference between them. The Arctic grayling is found in North America and Siberia, and the European grayling from Britain to the Black Sea.

▲ DOWN AMONG THE ROCKS
You can be almost certain of finding grayling in rivers with rocky beds, because the small creatures that they live on hide in the crevices. Grayling forage for nymphs, caddis larvae, shrimp, leeches, and even small snails.

▲ GRAYLING RAPIDS
Look for grayling in fast, rippling water, especially in summer when the fish are looking for insects brought down by the current. Schools of grayling lurk in slight depressions, sometimes just off the main current, ready to dart out and seize any small creatures that drift past.

GRAYLING IN WINTER

As winter begins, grayling make their way down from the shallower upland streams and begin to look out for deeper pools. Partly, this is to prepare for the coming floods of winter, which can make the shallow streams dangerous for fish. Also, a great deal of winter food is found in the slower water, especially in weedbeds that are dying back and among stones and bottom rubble.

At this time of year, grayling often gather in large schools, sometimes hundreds strong. Indeed, huge areas of water may be devoid of fish, while the whole grayling population is concentrated in a single hole.

Even in the coldest weather, grayling will still come to the surface to investigate any emerging insects. The fish may be seen rising periodically, often in the early afternoon, all through the dark months.

◀ DEEP POOL
Pools offer everything grayling need in winter. The water is deep and calm and can absorb a flood, but there are also plenty of invertebrates to catch among the stones and fallen branches.

▲ SPAWNING TIME
Around the month of March, grayling move toward their spawning grounds. They spawn on gravel, simply scattering their eggs on the river bottom. Fast waters are not suitable, because the grayling do not dig nests that would shelter the eggs from the current.

GRAYLING ANATOMY

The grayling has a slender, somewhat flat-sided body and a comparatively small head. The mouth is small, with tiny teeth. The upper jaw projects very slightly beyond the lower one.

The eye, which is very acute in low light, is "pear-shaped" – larger at the back and smaller in front.

As a grayling matures, its colors become bolder and the dark spots more pronounced. The fins take on a mauvish tinge, and the scales become slightly iridescent.

◀ FINS AFLARE
Grayling extend their fins like this at certain times: in courtship, when about to snatch a food item, or when trying to ward off a possible predator.

GRAYLING
Thymallus species
APPROXIMATE GUIDE TO WEIGHTS
AVERAGE 1 lb (0.45 kg)
TROPHY 2–3 lb (0.9–1.4 kg)
RECORD 6 lb (2.7 kg)

DORSAL FIN
Grayling is immediately identified by its very large dorsal fin.

TAIL WRIST
Gold-colored tail wrist identifies this specimen as a Mongolian grayling.

TAIL
Caudal fin is strongly forked.

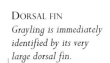

THE SUMMER GRAYLING

After spawning, grayling move back into the fast-flowing water. In this well-oxygenated environment, with its plentiful supply of insects and other food items, the fish recover from the stresses of spawning.

Summer grayling are fish of the rapids, seeking out their food under rocks and stones while being equally adept at finding the insects that hatch, fly briefly, and fall to the surface. They feed at dusk and, during warm periods, through the night. Besides rapids, they also frequent areas of weed growth.

◀ DANCING IN THE SHALLOWS
It is not unusual to see grayling move into very shallow water, especially early or late in the day. They grub among stones for shallow-water nymphs and for any fallen terrestrial insects. Grayling are vigorous diggers, often breaking the surface with their tails while working among the stones with their snouts.

▲ FAST WATER
No grayling angler could pass a place like this without casting a line! You could find grayling all along this "streamy" (fast and turbulent) stretch of water, but also look for them close inshore, behind rocks. Here they can shelter from the main current, darting out to chase any small creature that they see passing.

FISHING FOR GRAYLING

THE GRAYLING IS A REAL CHALLENGE for any angler. The take (a fishing term for the moment when a fish takes the bait and hook into its mouth) can be lightning quick, so watch your line with the utmost attention and strike the very instant you see signs of a bite. It is a feature of grayling fishing that many more takes are missed than hit.

The grayling also inspects a bait minutely and can take it with astonishing delicacy, so even detecting a bite can be a challenge. Also, in clear water especially, the grayling can be almost impossibly wary. Greed never outweighs its caution, and you will never find a grayling making the same sort of rash mistake as a trout. Finally, when the fish is hooked, that great dorsal fin makes it very difficult to turn in a quick current.

A FISH FOR ALL SEASONS

One of the great bonuses of the grayling is that it is catchable in both warm and cold weather. Unlike carp, it is an active feeder even in the depths of winter, searching for the scattered insects and other invertebrates that the water contains. In fact, grayling fishing often comes into its own in winter, when there is frost on the ground and even ice along the margins of the river.

▲ OUT IN THE FROST
The enchantingly beautiful River Dove, in the Peak District in northern England, was made famous by the 17th-century writer and fisherman Izaak Walton. Today, like then, the Dove is a fine grayling river, even on freezing winter days like this when the water from the fly-line froze in the rod-rings!

MONGOLIAN GRAYLING SESSION

The illustration and photographs here depict a grayling session in Mongolia, on which I was joined by another angler, Simon Channing. Mongolia is a wonderful fishing country, and no living angler knows a tenth of what it can offer; rumors of massive fish are rife. Mongolian grayling are quite extraordinary to look at. The dorsal fin is larger and more brilliantly colored than in any other subspecies. The ventral fins display vivid stripes. The body colors are fantastic, and the tail wrist is a brilliant gold or deep butter yellow.

SWIFT-FLOWING RIVER
The river surges over a jumble of rocks and passes through a "glide" (a gradual fall) into a deep pool where it slows to a steady current. The grayling congregate here, where they find a good depth, an easy-paced flow, and plenty of water-borne food.

▲ FOOTHILLS OF THE ALTAI
The rivers that flow out of the Mongolian mountains are stunning. They are quick and clear and, considering their high altitude, surprisingly full of natural foodstuffs. Grayling quickly grow large in these waters.

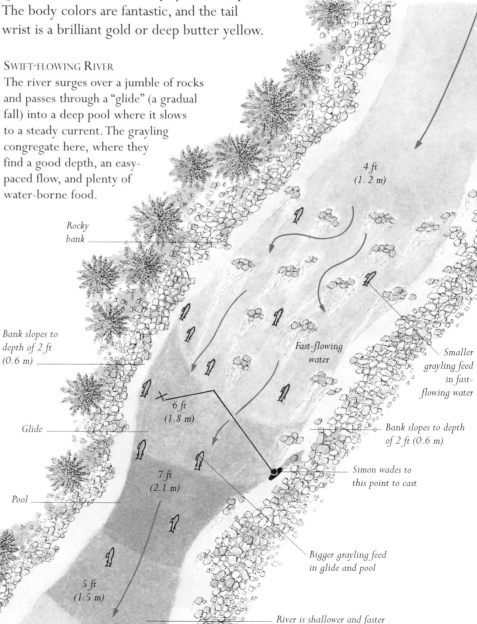

Rocky bank

Bank slopes to depth of 2 ft (0.6 m)

Glide

6 ft (1.8 m)

7 ft (2.1 m)

Pool

5 ft (1.5 m)

4 ft (1.2 m)

4 ft (1.2 m)

Fast-flowing water

Smaller grayling feed in fast-flowing water

Bank slopes to depth of 2 ft (0.6 m)

Simon wades to this point to cast

Bigger grayling feed in glide and pool

River is shallower and faster as it flows out of pool

HOOKING UP

1 CASTING INTO THE GLIDE
Simon wades a short distance from the shore so that he can cast easily into the deep water of the "glide," where the water begins its fall into the pool. He places his cast a little upstream and then mends his line (straightens out the slack) as the bait drifts downriver.

2 EYES ON THE INDICATOR
Grayling are quick on the uptake, and a bite indicator — a float placed a short way up the line from the nymph — helps prevent an unnoticed take.

3 AN INSTANT STRIKE
As soon as that indicator disappears or holds up in the current, Simon tightens his line. Grayling give no second chances, and every movement on the indicator has to be checked instantly. Even so, as we later found, his fish was hooked only on the outside of the lip.

TO THE HAND

3 COMING CLOSE
The colors of the Mongolian grayling sparkle in the sun. It is such sights that make anyone know why they are an angler . . . but beware of the hook-loosening head-shake at the final moment!

IN MARVELOUS CONDITION
This is a perfect virgin fish. Wilderness fishing at its best!

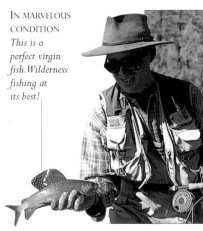

1 FAR FROM BEATEN
These strong, agile fish with their huge dorsal fins never give up a struggle. Mongolian grayling are particularly special in the way that they jump. Many of the bigger grayling will leave the water seven or eight times during a fight, often leaping more than their own length into the air. It is at such moments that the hook can easily be shed, and the fish is lost.

2 WADING ASHORE
Once the grayling is on its side and virtually beaten, Simon decides to move backward to the bank, where he can beach the fish easily. The classic way to do this is to hold the rod high and use the left hand to guide the line as the fish is brought into shallow water between the rocks. Once there, it will be an easy matter to unhook the fish and slip it back into the water.

4 PROUD MOMENT
Simon admires his grayling. Notice that great dorsal fin held up like a banner in the sunlight, and also that stunning golden tail — a characteristic quite unique anywhere in the world.

BAIT-CAUGHT FISH

THERE IS IMMENSE SATISFACTION IN BAIT fishing, and in many cases it is simply the joy of doing it well. But the subject of this chapter is wider than that. In past times, when fishing was either game or coarse, "coarse" fish were split into those taken on lures (predatory fish) and the rest, which were caught with bait. Nothing could be further from my way of thinking – for example, this book describes ways of catching sturgeon with flies, salmon with worms, and panfish with spinners. Nevertheless, for convenience, this chapter contains the fish that once were taken exclusively with bait.

A CAST AT SUNSET

Eels are among the hundreds of traditionally bait-caught fish that come out of their lairs at dusk to feed. Here, an angler makes his cast at the start of a nighttime eel session.

CARP

CARP INSPIRE VERY DIFFERENT PASSIONS around the world. In America and Australia, these fish are generally regarded as pests – excessively fertile, disgustingly greedy, and guilty of degrading the aquatic habitat. In Europe, however, carp are highly sought after, and everything is done to increase their numbers and preserve them from the slightest harm.

HEATHER, HERMAN, Sally, Eric . . . yes, carp in Britain are recognized as individuals and given their own names! This may seem ridiculous in America, but it is not difficult to understand how the British – and other Europeans – feel. Carp are large fish, and hard-fighting ones. Above all, they are clever fish, and it is doubtful whether any other species is so quick to learn.

You can watch an "educated" carp testing the water around the bait with its fins to feel if there is a line. A carp can pick up a bait, roll it around its mouth, and reject it if it feels the hook; this can happen without the angler knowing anything about it!

▲ MAN-MADE POOLS
Carp like to be in shallow water in warm, nutrient-rich pools. Many of the pools that contain carp were dug for the purpose in past centuries by monks, who relied on carp ponds as a food source.

◄ NATURAL LAKES
For carp anglers, great mysteries lie in huge lakes like this. Deep, nutrient-rich lakes in unvisited and unfished places, such as the quieter corners of Asia or eastern Europe, could hold monster carp.

CARP ANATOMY

All types of carp *(see p.130)* have acute eyesight, hearing, and sense of smell. They are tenacious of life and can survive in pools that have almost completely dried out or are heavily frozen. When introduced to a different location, carp always adapt well to new conditions and spawn prolifically. This explains their success as colonizers.

STRETCH LIPS
Mouth of carp is equipped with very sensitive lips. Bones of jaw are structured in such a way that when mouth opens, lips are pushed forward.

BARBELS
These are prehensile, fleshy whiskers that probe for food items in the silt.

▶ VACUUMING UP
The lips of a carp can be extended outward in telescopic fashion to suck up food items from the bottom. Carp can suck up even heavy items at a few inches' range.

CARP HABITAT

Carp are generally considered fish of deep, slow-moving, or stagnant water. In rivers, they tend to keep to the backwaters, side channels, or deeper pools. However, carp can surprise and often swim in quick water, where they hunt small aquatic creatures in competition with barbel and trout.

Carp enjoy warm water, and if they are to spawn successfully the average water temperature in summer must be 59–68°F (15–20°C). Shallow, weedy lakes and pools are favored. For carp to live in deep waters, there must be shallow bays where the water warms up quickly in spring. Another require- ment of carp is cover: they are rarely found far from weed, fallen branches, or snags.

Although principally a freshwater fish, the carp is found in slightly brackish (part salt, part fresh) water along the Baltic coastline.

▶ **AMONG DEAD BRANCHES**
All carp are very wary fish, highly aware of their need for security. Nothing gives them a greater sense of safety than a cage of dead branches, and it is in places like this that many carp will elect to spend the winter. Thus protected, they barely move until spring, passing two or three months in a semicomatose condition.

▲ **A LIKING FOR DEBRIS**
Carp are highly inquisitive and will forage anywhere. They are fond of exploring debris, such as the remains of fallen buildings on a lake bed. They turn over full- sized house bricks with their snouts in their search for the small creatures that live among the debris.

▲ **EMERGING FROM THE WEED**
Carp use weed as a spawning ground, a shelter from hot weather, a hiding place, and a place to hunt aquatic creatures. In very thick weed, carp will force their way through, creating a network of tunnels.

SCALE PATTERN
There are four categories of scale patterns in mirror carp: fully scaled, plated, linear (see small illustration, right), and scattered (shown here).

POWERFUL TAIL
The tail fin is the carp's "propeller."

MIRROR CARP
Cyprinus carpio
APPROXIMATE GUIDE TO WEIGHTS
AVERAGE 10–15 lb (4.5–6.8 kg)
TROPHY 20 lb (9 kg)
RECORD 70 lb (32 kg)

TAIL WRIST
A carp gets much of its power from its muscular tail wrist.

CAUDAL FIN
In all forms of carp, this fin is deeply forked, and the two lobes are relatively rounded.

CARP SPECIES

THE FAMILY CYPRINIDAE is one of the largest
fish families. As well as the various types
of carp, it includes many fish that are related
to carp, either closely or distantly. Scientists
estimate the total number of species to be
between 1,500 and 2,000. The most important of these, whether in terms of commercial
or sport fishing, are the carp themselves.

Carp have no teeth in their mouths but
have pharyngeal teeth (situated in the throat)
that grind food against horny plates. They can
eat a wide variety of foods, from bloodworms
to large mussels. Carp can tolerate waters
that are poor in oxygen or
even mildly polluted.

TYPICAL SIZE
*Carp average around
10 lb (4.5 kg) but
can exceed this many
times over.*

◀ WILD CARP
*This lovely fish is a typical example of the original,
wild population of carp that once was found all over
Europe. Today, cultivated fish have pushed these stocks
out of many of their strongholds, and wild carp tend to
be found only in remote areas.*

▲ COMMON CARP
*Like the wild carp, this fish has a fully
scaled body and a scaleless head. It can
be distinguished from mirror and leather
carp because it is the only one of the
three with scales on the flanks.*

DESCENDANTS OF WILD CARP

Centuries ago, the wild carp – the ancestral
European carp species – was domesticated.
Monks farmed and bred carp selectively for
strains that attained larger body sizes, grew
faster, and spawned more prolifically.

In some of these man-made varieties, such
as the leather and mirror carp, scales are
reduced or absent – an advantage in the
kitchen. The common carp is, however, fully
scaled, and many people consider it to be
the "main" variety, classifying the mirror and
leather carp as varieties of common carp.

These man-made forms have been introduced widely in the western world. In place
of the sleek, wild carp, which may attain,
say, 20 lb (9 kg), we now have deep-bodied
fish up to three times as heavy. Some have
even been derided as "footballs"!

SMOOTH OPERATOR
*The leather carp is completely
bare and scaleless, protected
only by a hard,
smooth skin.*

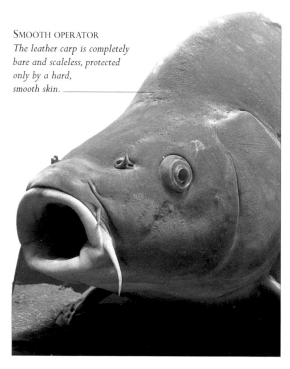

▲ MIRROR CARP
*The scale patterns on mirror carp are
unique to individual fish. This makes
it possible to recognize fish when caught
a second or third time. By monitoring
individual fish, experts have been able
to show that carp live for over 50 years.*

◀ LEATHER CARP
*Over the centuries, selective breeding has
removed any trace of scales from the
leather carp. The variety has also become
very fast-growing, so it is relatively easy
to find large, heavily built specimens.*

ASIATIC CARP

Many of the carp species of Asia look wildly exotic, and many (particularly the grass carp) have been introduced to western countries. Eastern Asia is the home of the goldfish and the koi carp. Both of these have been bred selectively over centuries, perhaps especially the koi. In Japan today, good specimens of some varieties and colors of koi are worth tens of thousands of dollars.

The grass carp, a Chinese species from the basin of the Amur River, is an exciting sport fish, capable of growing to vast sizes. It feeds almost exclusively on plant life.

Southeast Asia has its own, enormous local variety of the common carp, and China has another carp species, the blue carp. This, too, can grow to vast sizes.

▲ GRASS CARP
The grass carp has been introduced to many European and North American waters in order to crop unwanted weed. Its reception has been very mixed.

◀ KOI AMID THE SCHOOL
Koi carp are immediately recognizable in this school of darker carp (probably common) by their dramatic coloring. The most highly valued koi represent centuries of careful selective breeding.

▼ KARNATIC CARP
This beautiful karnatic carp was caught in the Cauvery River in southern India. It is shaped like the common barbel, another member of the Cyprinidae. These fish grow to about 20 lb (9 kg) in weight.

CRUCIAN CARP

This is a separate species from the wild carp and its man-made derivatives. However, it is quite similar in appearance, except that it is shorter and stumpier and lacks the barbels of the common carp.

Commons and crucians both spawn on plants, and they do so at the same time of year. The two species are able to interbreed, and so there are many hybrid forms.

Crucians have a greater tendency to school than other carp and form closely bonded groups that stay together throughout their lives. They prefer to keep close to the bank, in among jungles of weeds and tree roots. They seek out holes in the bank and hide in these until dusk. Food includes bloodworms, daphnia, and all small invertebrates.

▲ STAYING NEAR HOME
The crucian carp does not swim long distances but tends to glide and hang almost motionless in mid water, directing itself with odd twitches of the fins. A very alert fish, the crucian is aware of any bankside disturbance.

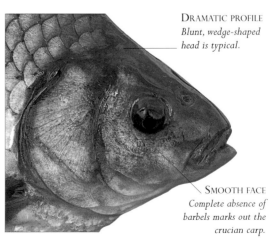

DRAMATIC PROFILE
Blunt, wedge-shaped head is typical.

SMOOTH FACE
Complete absence of barbels marks out the crucian carp.

▲ HEAD STUDY
The crucian generally feeds on the bottom, rooting out bloodworms and other small food items. It sometimes comes to the surface to intercept hatching insects.

CARP FISHING STRATEGIES

YOU NEED A CERTAIN TYPE of angling mind to catch a carp. It is a fish with a wide range of behavioral patterns. The first thing you will find out about carp is that they use all the water and are great investigators. Next, they have a truly catholic diet and will suck at just about anything they see. The third thing you learn is that despite their catholic diet they remain one of the most cautious of species, and once hooked they won't make the same mistake again.

This means that carp fishing is a cat-and-mouse type of game, especially in clear water. You will need a whole set of strategies if you are going to outwit these wily fish.

FLOATING BAIT

Carp are happy to take food from the water surface, and they will suck in fluttering moths or any struggling insects from the surface film. Floating baits once were fairly straightforward – commonly bread, cut into matchbox-sized pieces.

These days, many anglers bake bread especially for the purpose, often putting in scents that are attractive to carp. Commercial dry foods for dogs and cats are also important floating baits today. They come in a hard form and need a quick steaming to make them soft enough for baiting the hook.

▲ BREAD AND PET FOOD
A selection of floating baits: brown bread is as good as white; the pet foods can be steamed, and you can add flavoring and coloring if necessary. Variety is important for a long day's fishing.

SURFACE FISHING

Location is very important when surface fishing for carp. Take time to search out the right areas: look closely at the calmer bays, such as pools behind islands, which may be sheltered by trees or strewn with lilybeds. Carp love to rest in these areas, especially when the weather is warm. Backs out of the water, fins working idly . . . the perfect surface carp fisher's target.

There are also times when the carp patrol open water and accept surface baits. Cast the bait out into any ripple, after which you can either let it go with the drift or anchor a bait over a leger weight. Free offerings allay any suspicions, and it pays to slingshot out dog biscuits into the water. Do this over a half-hour period before fishing.

▲ A CONFIDENT FISH
The way in which a carp takes a piece of floating bait reflects its attitude. If the take is splashy and violent, the carp is suspicious of the bait. A slow take is a sign of a supremely confident carp.

▼ CAREFUL INSPECTION
Carp can often see a fishing line on the surface – this may stand out clearly as it leads to the bait. Sometimes a carp will deliberately investigate a bait by swimming around with its head out of the water, feeling for any line.

BOTTOM FISHING

For bottom fishing, many anglers use a "bolt rig," in which a leger sinks the bait and gives weight and distance to the cast, and a short length of slack line (the "hook length") carries the bait and hook. When a carp takes the bait, it suspects nothing since there is no tension in the slack line. The fish swims away but soon feels the shock of the tightening line. This makes the fish panic and turn against the tension, hooking itself firmly in the process.

▲ TELL-TALE MUD
When carp feed on the bottom, they dig for food items such as roots or worms, stirring up a cloud of mud, which becomes a useful giveaway for the angler. You may not see the fish, but you see the evidence.

▲ FISHING ON THE DROP
A useful alternative to the bolt rig is to weight your hook only lightly, so that it will take a minute or two to sink down to the bottom. Hungry carp often come off the bottom to pick out food as it drifts through the water layers. This way, you are basically bottom-fishing, with an option of getting a catch "on the drop."

◄ BAIT ON THE BOTTOM
In the final analysis, this is how you are going to catch most of your carp. They are very persistent scavengers and will not leave any stone unturned, literally, in their search for food that might have gotten away from them. Carp have highly sensitive nostrils and barbels, which they use in this activity.

FLOAT FISHING

Baits floating on the water surface are often rejected, and there is always a risk that a bottom-fished bait may sink into a tangle of roots and be ignored. However, a bait just touching the bottom under a float is a different proposition altogether, and it is frequently taken. Float fishing is a strategy that I find both fun and very efficient.

A driftbeater float *(see p. 162)* enables you to stalk carp around the margins and cast to them with great precision. You can put the bait exactly in the carp's path, and your float will register bites instantly. Whatever kind of float you are using, a tiny shot placed a short way up from the float will sink the line in a ripple and improve your control.

Sometimes it has been found that carp can show suspicion of a float lying on the water. At times like this, I find that changing from a regular float to an ordinary twig or even a feather can prove to be the answer.

SCALE PATTERN
This is a scattered mirror carp. Each individual mirror carp has its own recognizable pattern.

▲ SMALL IS BEAUTIFUL
When carp fishing, size is not everything. Although this fish was of modest size, it was a most welcome capture, especially coming from a very overgrown, snag-infested piece of water.

◄ A BRIGHT RED TIP
There is something good about watching a float just out from the rod tip. Floats present a bait very efficiently indeed, and any take is registered at once.

FLOAT FISHING FOR CARP

W HEN YOU FISH FOR CARP with a float, you are at close quarters with your quarry. If you make an unguarded footfall, it will immediately be felt or heard by the fish. If they are in clear water, the fish may be able to see you, so choose clothing with suitably subdued colors to enable you to merge with the foliage. You will also need to make every possible use of bankside vegetation, hiding from view behind trees, bushes, and even tall grasses. This is one of the times when the angler must become the active hunter.

ESTATE LAKE LOCATION
This beautiful lake is in a country estate surrounded by woodland. The water is shallow and clear, with lilies growing from a muddy bottom. Water flow is very slight: a small stream feeds the lake, flowing out under a footbridge.

▲ A BUBBLING CARP
There is no more encouraging sign for the angler than bubbles rising to the surface, indicating a fish feeding on the bottom.

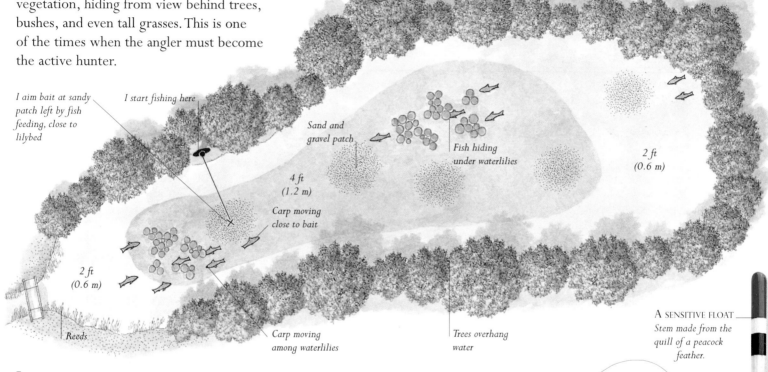

I aim bait at sandy patch left by fish feeding, close to lilybed

I start fishing here

Sand and gravel patch

Fish hiding under waterlilies

2 ft (0.6 m)

4 ft (1.2 m)

Carp moving close to bait

2 ft (0.6 m)

Reeds

Carp moving among waterlilies

Trees overhang water

▲ A SENSITIVE FLOAT
Stem made from the quill of a peacock feather.

Split shot

TIDBITS
Carp love any tasty food, and they seem to like variety. A cocktail of different baits can prove to be irresistible.

Corn

Live maggot

LAYING THE TRAP

1 PUTTING OUT THE GROUNDBAIT
Careful groundbaiting is an important part of carp fishing at any range. I use my slingshot to throw pouches of maggots and corn along the fringe of a lilybed, where carp are hiding from the sunshine. The smell of this bait could well draw them out into open water. Notice that I am partly hidden by foliage and camouflaged in green.

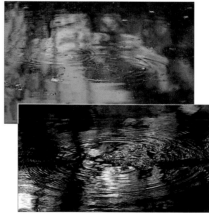

2 SPOTTING THE SIGNS
Fish drift out from under the lilies and begin rooting among the bottom debris for the bait. Bubbles rise (top), and one fish touches the surface as it maneuvers in the water (above).

▲ A FAVORITE RIG
It is important to make sure that the bait lies firmly on the bottom and that the float is not pushed around by the wind. This is achieved by placing a large split shot 6 in (15 cm) from the hook.

ENCOUNTER WITH A CARP

1 OUT OF THE LILIES
Now the carp are definitely scenting the food and feeling hungry. Fish that have just become active like this simply come out of their refuge, take one or two mouthfuls of food, and go back under the pads to chew and swallow what they have taken. One carp breaks the surface with a fin as it turns to go back.

2 SWINGING OUT THE BAIT
I flick out the float and bait and can tell immediately that all the carp are back under the lilies — otherwise I would see them dart away from the splash. Accurate casting is essential, because the carp will not venture far from the groundbaited area. I keep my eye on the lilies and the spot I am aiming for, avoiding catching the line in the tree.

3 THE FISH DROPS TO FEED
One particularly nice-looking carp looks more hungry than the rest and comes back over the groundbait for a third time. I see its stomach — it may look very faint, but that yellow gleam can mean nothing else — as the fish tips up in the water in order to get its head down to feed. The moment is close!

BATTLE IN THE WATER

1 THE SWIM EXPLODES
The carp takes the bait and I strike (jerk the line to catch the hook in the fish's mouth). A carp fooled like this is invariably an angry fish. My job is to keep the fish out of the lilies, where it could anchor itself or snag the line; a short but dramatic tug-of-war ensues.

2 GETTING IN THERE
With dense tree cover overhead threatening to catch the end of my rod or tangle my line, there is no way for me to land the fish from my original position on the bank, so, before I can begin the final landing process, I need to get myself out into the swim with the fish.

3 HELD IN THE EVENING SUN
I'm proud of this carp because I've exercised all the skills of the hunter to catch it — successful camouflage, ground-baiting, casting, and landing. Notice how I don't hold the carp under the stomach, where vital organs could be harmed. A quick photograph, then the fish is free to swim back to its home in the lilies.

LARGE-WATER LEGERING FOR CARP

SOME OF THE VERY BIGGEST carp in the world are to be found in the largest and deepest waters, where close-in float fishing is rarely possible. Legering is the most practical way to catch these fish. Instead of hanging your hook from a float, you anchor it on the bed with a sizable lead weight. Without a float, the rig casts well and enables you to cast long and fish deep.

Leger fishing for carp often involves long periods of waiting, and you cannot be sure of staying alert for long enough to see every bite. Self-hooking rigs, which respond automatically to a bite, will solve this problem. Whether it comes soon or late, the fight of a big carp at long distance in deep water is an extraordinary experience for any angler.

LONG-CASTING TECHNIQUE

Practice is the first requirement in learning distance casting; after that, the right gear: a powerful rod, a large-spooled reel, and a comparatively light line with a shock leader (stronger terminal length).

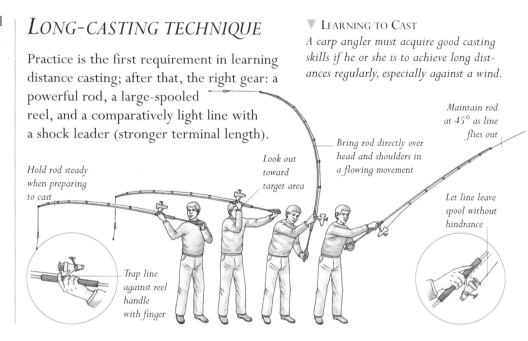

▼ LEARNING TO CAST
A carp angler must acquire good casting skills if he or she is to achieve long distances regularly, especially against a wind.

Hold rod steady when preparing to cast

Trap line against reel handle with finger

Look out toward target area

Bring rod directly over head and shoulders in a flowing movement

Maintain rod at 45° as line flies out

Let line leave spool without hindrance

WORLD-FAMOUS CARP WATER

One of the most famous of all large-water carp locations is Lac de St. Cassien in southern France. This lake, created by the damming of a river, is the home of some extraordinary carp and attracts enthusiastic carp anglers from all over the world. My Danish friend and colleague, Johnny Jensen, is just one of the many fishermen who have made a pilgrimage to this huge water.

LAKESIDE LOCATION
The illustration and photographs on these pages show some of the preparations and one catch made by Johnny Jensen in the course of a week-long carp session on Lac de St. Cassien.

LAC DE ST. CASSIEN

Johnny's position

◄ JOHNNY'S SWIM
Johnny chose a bay on the north arm to mount his attack. This spot is well known for its carp: the fish frequently patrol the drop-off from shallow to deep water.

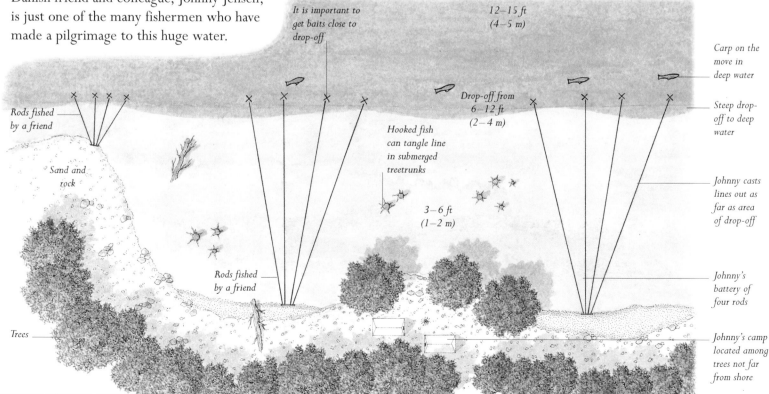

It is important to get baits close to drop-off

12–15 ft (4–5 m)

Carp on the move in deep water

Rods fished by a friend

Drop-off from 6–12 ft (2–4 m)

Steep drop-off to deep water

Hooked fish can tangle line in submerged treetrunks

Sand and rock

3–6 ft (1–2 m)

Johnny casts lines out as far as area of drop-off

Rods fished by a friend

Johnny's battery of four rods

Trees

Johnny's camp located among trees not far from shore

PREPARING TO FISH

1 SETTING OUT THE RODS

Johnny planned to set up a battery of four rods. He chose an armory of long, powerful rods capable of making the long cast and of landing a big fish from very long range. This is a situation in which choice of the right tackle is paramount. The picture shows the view that he saw during the days of waiting.

2 PREBAITING

You need to prevent carp from leaving your area on their patrol. The only way to do this is to lay down a large enough carpet of food to attract their attention and sustain their interest. Tiger nuts do this well but must be softened by soaking before use — fish consuming them in their hard state could come to harm.

3 HOOKBAIT

This hookbait consists of two tiger nuts separated by a piece of polystyrene that will keep them slightly buoyant. This is known as a "pop-up" and floats just off the bottom, swaying in the current — very enticing to a passing fish.

CATCHING THE CARP

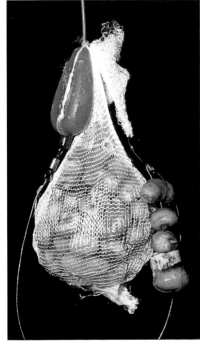

1 SOLUBLE BAG

Groundbait is carried out into the fishing zone in a PVA bag that Johnny attaches to his line. PVA is a plastic that dissolves in the water and releases the groundbait. Notice the stone — a handy weight to take this whole terminal rig directly to the bottom. A heavy rig like this is best taken out by boat.

2 THE SWIM IS COVERED

Fishing like this is very much a waiting game. The bait is out and the groundbait is being released from its bag. Any passing fish should be drawn down toward the bed and to the hookbait. You are left just hoping that fish will visit you before the end of your stay.

3 CARP OF A LIFETIME

No wonder Johnny looks so excited by this huge common carp, which gave him an unforgettable battle in the fading light of evening. This wonderful fish weighed 42 lb (19 kg), a true monster and a fantastic reward for the long journey to France from Copenhagen. It is at moments like this that all the planning, all the expense, all the effort, and all the hours and days of waiting are totally justified.

EELS

THE EEL TENDS TO BE THOUGHT unworthy of proper respect by many anglers, perhaps because of its snakelike looks. However, the eel is a fish just as much as any other, and has been appreciated as a nourishing food for many centuries. The ancient Greeks are known to have been fond of eel dishes, while 5,000 years ago in Egypt the eel was worshiped as a god!

STRONG TAIL
Tail can be wrapped around objects, anchoring eel immovably.

JOINED FINS
Anal and dorsal fins are both connected to tail fin.

THERE ARE MORE than 20 families of eel, but only one contains eels that occur in fresh water. This is the Anguillidae family, whose members are catadromous – they spawn at sea and grow to full size in fresh water (in contrast with salmon – *see p. 88*).

The American eel spawns in the Atlantic Ocean and migrates up the rivers of eastern North America, the Caribbean, and northern South America. The European eel spawns in the Atlantic and is found in all European rivers. The long-finned eel spawns in the Indian Ocean and migrates into rivers in Australia, Tasmania, and New Zealand.

European and American eels rarely weigh more than 10 lb (4.5 kg), but long-finned eels can reach 40 lb (18 kg) or more.

LIFE CYCLE

The European eel breeds thousands of miles from Europe in the Sargasso Sea, which is a region in the Atlantic Ocean just off the Gulf of Mexico.

The larva starts as a tiny, leaf-shaped creature that drifts northeastward in the Gulf Stream. Some three years later it appears on the shores of Europe as an elver, a tiny eel about 2–3 in (5–8 cm) long.

The elver travels with millions of companions up a river. Those that are not taken by predators or caught in nets make their homes in ponds or rivers, where they live for anything up to 50 or 60 years before returning to the Sargasso Sea to spawn and die.

▲ INVASION OF THE ELVERS
The springtime elver invasion is a remarkable sight. The elvers tend to follow the margins of the river, where they do not need to face the main current. They frequently stop to rest among clusters of rocks or within chinks or hollows in brickwork.

BACK FROM THE SEAS

Elvers must utilize currents and tides in their long journey across the ocean, often drifting hundreds of miles along with the Gulf Stream. At this age they are very small and are not strong swimmers: the long distances involved would exhaust them. High tides are especially useful when they reach estuaries, for they sweep the elvers up against the flow of the river. Even on a strong tide, the elvers will swim close to the banks, where they find the push of fresh water weakest. By the time eels reach adulthood and need to return to their spawning beds, they have no such worries. At this stage, they will have become confident in the water, swimming with a slow, powerful motion that they can maintain for days.

▲ THE ESTUARY
The elvers leave the sea and swim into estuaries. Here, all manner of dangers lie in wait for the young eels. Predatory fish include bass and sea trout. Many species of seabird also feed from the estuaries, and thousands of elvers are taken as they move up with the tides.

▲ THE MARSH
Many estuaries pass through a salt marsh like this one, and some elvers leave the estuaries here to find creeks, where they will make their homes before returning to the Atlantic. Most, however, pass through the marsh, following the brackish river into true fresh water.

DORSAL FIN
Dorsal fin forms unbroken line down back of eel, joining with tail and anal fins.

YELLOW UNDERSIDE
Belly shading is yellow-green. This becomes silver as spawning approaches.

TINY SCALES
Scales are small and oval, deeply embedded in skin, and covered with mucus. Mucus may help eel to slip away when seized by a predator.

EUROPEAN EEL
Anguilla anguilla
APPROXIMATE GUIDE TO WEIGHTS
AVERAGE 1–2 lb (0.45–0.9 kg)
TROPHY 4 lb (1.8 kg)
RECORD 10 lb (4.5 kg)

PECTORAL FINS
The only paired fins on the eel are the pectorals. These are comparatively small for a large fish.

EEL ANATOMY

An eel is a fish that has evolved an elongated body plan and long dorsal and anal fins. Most other fish have a pair of pectoral fins at the front of the body, a pair of pelvic fins close to the belly, a single or double dorsal fin on the back, and an anal fin underneath. Eels are unusual in that the pectoral fins are relatively small, and pelvic fins are absent. Another unusual feature is the difference in size between the sexes: females of the European and American eels, for example, grow up to three times longer than males.

▲ **COVER UP!**
An eel tends to spend much of the daytime with its body entombed under a rock or covered with weed. Only the head sticks out, swaying slightly as the eel surveys the scene.

SHARP EYE
Eyesight is good; eye itself grows considerably before the return spawning migration.

POWERFUL SNOUT
Muscular snout can be used for digging in bottom silt for invertebrate prey.

▲ **LOCK GATES**
Lock gates are no obstacle. The elvers will swarm through any cracks and openings and will sometimes leave the water altogether, scaling the brickwork instead. They make easy pickings for birds and rodents and, at night, foxes and badgers.

▲ **UP THE STREAM**
The elvers will follow the smallest of water channels, constantly nosing forward, looking for their destined homes. Somewhere they will find sanctuary. If they find a chain of interconnected lakes, the elvers are likely to favor the topmost one.

▲ **ACROSS THE MEADOW**
Not all eels stay in the pond or stream that they chose as elvers. Mature eels sometimes seek a new home, traveling at night. These eels usually follow streams, but after rain or in thick dew they can also travel short distances across land.

▲ **NEW HOME**
A secluded pond with plenty of cover provides an ideal home for many years. However, the mature eel still has its predators even in this haven, especially pike which find winter food by digging eels out of the silt at the bottom of the pond.

FISHING FOR EELS

TACKLE FOR EELS needs to be robust: you need strong hooks, and your line should have a minimum breaking strain of 10–15 lb (4.5–7 kg). Strong tackle is vital if you are to be able to drag an eel out of its lair, because once that tail wraps itself around any sunken obstacle, the game is over.

Rigs need not be too sophisticated but, whether using leger or float, it is essential that the eel feels little or no resistance. The eel is a sensitive fish, and it will drop a bait quickly if there is not plenty of slack in the line. It must suspect nothing.

TIMING

Eels are known for their tendency to become active in warm weather, and close, muggy periods seem to produce the best catches. Eel sessions that happen to coincide with thunderstorms are often highly successful.

Most eel fishing is done at night, since that is the time when the eels are at their most active. However, good catches can be made in the daytime if baits are laid close to the places where eels like to live.

WHERE TO FISH

Eels can be found anywhere that has good enough access from the sea. Their favorite places are millpools, where there is usually plenty of rubble on the bottom in which eels love to hide.

All still waters will hold their stock of eels, and so do most rivers, but the biggest eels often tend to be in the most remote places. The more difficult it is for the elvers to get into a water, the more difficult it is for the mature eel to return to the sea, and this is why some big eels occur in these locations.

Eels love snags – features that stick up from the bottom or out from the bank – as well as islands and gulleys. However, if the water has been netted by commercial eel fishermen, your chances of good sport are slim.

▲ EXPLORING A CREEK
Some eels do not travel far upstream but make their home close to the sea. This means that there can be good eel fishing as near to the sea as in this creek, which is close to the estuary. Remember to explore any deeper areas and places where boats are moored.

▲ AS THE SHADOWS FALL
There is no doubt that eels begin to move as soon as the sun sets and the shadows fall across their waters. This is when they come out of their lairs and feed in earnest. An early-feeding eel that came out when the sun was still above the horizon is seen being caught here.

▲ CLOSE TO WEED
Eels rarely stray very far from water weed, where they can find excellent cover among the roots and a plentiful food supply in the water snails and small fish that tend to shelter amid the stems and leaves.

► KEEP THE HEAD UP
If you hook an eel in the weed, keep its head up. Your line will inevitably break if you let an eel get caught in the fronds.

EEL BAITS

Eels hunt largely by scent, so use bait that give off an aroma *(see p.178)*. However, do remember that eels like only fresh baits and will not take those that are old or stale.

In the wild, eels tend to eat either small foodstuffs like bloodworms, snails, daphnia, or leeches. Alternatively, some eels prefer larger prey – particularly small fish.

The experienced eel catcher will consider using both large and small baits, trying maggots before larger baits such as dead fish or a bunch of lobworms.

Strong-scented groundbait can draw eels to your hook bait. Try packing a feeder with a blood-soaked rag (from cutting up deadbait). This attracts fish without overfeeding them.

▲ PARTICLE BAITS
A maggot is a fly larva, and a caster is the chrysalis in which it will change. Both of these are known as particle baits and are perfect for eels, especially small ones. An eel will browse for a long time over a bed of maggots, sending large, fizzing bubbles to the surface.

▲ DEADBAIT
Any small dead fish makes good bait for eels, but the favorites are gudgeon, dace, and roach (a dace is shown here). If you are using large fish as deadbait, cut them into chunks about the size of a matchbox.

▲ LOBWORMS
Eels love lobworms and like them to be fresh and lively. You can try just a single lobworm, but very frequently bunches of four or even six worms attract the biggest fish.

CARE OF THE CATCH

A big eel is invariably an old eel, and in many waters a real specimen is rare. (A specimen is a catch of record-breaking size or of a size that is for any reason worthy of note.) If we are to enjoy catching more of these prize eels, we must take the greatest possible care of all the stock.

Remember not to grip an eel too tightly when removing the hook, or vital organs could be damaged. If you catch your eel at night, put it in a sack to be unhooked in the morning light. Keep the sack in deep, weed-free water all night: weeds give off carbon dioxide, which could kill the eel. Some eel anglers cut a narrow trench in the bank and lay their overnight catch in this to prevent damage from wriggling. Do remember, however, not to keep an eel out of water for long, especially in warm weather.

◀ PERFECTLY HOOKED
Hook your eel so cleanly that you will be able to release it easily and painlessly. To achieve this, you must strike immediately the moment the bite begins. The only possible disadvantage is that the hook may slip out of the eel's mouth. Waiting for bites to develop means that you might hook more fish but so deeply that they might not recover.

CATFISH

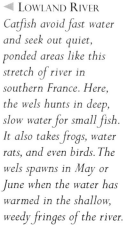

MY WIFE AND I, with three Nepali guides, were rafting down a Himalayan river. As our craft was floating gently across a clear pool, an enormous underwater shape came toward us. It was so large that our craft was lifted up 1 ft (30 cm) or more by the water that it had displaced. The great shadowy shape disappeared upstream. That was a catfish!

THOUGH CATFISH may not be the most beautiful of fish species, their vast size gives them a mystery of their own. Take, for instance, the colossal goonch of Asia — the fish that I have just described. Fish of this species commonly grow to 200 lb (90 kg) and are reputed to attain four or five times that weight in remote, unexplored streams.

Another giant is the pla-buk catfish of the Mekong River in southeast Asia. This fish grows to such an enormous size that whole villages set out to catch one, every inhabitant dreaming of becoming rich when the fish is sold at the market.

Two further examples are the piramutaba catfish of the Amazon and the wels of the Danube drainage area, both of which, at their largest, are the stuff of dreams.

◀ LOWLAND RIVER
Catfish avoid fast water and seek out quiet, ponded areas like this stretch of river in southern France. Here, the wels hunts in deep, slow water for small fish. It also takes frogs, water rats, and even birds. The wels spawns in May or June when the water has warmed in the shallow, weedy fringes of the river.

CATFISH FAMILIES

Worldwide, there are over 30 families of freshwater and marine catfish, containing about 2,250 species. North America has one major family of freshwater catfish, which contains about 50 species; there could be 20 times that number in the huge river systems of South America.

There are many species of freshwater catfish in Africa and Asia. Europe has just two, the wels and the tiny Aristotle's catfish, which is confined to Greece.

In poor countries, large catfish are of economic importance, and fishing there can be so intensive as to place these species at risk. The pla-buk of the Mekong River is just one example of a catfish species in danger.

▲ WEIRD AND WONDERFUL
Anglers often travel the world to fish for catfish. There are plenty of warm-water rivers where a bottom bait with a strong scent will attract a bite from some weird and wonderful species of catfish.

▶ HOME OF THE GOONCH
This stretch of the Brahmaputra River in northeast India is 1 mile (1.6 km) wide and contains freshwater dolphins, colossal mahseer — and the goonch catfish.

BARBEL
Wels has six or eight long, sensitive barbels. Numbers of barbels vary between species.

TAIL
Tail of wels begins here and makes up three-fifths of body length.

MUSCULAR PHYSIQUE
Catfish are more powerfully built than most other kinds of fish.

ANAL FIN
Anal fin almost joins tail fin and is proportionally longer than that of other catfish.

CATFISH ANATOMY

All catfish have long bodies with large heads, scaleless skin, and a series of pairs of fleshy barbels surrounding the mouth. The young wels shown here displays two features that are characteristic of its species: the anal fin is very long, and the eyes are very small. The wels has a black back and very dark sides that are marbled with white or yellow.

DORSAL VIEW
This view shows the width of the mouth, which enables the catfish to take big prey.

WELS *Silurus glanis*
APPROXIMATE GUIDE TO WEIGHTS
AVERAGE 10–20 lb (4.5–9 kg)
TROPHY 30–40 lb (14–23 kg)
ROD-CAUGHT RECORD 400 lb (180 kg)
COMMERCIALLY CAUGHT RECORD 700 lb (320 kg)

▶ **BLUE CATFISH**
This is the largest species of catfish in North America. Its average weight is 50 lb (23 kg) but it can exceed 100 lb (45 kg). Unusual for a catfish, it has a preference for swift-flowing, clear rivers.

CATFISH SWARMS

Large numbers of catfish sometimes come together, either where food is particularly prolific or where water conditions are particularly suitable for them.

In slow rivers, a deep hollow in the bed can often attract great numbers of catfish, especially during the daylight hours. The catfish will emerge from the hole at dusk to wander and feed throughout the night.

Numbers of catfish come together to feed on other fish species when they are spawning in reedbeds. In the Volga Delta in the south of European Russia, mass migrations of frogs or toads regularly attract swarms of catfish.

Even the massive goonch catfish *(see opposite)* sometimes swarms. Legend has it that gangs of goonch cooperate in killing large prey fish such as mahseer or even a small deer drinking at the waterside.

▲ **YOUNG SWARM**
Baby catfish stay together in compact schools. This is a form of defense against the many predators in the environment. The fish seen here are only a few months old, but a large part of the original school has already been taken.

▶ **ADULT SWARM**
Adult catfish are forced to swarm if river levels fall and the fish are marooned in shrinking lagoons. The catfish are adept at surviving with little water and can do so for many days as long as they manage to keep themselves moist.

FISHING FOR CATFISH

WHEREVER YOU FISH in the world, the really big catfish are found only in the really big rivers. The Volga, the Ebro, and the Amazon are all superb catfish rivers.

To be a catfish angler you are going to need to think big and do things on a scale as grand as your intended quarry. You are almost bound to need to do some traveling, and once you have arrived at your chosen location, which is usually a remote one, it is up to you to make sure that all the right tackle is present and correct.

A boat is almost certainly needed. You are probably going to need big baits and the right weights to enable you to sink them deep in swollen currents. Small catfish from pleasant pools are one thing, but to fish for monstrous, fully grown examples demands a completely different approach.

THE RIGHT TACKLE

Anybody looking to land a catfish of 100 lb (45 kg) or more from a deep, swirling river must not leave a single thing to chance when choosing tackle. The rod must be strong and short and yet beautifully flexible. An uptide sea rod (see p. 171) is almost certain to be the ideal weapon, probably with a roller fitted on the top ring to avoid line friction.

Use a multiplier reel, and pick one that is sufficiently strongly geared to cope with the strains involved. The breaking strain of the line should never be less than 40 lb (18 kg). Your hooks should be stout: try the forged and sharpened hooks that are used for moderate-sized sharks. You must fit a heavy enough weight to get the bait right down on the bottom: catfish weights can be fist-sized.

An added extra that could prove important is a butt pad (see p. 74), which is strapped around the waist to give you valuable extra leverage when you are trying to get a monster off the riverbed.

▲ BIG AS A MAN
A catfish this size is capable of fighting for an hour or more, plunging and surging in a deep river with a powerful current. Both tackle and angler must be up to the grueling job.

▼ BOATED
A mottled giant lies in the boat well. You must keep the fish wet while it is being unhooked and return it to the river as soon as possible.

▲ IN THE NET
A fair-sized African catfish fights all the way to the boat, where it is scooped out of the water with the aid of a voluminous net. The trouble is that African catfish can be a lot bigger than this, and an angler who hooks one of the heavyweights faces a major challenge!

PLAYING A LARGE FISH

Let us assume that you have the physical strength for the job and concentrate on the psychological factor: a battle with a big fish is likely to be a prolonged one, and you must keep both your nerve and your patience. I have seen anglers crack under the strain when half an hour has gone by, and still there is no sign of the fish weakening.

Commit yourself to the catch, and play the fish hard with determination. Once you have stopped what might otherwise have been a tearaway run, the key is to wind the fish in little by little. Keep trying to put just a yard or two of line back on the reel each time. You are not going to budge the fish much at a time, but providing you keep winning just a little, the fish will eventually come!

You must take care when the fish is near the boat, because when it sees daylight and feels the air on its whiskers, the struggle is almost bound to erupt all over again. You will need to bring the fish to the surface, but first maneuver it close in to the boat, where you can lay hands on it easily.

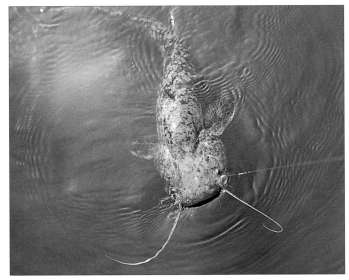

▲ PUMPING HARD
The technique known as "pumping" consists of lowering the rod, reeling in line, and leaning backward, winning a little line each time. The fish will yield slowly.

◀ THE END IS IN SIGHT
Here comes a big fish, gasping in the daylight. Take care now, because it might make one last run and could break your tackle. Give the fish line if it wants to dive.

BAITS

Catfish are not simply scavengers that eat anything – indeed, they can be very choosy in what they take. When at all possible, use perfectly fresh baits. Do not be afraid to experiment with new types of baits; offer fish and other creatures that the catfish have probably never seen or tasted before in their native environment. Normally it is quite effective to use large baits, but, if the fish are being cautious, you can be successful with very small ones; a simple idea such as a dead frog can often land the biggest catfish of all.

◀ THE PREDATOR
Never has a photograph proved so conclusively that the catfish is a big, mean-looking predator, happy to hunt anywhere in its huge environment.

▲ SQUID
Experimental baits pay off. There are not many catfish that have seen squid in their natural environment, but it turns out that they love them!

BARBEL & MAHSEER

BARBEL ARE A VARIED GROUP of fish belonging to the carp family. Over 100 species are distributed in Africa and Asia, including the mahseer, an Indian sport fish. Europe has three species, of which only the common barbel is widely fished. The mouths of all European barbel are equipped with sensors, or "barbels," from which the name of the fish is derived.

COMMON BARBEL

THE DISTRIBUTION of the common barbel extends from England across Europe as far south as Italy. This species grows to a maximum weight of 18 lb (8 kg). A smaller barbel, *Barbus meridionalis*, found in southern Europe, grows to a weight of ½ lb (0.25 kg) or thereabouts. A third species, which lives in Spain and Portugal and is distinguished by its large scales, grows to 25 lb (12 kg).

Common barbel spawn in May or June in fast-flowing, shallow water over gravel. The species lives mostly in schools of equal-sized fish, while large individuals are often solitary.

The name "common barbel" is scientifically correct in formal contexts, but I shall call this fish by its more usual name – "barbel" – where it is clear which species is meant.

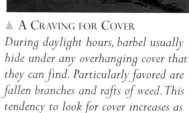

▲ A CRAVING FOR COVER
During daylight hours, barbel usually hide under any overhanging cover that they can find. Particularly favored are fallen branches and rafts of weed. This tendency to look for cover increases as angling pressure grows stronger.

◄ WEED OVER GRAVEL
Gravel holds much of the food that barbel seek, and the flowing tresses of weed give the fish some shelter from overhead predation. With their large pectoral fins and streamlined body shape, barbel hold their position without difficulty in fast-flowing water.

BARBEL ANATOMY

The body and head of the barbel are long and cylindrical in shape. The mouth is low and underslung and is surrounded by four barbels. These are flexible, fleshy sensors that are used to locate potential food items.

The eyes are situated high up on the head and are directed slightly upward. The tail fin is large and deep and the body very muscular. Coloration varies widely, even among fish within a single school: flanks can be anything from ivory (rarely) through to gold and a dark chocolate-brown.

COMMON BARBEL
Barbus barbus
APPROXIMATE GUIDE TO WEIGHTS
AVERAGE 5–7 lb (2.3–3.2 kg)
TROPHY 10 lb (4.5 kg)
RECORD 18–22 lb (8.2–10 kg)

MOUTH
Mouth is underslung, with protruding lips.

PECTORAL FINS
Pectoral fins are large in relation to body size. They help hold the fish at the bottom in fast currents.

FRONT BARBELS
One pair of barbels is at the front of the mouth.

BACK BARBELS
One pair of barbels is at the back of the mouth.

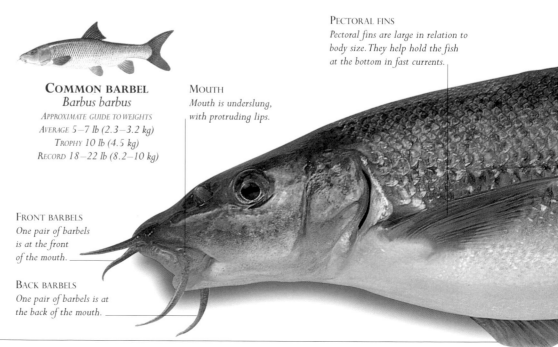

FEEDING ON THE RIVERBED

The barbel lives on foods that are plentiful in its habitat: caddis larvae, nymphs of all types, leeches, shrimp, and snails, all of which are often found on the riverbed.

The barbel uses its pairs of sensors in the search for food. These barbels carry a large number of taste and touch cells and act like external tongues, allowing the fish to test items for edibility. Anglers will also confirm that the barbel is able to examine a bait, together with the hook and line, with equal care and caution!

The barbel is often regarded as a nocturnal feeder, and to a certain extent this is true. However, in any barbel waters that are not fished, the species is very active all through the day. Night feeding is probably little more than evasive action in response to growing pressure from anglers.

▲ RICH LARDER
Here is a very pleasing sight to a barbel — a small hollow in a riverbed, covered over with weed and swarming with minnows. The barbel would also like the look of those stones, for it uses its strong snout to overturn objects as it grubs for food. There could be a feast of invertebrate life under there.

◄ HUNTING AT DAWN
Very early in the morning, barbel will be found in the shallows, hunting for all types of aquatic food. The dorsal fin often breaks surface. Sunrise, and with it the first anglers, sends the fish gliding back to deeper water.

HUNTING ON THE SURFACE

Though barbel often feed on the riverbed, it would be a mistake to think that they feed there exclusively. They do not! In areas of thick weed, barbel of any size will readily come to the surface to take luncheon meat and other bait from the surface.

Larger barbel come to the surface when hunting small fish. A lot of splashes that are attributed to trout or even salmon are made by barbel breaking through the surface in pursuit of small fry, minnows, or bleak.

▲ PREDATOR
A 7 lb (3 kg) barbel rises toward the surface, shepherding small fish before it. At the surface, it will attack the school with great speed and ferocity, seizing any fish unfortunate enough to be in its path.

▲ PREY
The small fish are now silhouetted against the surface. One or two of them will suffice to make the raid worthwhile.

BODY SHAPE
Barbel has a torpedo-shaped body, streamlined for life in fast currents.

TAIL WRIST
Tail wrist is very muscular and provides much of the barbel's swimming power.

TAIL
Caudal (tail) fin is deeply forked (see illustration opposite) for maximum power and maneuverability.

MAHSEER

THE MAHSEER BELONGS to the carp family, but, as far as we anglers are concerned, it can be regarded as a mammoth barbel. For a century and more, anglers from all over the world have considered this one of the most exciting sporting fish imaginable.

The mahseer inhabits huge areas of Asia, and its various subspecies can be recognized by shape or color. Mahseer of the Himalayas are long and slim, presumably in response to the torrents of water found there. Mahseer of more southerly waters, which are deeper and slower, are fatter and shorter and are shaped like carp.

Gold is the most common color for mahseer, but you also find dazzling silver, turquoise, and glowing copper mahseer. The most exotic color is black, which is found as a body color, setting off pink and coral fins. Rarest of all is the chocolate variety, found in a very few Himalayan streams.

TYPICAL WATERS

The mahseer is a lover of fast, cool, well-oxygenated rivers. It is found in the slower water where rivers are held back by dams, but it does not thrive there, and the fishing in these two habitats does not compare.

Give the mahseer a swirling torrent any time! Look out for the necks and tails of mahseer in big, streamy pools. If the weather is warm, you will find mahseer even in the most boiling, white water imaginable. In a cold snap, they may sink to the bottom of the deepest pools. Look for them around boulders and large rocks and anywhere where there is a gravel or stone bottom.

Confluences have always been traditional mahseer fishing sites, especially when there is a difference in color between the two streams. Mahseer are not lovers of mud or silt, so you won't find them feeding there.

▲ SPAWNING GROUNDS
The mahseer is a river migrant and can move many hundreds of miles up into tributaries to find its spawning redds. These are often in comparatively small, gravelly streams, too shallow for a mahseer to swim in except during the height of the monsoon.

▲ NIGHT SESSION
With those big eyes of theirs and their sensitive barbels that can dig out crabs and other prey that hide in the bottom gravels, mahseer are quite capable of feeding at night. Beware the roaming tiger, however!

▲ LOWER REACHES
A perfect mahseer pool! The water is deep, the current glides, and the pool is bounded by rocks that harbor numerous prey fish. The scene looks gentle, but wait for the explosion of the take!

◄ WHITE WATER
Big mahseer are found in swirling rapids like these. They hide behind rocks and wait to pounce on any smaller fish or other aquatic creatures that might pass by, disoriented by the rapids.

ANATOMY

The mahseer is a magnificent fish and absolutely vibrates with power and vitality. Its scales are massive, almost the size of a man's palm. During the British occupation of India, officers used them as playing cards because they were the right size and were durable enough for this purpose.

The fins are large in relation to body size and help the mahseer cope with the rush of water that it faces during monsoon rains. The pectoral fins are particularly large and can clamp the fish to the bottom, no matter what power of water flows over its head. Look, too, at those huge tail fins, which can thrash the fish up the most powerful of rapids. The tail wrist is immensely muscular and generates enormous strength.

The eyes are large, enabling the mahseer to hunt at night and, as it frequently does, in very turbid water: most mahseer rivers run comparatively clear, but during the monsoon floods they can run as dark as chocolate.

The monsoon is a very important part of the mahseer's life because the fish generally choose this period to ascend the smaller streams to their spawning grounds. Once the rainfall begins to tail off, the mahseer leave the shrinking highland waters and make their way back to the parent river.

▲ CLOSE-UP PORTRAIT
This mahseer was caught in the heat of the day, in white water. The scales glow with a magical appearance. The fish has the same kind of hues that you see on many things in India, from clothing to paintings and landscapes.

◀ POWERFUL PHYSIQUE
This fish fought against my wife, Joy, for over 40 minutes, even though the action took place in a deep, slow pool. It took both Joy and our guide, Bola, to hold the fish still for long enough to enable me take the most speedy of photographs.

HEAD AND MOUTH

The head of a mahseer is an enormous creation. In many specimens it makes up a third of the fish's length. When the mouth opens, the lips extend forward like a funnel, creating an inward current that the mahseer uses to suck in much of its food.

The mahseer's head is also extremely bony and tough, and large specimens can dislodge heavy boulders with their snouts in order to search for prey beneath.

The teeth are awesome. Like all carp, these are situated in the throat, not the mouth, but have a crushing power that is unknown in any other species. Tales of crushed spoons and pulverized plugs abound.

▶ POWERFUL LIPS
Here, a recently caught mahseer displays a strongly made mouth. Quite apart from the jaws, the mahseer's lips are themselves extraordinarily strong, and anything held between them is unlikely to escape. The skin of the lips is slightly roughened to enable the fish to gain a better grasp on small fish or crabs.

◀ A CATHOLIC TASTE
There are few foods that the mahseer will not tackle. India's many scorpions, snakes, and crabs, as well as all manner of fish and mollusks, are on the menu.

TOOTHLESS
Mouth consists of jaws and lips only. Mahseer has pharyngeal (throat) teeth, not seen from the outside.

FISHING FOR BARBEL

BARBEL FISHING IS CONSIDERED a sport for the warmer months, but these fish can still be taken when the temperature drops below 43–46° F (7–8° C). If you fish in winter, wait until after dark, when the barbel begin to move and feed for short periods.

Nocturnal sessions can be productive in the warmer months, too, but that is the time of year when barbel are very willing to feed throughout the daylight hours.

Location is of paramount importance to successful barbel fishing. In my experience, snags are the key, the most important of these being large rocks.

There are plenty of baits for barbel. Most anglers readily use luncheon meat, sausage, maggots, casters (fly chrysalises), and corn. All these baits work. Other natural baits are also good: lobworms, minnows, and caddis grubs. If the barbel are wary, then try a combination: a kernel of corn with a dead minnow mounted by the head often proves to be an irresistible cocktail.

BARBEL SESSION

The illustrations and photographs depict a four-day session on the River Wye in England in June. Bright sun and warm temperatures might seem to augur badly for barbel. Not so! My friends could pinpoint each fish in the clear water and put a bait on its nose.

IAN'S SWIM
Anglers Ian Whitelaw and Simon Rolph have picked a good spot. Two-thirds of the way across the river, a group of rocks breaks up the current and provides sanctuary for barbel. The rocks are situated close to a deeper channel in which the water runs at a pace over a bed of sand and gravel.

▲ SWIM-FEEDER IN ACTION
A swim-feeder (see p. 178) is attached to the line near the hook. It scatters feed in the area of the hook, attracting fish.

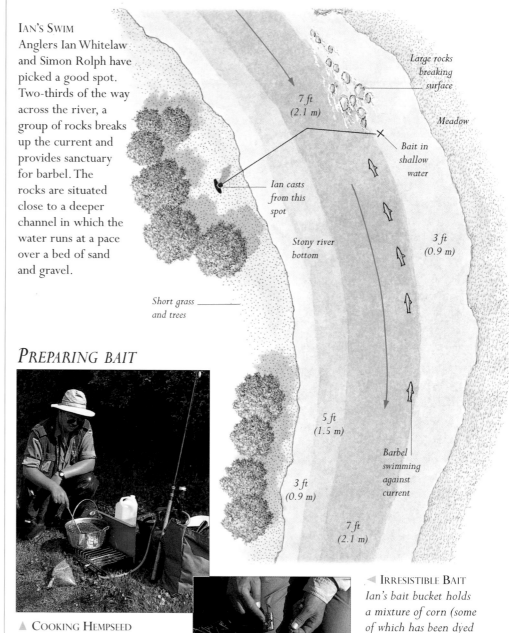

Large rocks breaking surface

7 ft (2.1 m)

Meadow

× Bait in shallow water

Ian casts from this spot

Stony river bottom

3 ft (0.9 m)

Short grass and trees

5 ft (1.5 m)

Barbel swimming against current

3 ft (0.9 m)

7 ft (2.1 m)

PREPARING BAIT

▲ BIG RIVERS, BIG BARBEL
Frequently, the larger rivers of Europe seem to produce the larger barbel. This is not always the case, and much depends on the food available as well as on the number of fish in competition for it. For the record, this 10 lb (4.5 kg) fish was taken from the Wye.

▲ COOKING HEMPSEED
Barbel adore hempseed. In the course of his four-day session, Simon used so much of this bait that he cooked it (to release the flavors) on a daily basis.

◀ IRRESISTIBLE BAIT
Ian's bait bucket holds a mixture of corn (some of which has been dyed red) and hempseed. The combination of smells, colors, and textures fascinates barbel. Ian loads the bait into a swim-feeder (see above).

HOOKING THE FISH

1 TOUCH LEGERING

This style of fishing enables you to detect the faintest of bites. Sitting on the bank, you point your rod at the bait, ensuring that the line from rod tip to swim-feeder is as straight as possible. Hold the rod, perhaps resting it on your knee, and with your other hand take the line and lay it around your index finger.

2 INSTINCTIVE STRIKE

This is the moment of the strike. When Ian detects a bite by a movement of the line around his finger, he tightens the line to secure the hook in the fish's mouth. When touch legering, it is often impossible to know exactly what made you strike. Suddenly, the line does something at your fingertips, and the next second your rod is hooped around and you're playing a fish (inset).

LANDING AND RELEASE

NET AT THE READY
A good netsman never chases a fish but lets it be drawn in over the rim of the net.

EASING BACKWARD
Ian moves gradually up the bank, forcing the now tired fish to follow.

1 INTO THE SHALLOWS

The barbel has been drawn from deep water into the shallows where it sees the netsman. There is a commotion on the surface as the fish turns around to head back to the open water. Be prepared to let the fish go some of the way, or the line is likely to break.

LIFTING THE NET
This is a medium-sized barbel. If you need to land a big one, lift the net by the rim rather than the pole, which could break under the strain.

2 NETTING THE CATCH

The barbel's attempt at escape was short-lived, and Ian was able to turn the fish back after 9–12 ft (3–4 m). Ian reeled the line in and slid the fish over the rim of the net. Simon could now lift the net, knowing that the barbel was safely held.

3 RELEASING THE BARBEL

A barbel suffers if taken from the water, especially in warm weather. Unhook it in the net, then hold it against the current until it has the strength to swim away.

FISHING FOR MAHSEER

A JOURNEY OUT TO the wilderness in search of mahseer is, for most of us, going to be a long, tough one. Before that, there is homework to be done. The timing is crucial, because mahseer migrate at different times on each and every river, perhaps influenced by the filling of streams with monsoon rain or by the melting of mountain snows.

Do plenty of research about the river (or rivers) that you are considering. These days, not all rivers in India hold mahseer. Great damage has been done to stocks of these fish by deforestation, dams, and illegal fishing.

Take with you everything you are going to need – there will be nowhere to buy tackle or replacements once you are there.

Plan your personnel in advance. You will need local people to help run your camp and ensure good relations with nearby villages, and you will need an expert fishing guide, especially when it comes to playing or landing the fish. There is no net in the world that can cope with a mahseer and so, at the end of the struggle, somebody will need to wade into the river and lift the fish ashore.

PREPARING TO FISH

Tackle is of huge importance in mahseer fishing, probably more than with any other freshwater fish in the world. Mahseer are immensely powerful creatures, living in unforgiving places, and any tackle weakness is bound to show up at once.

A powerful rod, a multiplier reel, and line of 30–40 lb (13–18 kg) breaking strain are all essential. Fit your lures with the strongest hooks – the ones fitted as standard will be too flimsy. All the swivels linking line and lures must have a breaking strain of 100 lb (45 kg). A butt pad (see p. 75) is a good idea, and remember to wear a big sun hat: the fight could be a long one, in burning heat.

▲ HOOKING UP DEADBAIT
Deadbait is always very effective with mahseer, but you must make sure that the hook is immensely strong and very firmly tied. Make sure, too, that you hook the bait very securely, because you will be casting it into wild, white water where it is bound to be tossed about.

▲ ANYTHING CAN HAPPEN
Mahseer waters are full of the strangest beasts, and it is not unusual to hook a turtle – or even a crocodile, for that matter! I have even had panthers coming to visit me while fishing for mahseer.

▲ NATURAL BAITS
For deadbait fishing, it is easy to find suitable bait fish in small pools or fast-moving shallows. Here, a fisherman demonstrates the skill of using a drop-net. This is a traditional and very efficient way of making a haul.

◄ MAHSEER BAITS
This selection of mahseer baits includes fish for use as deadbait, large lures, and a lump of paste bait. The paste is made to the angler's own recipe and is useful in the slower waters of the more southerly parts of India.

HOOKING AND LANDING

Generally, you will know when you have hooked a mahseer! The rod buckles in your hand and the reel begins to scream. If you are very lucky, your mahseer will have taken the bait in a very large, placid pool, where you will be able to play it out to the finish.

This, however, is not normally the case. It is more normal for the angler to be unable to restrain the fish at all. It is no use trying to hold a mahseer back – strong enough tackle does not exist – so you must let it have its way, and give plenty of line.

Mahseer anglers often need to follow their fish for long distances. There are plenty of stories of anglers being towed downstream through rapids. Do not attempt this on your own, but you should be safe enough with a fishing partner or guide, preferably both.

Do not despair if you find yourself in this situation. The worst that can happen is that the fish may anchor itself behind a rock or branch, and there is every chance that you will dislodge it if you can get close enough.

▲ CHASING THE FISH
Here we go! A mahseer has left the pool where it was hooked and is heading off to the sea. The angler on the left has hooked the fish, and the one on the right follows, rod still in hand, to give assistance.

▶ CLOSER ACQUAINTANCE
You will catch a mahseer in the end if you stick with the job. This fish pulled my companion Johnny Jensen through over half a mile (more than a kilometer) of white water, but the look on his face suggests that it was worth the pain!

HANDLING THE CATCH

Mahseer are massively strong creatures in the water but, like any other fish, become vulnerable once defeated. Remember that, under India's powerful sun, it is important not to remove the fish from the water for long: the heat would quickly dry its scales.

If you look at all the photographs on the pages on mahseer in this book, you will see that the fish are never taken onto the bank, and this is very important. Keep them in or over water at all times. When photographing, keep dipping them in the river to make sure there is a constant supply of water flowing over their scales. If you take them onto the bank, besides the threat of dehydration there is a danger that they will twist themselves free of your grip and fall on the rocks.

Always have your "stringer" (string tether) in your pocket, because it is the first thing the guide will ask for. He will use it to tie the vanquished mahseer to a rock or branch while it recovers in the water.

◀ PLAYED-OUT MAHSEER
This fish has just been landed, and the stringer has been slipped through its gills so that it can be tethered in the margins while it recovers, rather like a dog on a leash. Only when it is beginning to show real signs of recovery should you take those last, quick photographs.

▲ RECOVERY
Fisherman Steve Harper is seen here holding his huge 104 lb (47 kg) mahseer in the correct way – half in and half out of the water. This fish was recognized when it was recaught two years later, proof that his careful handling had been successful.

STILLWATER FAVORITES

EVERY ANGLER HAS TO BEGIN somewhere, and in America it is generally with panfish, while in Europe it is usually the fish we know as "stillwater favorites." Small these fish may be, but they still present a challenge. In both America and Europe there are specialist anglers who never feel the need to go for the big fish, sticking with the species of their youth.

▲ UNDER THE PADS
Lilypads are particularly attractive to tench and rudd, two species that like to hang underneath the canopy of leaves and escape from the summer sun.

EUROPEAN SPECIES

THERE ARE MANY SPECIES of smaller fish in the still waters of Europe, but I shall concentrate on what are popularly seen as the favorite four: bream, tench, roach, and rudd. These are traditionally summer fish, although roach and bream can be caught in winter if you are feeling hardy! All four are springtime spawners, and they are not too happy in rivers or strong currents. All these species are very widespread.

There is much variety in sizes. Bream can reach 20 lb (9 kg) in Poland but will not exceed 3–4 lb (1.4–1.8 kg) in an English pond. The rudd of the Irish loughs can reach 4 lb (1.8 kg), whereas one of only a tenth of that weight would be a good catch in many farm ponds. One of the limiting factors to

growth is overstocking, and all four species are prone to this if sufficient predators are not present. Perch, eels, pike, and zander all serve an important function in thinning out the small fry every spring.

The habitat of these species has expanded in recent times with the digging of large pits for gravel extraction. These deep, clear, rich waters are too big to become overstocked. They are, however, relatively hard to fish, and the beginner would do well to serve an apprenticeship on smaller, cloudier waters.

▶ IN THE BAYS
The shallow, warm, silty bays of lakes are favored by tench and bream in particular. Tench love to wallow in the silt, sifting out bloodworms or sucking in the clouds of daphnia that always drift into such places.

BREAM

It is the bronze bream *(shown here)* that interests the angler, rather than its small cousin, the silver bream. Bream are schooling fish, feeding on small food items in the silt. They also sip flies at the surface and are often seen doing this at dawn or dusk, rolling in the water as they feed.

LARGE EYE
Bream has a comparatively large eye, which enables the species to feed avidly on the darkest of nights.

BREAM SHOULDER
Adult bronze bream have strikingly humped "shoulders" that rise up steeply from the head. The older the bream, the bigger the hump.

DEEP BODY
Some bream are so deep in body that they are almost round in shape, hence the nickname "dustbin lid."

DORSAL FIN
This fin is lighter in color than pectoral or pelvic fins. Dorsal can be grayish or lightly tinted with brown.

LONG ANAL FIN
This fin is exceptionally long. Roach/bream hybrids are often very like roach, but can be identified by the breamlike anal fin.

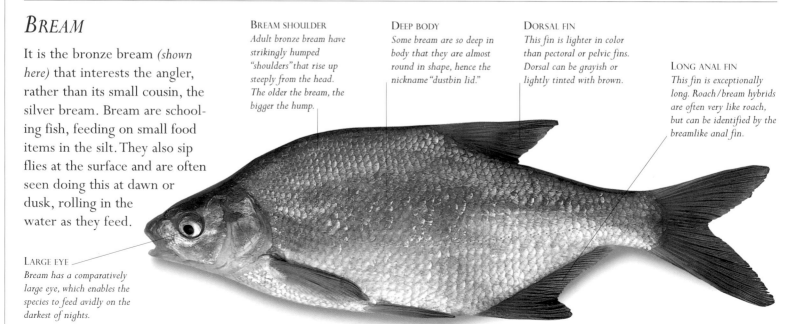

ROACH

The roach has a claim to be the most popular fish in Europe. It is a delight for children, match fishers, and specialist anglers alike. A big roach is a true prize, and one of 2 lb (0.9 kg) or more is something to be proud of. Indeed, there are many roach specialists who devote their life to catching these blue-scaled giants. Big fish are most active in the twilight hours when they will feed on all manner of nymphs, bloodworms, and snails.

TOP LIP
Upper lip projects noticeably over bottom lip. Level lips are signs of roach/rudd hybrids, which are often encountered.

DORSAL FIN
Dorsal fin is set high on the back, almost vertically over pelvic fins. A dorsal fin nearer to the tail is a sign of a roach/rudd hybrid.

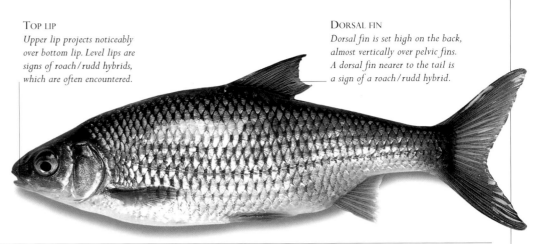

◀ **QUIETLY GRACEFUL**
The rudd is a serene, athletic fish and looks at its best when seen drifting through clear water or gliding through weedbeds in sunlit water. The rudd may not look like everybody's idea of a predator, but it often feeds on its own fry and on the young of other fish.

BOTTOM LIP
Bottom lip protrudes visibly beyond top one: an important recognition feature.

DEEP BODY
Young rudd, like this one, are slender; their bodies grow deeper as they mature.

RUDD

Rudd are quite glorious fish: they are deep-bodied, with brassy golden scales and vivid red fins. Their schooling behavior has earned them their country nickname, the "starlings of the water." The schools feed as readily on surface insects as they forage for aquatic life in midwater or on the bottom.

Rudd thrive in clear, weedy, nutrient-rich waters, and the limestone loughs of western Ireland are perfect for them. Rudd are active at night and spend much of the day hiding under weeds or deep in reedbeds. They occur throughout Europe, except only Scotland, northern Scandinavia, and southern Greece.

TENCH

The tench is a stunningly beautiful fish with a distinctive red eye, great paddle fins, and tiny, olive scales bedded into a smooth, silky skin. A golden form exists, which is beautiful but very rare and is not often seen in the wild. The distribution of the tench covers all of Europe, except northern Scotland and the southern part of the Balkan peninsula.

In some countries, tench are kept as food fish with carp. They can survive on very low oxygen levels and can be transported alive, wrapped only in damp moss.

▶ **COMPANIONABLE FISH**
Tench tend to form loose groups, the sexes generally keeping apart until spawning actually begins. Sometimes tench schools are very few in number, consisting of no more than two or three fish that choose to live and feed together. Sometimes large females adopt a solitary lifestyle.

SMALL SCALES
Though small, scales are visible to the naked eye.

LARGE FINS
Much of the swimming power of the tench is derived from its fins, especially the strong tail fin.

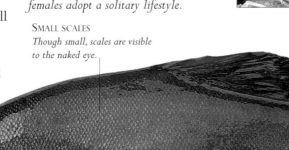

RED EYE
This is a recognition feature. Eye is small, and tench has relatively poor vision, feeding largely by feel.

PANFISH

THE NAME "PANFISH" is used by anglers to refer to a number of American species, most belonging to the sunfish family (though four belong to the bass family), that are too small to count as game fish but are still worthwhile quarry. Though small, they bite cunningly, fight hard, and, at least according to tradition, taste good cooked in a pan!

The largest panfish are the white and black crappies, which weigh around 5 lb (2.27 kg). Almost this size, but not quite, is the largest of the sunfish – the redear.

Closely related to the sunfish is the bluegill, the best-known panfish. The four species of bass are unrelated to other panfish.

Panfish species are not always easy to tell apart. Related or not, all have short, squat bodies and very similar fin alignments. Many species vary in color from place to place – bluegills can be anything from dark blue to yellow, and some are almost transparent.

Small differences in the shape of the gill covers can help in identification. The crappies can be distinguished by counting the spines on the first dorsal fin: the white crappie has six spines, the black seven or eight.

WHERE TO FISH

Panfish usually lie under cover, so look for them among weed and brushwood and under man-made structures, such as docks.

Beyond this, panfish seem to follow no rules: small bluegill spawn in the shallows, while large ones spawn at depths of 6–9 ft (2–3 m). Foraging bluegill may splash about in the surface layers or swim deep in the water. Crappies are inconsistent, too: "blacks" need clearer water than "whites," which tolerate murky conditions.

▲ WEED-FILLED WATER
Weeds often hold the food panfish need – aquatic insects and the like. All panfish do well in the shallow, weedy bays and fringes of reservoirs.

◀ GOOD LOCATION
Docks attract panfish. An overgrown creek nearby, with large beds of water-weed, or a submerged island with steep under-water banks, will also bring panfish to the site.

BLUEGILL

Originally, the bluegill was common only in the eastern states of America, but it has now been introduced to quiet, weedy ponds all over the country. Males can be seen guarding their spawning nests and chasing off any fish that approach. The bluegill is often considered a daytime feeder, but in summer it often feeds at night. Natural foods of the bluegill include all aquatic insects, crickets, spiders, and worms, while large individuals will strike at fry of any fish species.

◀ SPAWNING BLUEGILL
The bluegill spawns in May, when water temperatures reach about 68°F (20°C). Average sizes are a few ounces, but big bluegills weigh 4 lb (1.8 kg).

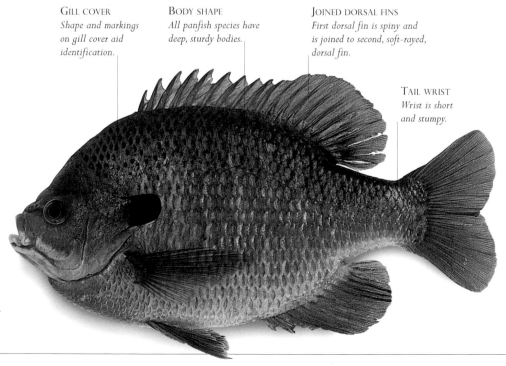

GILL COVER
Shape and markings on gill cover aid identification.

BODY SHAPE
All panfish species have deep, sturdy bodies.

JOINED DORSAL FINS
First dorsal fin is spiny and is joined to second, soft-rayed, dorsal fin.

TAIL WRIST
Wrist is short and stumpy.

SUNFISH

Sunfish species include the green, redear, spotted *(see right and below)*, orange-spotted, and redbreast sunfish, and the pumpkinseed.

Sunfish like waters containing weed and snags – any protruding objects, such as submerged branches. The fish hunt for larvae of insects, fish fry, and small mollusks. Snails are a favorite food of the redear sunfish, which is nicknamed the "shell cracker."

Few sunfish species attain weights of over 1 lb (0.45 kg), although redear weighing up to 4 lb (1.8 kg) are sometimes encountered.

BODY SHAPE
Bodies of sunfish are more elongated than those of other panfish species.

TAIL
Tail is rounded in profile and comparatively small.

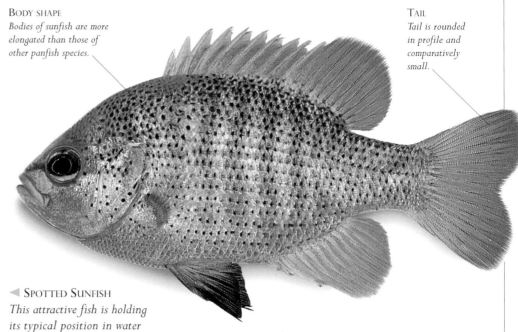

◄ SPOTTED SUNFISH
This attractive fish is holding its typical position in water plants. Mayflies and stoneflies are important foods for sunfish, which take larvae and occasional adult flies that have fallen into the water.

► ORANGE-SPOTTED SUNFISH
This vividly colored species is not the most common panfish but can be found in small numbers all down the eastern side of North America, from Canada to Mexico.

SMALL BASS

The warmouth bass *(shown here)* and the rock, white, and yellow bass belong to the bass family, the Moronidae. It should be pointed out that despite their name, the large- and small-mouth black bass *(see p. 54)* are not "true" bass, for they belong, like the other panfish, to the sunfish family.

These small true bass are schooling fish and, once found, provide good fishing. Look for them on the fringes of shallow water, along steep underwater banks and rocks, among submerged brushwood, beneath tree stumps, underneath bridge pilings, and in dense beds of weed. Most of the small bass prefer clear-water lakes, but the warmouth bass thrives equally well in murky waters.

PECTORAL FIN
Fin is fan-shaped.

FLANK
Flank is mottled for camouflage.

TAIL
Lobes of tail are very rounded.

FISHING FOR BREAM & TENCH

BREAM AND TENCH are best fished for in warm, settled weather; both species will stop feeding in periods of cold wind and rain. Bream tend to be nocturnal, starting to feed at last light and continuing through the night until dawn. Tench are not so strictly nocturnal; it is more typical of them, especially in larger waters, to feed from first light until mid- or late morning.

With bream and tench, fishing success depends on preparation of the swim – the water containing the fish. But before you can prepare it, you must find it! This is done by observation. If the fish are present in a water, you will see them rolling or bubbling at the surface. Look for fish in waters that have beds of lilies or bulrushes interspersed with open water areas.

Preparing a swim often involves clearing weed. Special cutters *(see below)* are made for this job. Otherwise use a rake, which has the advantage of stirring up the bottom mud and the small creatures that live in it – this helps attract tench all the more.

Your other preparation is to prebait the water: hempseed or rice are good baits to use. Experience will tell you whether this is best done hours, days, or weeks in advance.

▲ USING A WEED CUTTER
Clearing weed makes an area attractive to bream, so prepare your site if you can. My friend Nick and I decided to deweed our swim early in the day, so that the water would have all day to settle before the start of our bream session that evening. The weed cutter is a large, curved blade with a rope attached to either end for dragging the implement across the bed.

FISHING FOR BREAM

Bottom-fishing is the usual strategy to catch a bream. You can use a leger *(see p.136)*, but swim-feeders *(see p.178)* are more common. Corn, maggots, casters, bread (the inside of the loaf, not the crust), or pieces of worm are all great bream baits.

The important thing with bream is to use a light rig. Bream are fickle fish and will drop a bait if they feel resistance. A delicate hook and a long hook-length (the final section of the line, usually the thinnest) can play an important part in inducing the fish to take the bait properly into its mouth.

Before the bream begin to feed properly, you will probably see them rolling about in the surface waters of their swim. You may experience "line-bites" (fish brushing against the line, not mouthing the bait). Don't strike at these, or you will scare the school away.

▲ NETTING THE CATCH
In bream fishing, the moment when you draw the fish close to your net is critical. Bream are rarely deeply hooked, and a fish can free itself with a single shake of its head. Take care, and make sure your landing net is big enough.

▼ PLAYING A BREAM
A hooked fish breaks the surface for the first time: another moment when the fish can drop the hook. If that doesn't happen, the fish could gulp in air, and this will help you. The air makes the fish more buoyant and less able to dive deep.

FISHING FOR TENCH

The illustration and photographs here show how I caught a tench in a summer session on an estate lake. Tench fishing is generally associated with misty summer dawns on lakes where you can be at close quarters with the fish. The strategy I decided upon was float fishing, and my baits were soft bread, maggots, and lobworms. Tench are wary fish, so I kept a low profile and made good use of the cover.

ESTATE LAKE LOCATION

Old estate lakes are havens for tench, which grow big on bloodworms and swan mussels that they find in the silt. There are lakes in which tench have been resident for over 200 years.

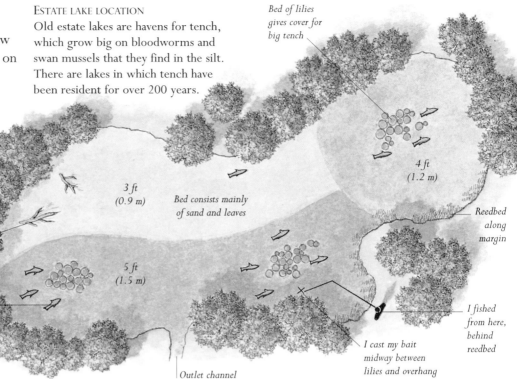

Bed of lilies gives cover for big tench

4 ft (1.2 m)

3 ft (0.9 m)

Bed consists mainly of sand and leaves

Reedbed along margin

Fallen tree lying in water

Tench frequenting clump of lilies

5 ft (1.5 m)

I fished from here, behind reedbed

I cast my bait midway between lilies and overhang

Outlet channel

A SUMMER SESSION

1 PLACING GROUNDBAIT
I used a slingshot to sprinkle the surface of the swim with a variety of tidbits, in order to entice the tench off their natural diet. Soaked bread (see inset), or some corn or maggots, should do the trick.

2 WATCHING FOR SIGNS
I cast my float rig and waited; before long I began to see air bubbles (see inset) and small clouds of stirred-up silt around the float. These were signs that tench were definitely active in the area.

3 LETTING THE BITE DEVELOP
A bite came, but I knew that a tench can take a few seconds to get hold of the bait properly. I waited until my float submerged completely. Then I struck, tightening the line to fix the hook in the fish's mouth.

LANDING AND RELEASE

1 FIGHTING A TENCH
Any tench, once it is hooked, will head straight for weed or snags, but I had made a mental note of these before starting. I kept a tight grip on my line. With tench, hookholds are usually sound, so there is less danger of losing the fish than there is with bream.

2 CARE WITH RELEASE
I always return tench straight to the water, especially in warm weather when oxygen levels are low. I supported this fish until I could feel that it had the strength to move off of its own accord. After release, tench often lie motionless for an hour or more in the margins. This is their way of recovering.

FISHING FOR ROACH & RUDD

SMALL ROACH AND RUDD can take the bait in suicidal fashion when feeding competition is intense in a big shoal. Mature roach and rudd, however, behave quite differently, and can be very wary adversaries indeed.

Roach can examine a bait with eagle-eyed caution, and an entire shoal will vacate the swim if it senses anything amiss. So, if you are after big specimens, you have to think carefully about your tactics, your bait, and your general approach. Sometimes you will be mobile, sometimes you will sit tight in ambush – the challenge remains the same.

▲ FISHING FOR ROACH
You need to be under cover to catch roach. This fisherman has a weedbed to his right and a large overhanging oak tree to his left. Calm and composure, in body and mind, are important too.

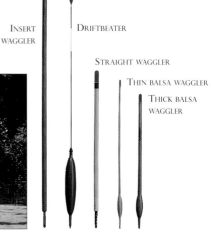

INSERT WAGGLER
DRIFTBEATER
STRAIGHT WAGGLER
THIN BALSA WAGGLER
THICK BALSA WAGGLER

▲ STILLWATER FLOATS
The roach angler never sets out without a selection of floats for all conditions.

FLOATS AND SHOTTING PATTERNS FOR STILLWATER FISHING

Think carefully about the depth at which the fish are likely to be found. How will you set your float? What should your arrangement of weights (shotting pattern) be? Do you expect fish to take the bait as it sinks ("on the drop") or only when it is on the bottom? If bites are not forthcoming, then experiment constantly. You can alter the shotting pattern to adjust the depth at which the float sits in the water, or the speed at which the bait sinks.

▼ FIVE FLOAT-FISHING RIGS
Rigs are designed for varying conditions such as wind speed, water temperature, and water clarity. Shot weights in grams: SSG = 1.89, AAA = 0.81, BB = 0.4, No. 4 = 0.17, No. 6 = 0.105, No. 8 = 0.063, No. 10 = 0.034.

▲ LOOSE BAIT FALLING
One of the arts of float fishing is to keep loose feed falling in the target area. Do not put in too much bait, as this would overfeed the fish. If you throw in too little, however, you might not attract enough fish, or those fish that do come may not stay in the area long enough for you to catch them.

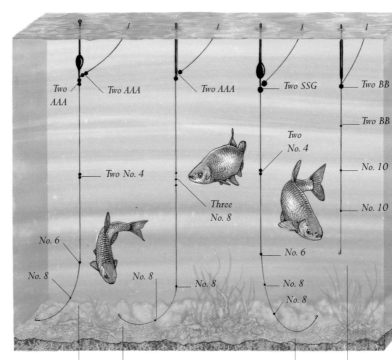

Two AAA
Two AAA
Two AAA
Two SSG
Two BB
Two BB
Two No. 4
Two No. 4
No. 10
Three No. 8
No. 10
No. 6
No. 6
No. 8
No. 8
No. 8
No. 8
No. 8

Float is held in vertical position by SSG
Float rises and then lies flat
Hooked fish lifts SSG
SSG

STRONG WIND
The driftbeater float is designed to hold its position in the water in spite of strong winds and forceful undercurrents. The body is very buoyant, and will carry plenty of shot.

LIGHT WIND
This rig is fished at close range when the wind is light – good conditions for catching fish on the drop. The rig consists of a thin balsa waggler and a light shotting pattern.

LONG RANGE
For a long cast you need the momentum of a well-shotted rig. This float is buoyant enough to work despite the SSGs. Nearer the hook, three weights sink the line fast, before it can tangle in weeds.

SHALLOW WATER
In shallow water it is best to keep the bait clear of the bottom. An insert waggler is used, and small shot is spaced between float and hook. No. 10 shot may escape the notice of wary fish.

LIFT METHOD
In this rig for catching bottom-feeding fish, an SSG is used to hold the float in an upright position. If a fish bites, it lifts the SSG, allowing the float to rise through the surface and fall flat.

FISHING FOR RUDD

Rudd are highly nomadic fish and rarely stay in a swim for long periods. This means that the wise angler will be mobile and probably fish many places during the course of the day. It pays, therefore, to travel fairly light, although a pair of binoculars is absolutely essential. Use them to scan the surface for any sign of rudd rolling or splashing – they are avid top-water feeders.

As soon as you have located rudd, you must act quickly. Cast your bait to them from a distance and with as much delicacy as you can, to avoid alarming the fish. Try a floating bait – a walnut-sized piece of bread perhaps; or use a piece of bread (the soft, inner bread without the crust) and weight it lightly so that it will sink slowly, under a float.

Casters (chrysalises formed by maggots) can be fished either as floating or as slowly sinking baits, and they often have the right properties to tempt a big, wary fish.

You will need light line, because it enables you to cast long and because it is thin enough not to scare the rudd. Don't go too light: big rudd are rarely far from snags, and they can charge powerfully when hooked.

▲ WATCHING FOR A BITE
The moment you have spotted rudd, you must cast without delay. Rudd delight in surfacing to feed on insects, and you will learn to recognize their way of splashing at the surface (see inset). This activity is different from the gentle, porpoiselike movements of tench or bream. You can also recognize rudd by the flash of their golden scales or of their red fins.

▲ GENTLE RELEASE
Rudd suffer if handled excessively, or if kept in a net for too long in warm weather. Numbers of big specimens are limited, so treat all rudd with respect.

STILLWATER BOTTOM BAITS

There are times, such as when the water is cold, when you need to get your bait right down on the bottom. Success depends on using the right bait and the right delivery system for the occasion.

Your first action should be to lay down a carpet of groundbait (unhooked bait that attracts fish and keeps them in the area during the time in which you are fishing).

When you cast your hookbait, also cast small amounts of groundbait in a "feeder" (container) attached to the line close to the hook. If you are not using an attached feeder like this, you will need a leger *(see p. 136).*

▶ CAGE FEEDER
This is a piece of equipment for delivering groundbait at long range (see p. 178). It is often used for rudd or roach and is attached to the line and cast to the fish. The feeder is packed with layers of different baits.

◀ BOILIES OVER HEMPSEED
The pink balls are boilies (see p. 179), and this picture shows an excellent way to present such large hookbaits – on a carpet of hempseed. Roach, rudd, and other fish are attracted by the seeds, smelling them from far off because they contain an aromatic oil. Once in the area, the fish stay for long periods, nosing about on the bed for the seeds.

▲ MAGGOT FEEDER
Like the cage feeder (see left), this device is attached to the line and cast with the hookbait. The feeder is a perforated bottle with holes large enough for the maggots to escape, attracting fish.

FISHING FOR PANFISH

PANFISH ARE FAVORITES for many anglers. This may be partly because of childhood memories of learning to fish, with panfish as the quarry. Another reason for liking panfish is that they present a challenge far beyond their size. Indeed, there are those who would suggest that a big bluegill is one of the hardest of all trophy fish to catch, more difficult even than a steelhead or a brown trout.

Another appeal of panfish is that you can fish for them using virtually every method in the fisherman's encyclopedia. You can jig for them *(see p. 58)* and do so with several types of lure *(p. 174)*, including soft plastic, feathered lures, or small spoons. You can troll *(p. 81)* with a small spinner. You can fly fish. You can bait fish, using a small fish either as live- or deadbait, or a worm. You can use other natural baits, such as crickets or crayfish. You can fish in spring, summer, or autumn, or even through the ice in winter. In short, the panfisher who knows everything, has tried everything, or has caught everything just does not exist.

BAIT FISHING

Worms make good bait for panfish. You can fish a worm on the bottom, using weights to take it down; you can do this and use your reel to twitch the worm enticingly in the water; or you can hang the worm at any depth from a float. Watch for gentle, nipping bites. Fish one area after another, exploring slowly, taking care not to disturb the fish.

Small fish are an excellent bait, presented live or dead. If you use a float, watch to see it rising or leaning over, for this is what happens when crappie attack from below.

All "natural" baits *(see p. 178)*, from shrimp to crayfish, are worthy of experiment. You must use great care in hooking and presenting them. Don't expect big bites; strike at any unusual resistance or float movement.

▲ SIPPING FROM THE SURFACE
There are times when bluegill come to the surface and feed on insects that the wind has blown off nearby vegetation. Crickets are a favorite, so catch some yourself, hook them, and fish them under a float. Try craneflies, mayflies, or anything else that bluegill find interesting.

▲ FIGHTING ALL THE WAY
Panfish are small, but they tend to fight hard. You need lightweight hooks and line, for they may notice anything too heavy, but your tackle must be strong enough to hold back a fish that threatens to tangle your line on a snag.

◄ WILD THING
You do not need to catch monsters to experience excitement when fishing — even small fish can fight well and give great sport. Very often the fight of a small fish, close in on delicate tackle and a wand-like rod, is simply thrilling. It is every bit as wonderful as battling it out with a huge fish on heavy-duty gear that would land a juggernaut.

▲ ESSENTIAL BOAT
The bonus of a boat is that it gives you the ability to row yourself very close to a prime, "snaggy" location. Underwater snags such as branches are hard to see unless you can explore in a boat. Take care on your approach, because any noise will upset the residents!

FLY FISHING

Like other fish, panfish can learn to recognize lures for what they are. If this happens where you are fishing, it is time to offer the panfish something that imitates their natural diet a little more closely.

This can mean fly fishing. Since panfish live in or near weedbeds and brushwood, it pays to imitate the type of food that they find there. Dragonfly larvae, minnows, freshwater shrimp, and water boatmen are all on the natural menu and have been imitated very realistically by the makers of fishing flies.

Allow the fly to sink slowly, and then twitch it back: you can either make a series of short, vertical lifts of the rod, or you can retrieve the fly by winding it in with the reel. Make frequent pauses, too, for this will also trigger strikes from panfish as they follow the fly down. Weighted flies are useful on those hot days when the fish are deep down.

▲ AVID INTEREST
Some fish inspect everything that they find. Use your imagination and learn to "work" the fly to make it look lifelike and fool the fish.

► ALL TO PLAY FOR
Infuriated, the fish turns back toward the cover that had been its sanctuary. This is a crucial moment: provided all the tackle holds together, the prize will be yours.

► HANDLING
Many panfish make superb eating, hence their more than appetizing name! If fish are destined for the kitchen, keep them cool; if they are not, let them go as gently as possible. With smaller fish, you may decide not to take them from the water at all.

◄ LATE SUCCESS
As the day advances, panfish move less and less into open water, and you too should keep to cover. If the fish start rising to take food from the surface but you see no flies in the air, the panfish may be taking larvae that hang from the surface film. If so, fish with a "suspender midge" fly (a pattern of trout fly) for best results.

JIGGING

Fishing with jigs *(see p. 58)* among brush and timber is the ideal way to take panfish. Jigging spoons work well because their shape makes them twist and turn as they fall, attracting the fish. Small jigs tipped with soft plastic *(see p. 174)* are a common choice. Jig designs to try are Paddle-tails; soft plastic designs are Wiggly-tails and Octopus legs.

The art is to get the jig as close as possible to where the panfish are lying. This is important in cold weather, when panfish are practically motionless all day long.

► KEEPING WATCH
You need to be in constant contact with your bait, and that is where a float really makes a difference. Put the correct weights on the line, then strike at the first sign of a bite. You can use a float to suspend the bait at any depth, often just off the bottom to catch crappies or bluegills. A float can also help to indicate water depth — vital if you want to start jigging.

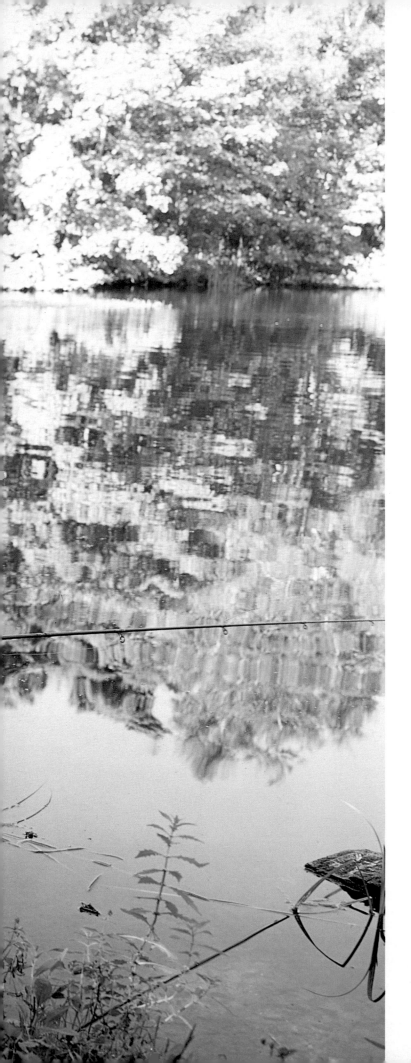

EQUIPMENT & ACCESSORIES

DESPITE COUNTLESS TALES OF CHILDREN catching trophy fish with string and a bent pin, having the right tackle is important. It is a foolish angler who takes no interest in the tools of the trade, and nothing is worse than being let down by equipment at the end of a battle with the fish of a lifetime. Believe me, you don't get over that, ever. There is great joy in using tackle that you are happy with and can trust in every situation that you're likely to meet. And it is said that choosing a rod is like choosing a spouse – one hopes that the relationship will be lifelong!

FISHING WITH CONFIDENCE
Being equipped with a good-quality rod and reel, and having the right accessories, brings real satisfaction. The equipment should be a pleasure to use and appropriate for the water you are fishing.

RODS & REELS

IN HIS CLASSIC BOOK, *Fishing from the Earliest Times*, William Radcliffe states that 4,000 years ago the ancient Egyptians were using four methods of fishing: spear, net, hand-line – and rod. How many rods have been built since those distant times? How many have bent to the thrust of a fish and have perhaps been broken by monsters? The roots of our sport certainly go a long way back into history.

RODS

NATURAL MATERIALS have been used for rod building over the millennia, and those weapons wielded by the ancient Egyptians were surely made of papyrus reed gathered from the banks of the Nile. Since then, any number of natural materials, mostly wood, have been used. Cane, ash, sallow, beech, hazel, poplar, greenheart, hickory, and lancewood have all proved their worth over and over again, even if most have had some inherent flaws. Immense ingenuity has been shown along the way. Rods have even been fashioned of whalebone, and after the Second World War, thousands of unused tank aerials visited the river banks! There are many anglers who still swear by split-cane rods, but modern materials have generally proved the best of all. Solid glass tended to be heavy and unresponsive, but some hollow glass designs were excellent. And now we have all manner of space-age fibers at our fingertips. These make rods so powerful, light, and delicate that they would be the envy of any ancient Egyptian.

SALMON ROD

The British salmon angler has always tended to go for the traditional, long, comparatively heavy, two-handed rod, while the Americans have favored a much lighter approach. As in most debates, both sides have points in their favor. The big British rod does have its moments, especially on large rivers that are carrying extra water. With these rods it is easy to "Spey" cast, punching out the line 130 ft (40 m) or more with relatively little effort, and rods like this can cover big pools easily once the angler has found the rhythm. The small American rods also have a lot going for them. Their lightness means that the angler can be infinitely mobile, aiming to get close to the fish and placing the line with delicacy. This is real, up-close fishing, although a good American caster can still make the line absolutely zing out.

▲ AERIAL POWER
Salmon just do not give up, and their leaps can be awesome. This is where a good rod comes into its own — strong enough to put some pressure on the fish, responsive enough to go with the flow, and too flexible to allow a hook-hold to jerk free.

LENGTH
This is a traditional British salmon rod, around 16 ft (5 m) in length and often considered the ideal tool for big salmon rivers.

ACTION
This would be considered an all-action rod, capable of being bent into a perfect quarter circle.

◄ COMFORT
Although the traditional salmon rod is long and comparatively heavy, it need not be tiring for the angler. It develops a rhythm all of its own, and even when fishing out the cast, it is possible to hold the rod comfortably. Tuck the butt under your armpit and hold the rod above the corks, close to the first ring.

BUTT
The handle of the salmon rod should be comfortable to grip, neither too thick nor too slender, and of a good length.

TROUT ROD

Trout rods are an absolute delight to hold and to fish with. At their best, they are light as a fairy's wing and flick out a beautiful line. You should check out every single rod for yourself before you buy. Go to a big dealer who will allow you unrestricted casting practice on an artificial pool.

▶ TAKE GOOD CARE
A fly rod should last a lifetime, providing it is well looked after. Always make sure the ferrules (joints between the sections) fit nicely, and clean away any grit or dirt at the end of a fishing session. Good rings are vital. Once you see they are becoming grooved through wear, replace them at once. Otherwise, your casting and the fly line itself will suffer.

MATERIAL
Carbon is the most commonly used modern material, but it is hard to beat the action of old split-cane.

ACTION
The perfect action of a fly rod under pressure is a nearly exact quarter circle. Let the rod do the work when you are casting the fly line. More effort can mean less distance.

▲ FISHING A WEIR
Being equipped with a light rod like this gives the angler increased mobility. At times of year when the water is low, you can use a trout rod perfectly well to catch salmon, with light line and a small fly.

JERKBAIT ROD

A jerkbait rod needs to be flexible, but it must also be very firm if it is going to pull a big, aggressive lure properly through the water. You need to make the predator believe that the jerkbait is alive, and this means putting some really lifelike movement into the retrieve. A very flexible rod would not be able to achieve this effect.

TOUGH RINGS
Rings should be made of (or be lined with) hard metal, or the line will wear grooves in them and render them useless.

◀ LIGHTNESS AND POWER
A good jerkbait rod will be light and easy to handle but will have a lot of firmness for its weight. A rod any softer than this would not be able to pull a big lure through the water at any speed or depth. The rod would just lock into a bowed position, and the lure would appear lifeless.

STURDILY BUILT
Even under heavy pressure, the jerkbait rod maintains its shape and power.

THE RIGHT REEL
Jerkbait rods work well with multiplier reels, whose gearing can take the strain of working a heavy lure.

▲ UNDER PRESSURE
Rods are built to work hard, so don't worry if you need to apply pressure toward the end of a fight. More fish are lost by being gentle. Set the clutch on the reel sensitively: this will enable you to give line as soon as there is a take. Fish are easily alarmed at close quarters, and a taut line at first bite scares them off.

PIKE ROD

It is very difficult to nominate an average pike rod because there are so many different types of rods for different purposes. However, at around 10–12 ft (3–4 m), with a good action and lots of power, this would be a good general rod. Pike rods take a lot of strain, especially in boats in the winter, so durability is an important consideration.

ACTION
The action of the pike rod is progressive, allowing you some feel during the fight but still giving the power to cast a bait a long way.

◀ LOW FRICTION
The rod rings on a pike rod are large and widely spaced. This helps cut down friction when casting a big bait a long distance. Choose a rod with tough and secure rings to withstand hard knocks against the side of a boat.

POWER LOW DOWN
Notice how the bottom section maintains rigidity under tension – vital when a big fish is running.

A GOOD HANDLE
Make sure that the pike rod gives you plenty of grip. You will need it when casting and when playing a big fish.

▲ NOT JUST FOR PIKE
A pike rod is a very versatile tool, and it can be used for most big fish. Here it is doubling for carp fishing. The combination of strength and action makes it quite capable of holding a running fish away from the lilies.

SPINNING ROD

A spinning rod should be light and responsive so that you don't tire after a long day. A rod that is too long prevents you from flicking the bait here and there under low-lying tree cover. A delicate tip allows you to put more life into the lure as you work it back past snags. This is critical: a rod that is heavy and unresponsive is never going to work that lure in quite the most realistic fashion and is unlikely to bring success.

SENSITIVE TIP
The top section of the rod is very responsive, quite capable of imparting life to a light lure fished in a snaggy situation.

A LIGHT MULTIPLIER
A light baitcasting reel is pretty well all you need for this sort of rod. Casting is very easy, and the clutch is highly efficient.

STIFFER MIDSECTION
Power develops lower down the rod. This helps with casting, striking, and playing the fish.

◀ POWER WHERE IT COUNTS
Down toward the butt, the rod really shows its mettle. Here, in the spine, the real power is to be found. Rods like this have been carefully designed over many years to provide everything that the lure fisher might want – delicacy, lightness, and power when it matters.

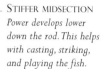

▲ BATTLE ON
Trout, bass, and smaller pike are all perfect targets for this type of gear. You experience every thrill of the battle when you are playing them on a spinning rod that is not too long or heavy and has the sensitivity to transmit every tug and turn.

STURGEON / UPTIDE ROD

This really is a beast of a rod – heavy, powerful, and totally unforgiving. In fact, it only just has a place in fresh water at all, and then it is for real monsters. Usually, you would see a rod like this out over a wreck at sea, perhaps winching up a string of cod or a monster conger. Nevertheless, with a really big fish like the sturgeon, you just cannot lever it off the bottom with any lighter tool.

ROD RINGS
The rings on the uptide rod are built for power and are whipped on strongly. The top ring may well have a roller to reduce friction on the line.

BOTTOM SECTION
There is enormous power down here, allowing you to lean into the fish and give it every bit of strength you possess.

◀ **COMFORT FIRST**
You are going to need to lever the rod against your body to get the power you need to control a large fish, so it is a good idea to use a butt pad. Otherwise, you will end up badly bruised!

▲ **THE ROD IN ACTION**
Here, Danish traveler and angler Johnny Jensen strains to bring a sturgeon to the bank. It is a mighty fish, and it demands serious tackle. When a 260 lb (120 kg) fish runs, try stopping it on a lesser rod!

REELS

REELS ARE A COMPARATIVELY late development. Before they appeared, a line was tied to the end of the rod. Casting was therefore limited, and line could not be given to a running fish. The first reel probably appeared about 1,000 years ago, and it was quite primitive in design, with none of the features that we demand today. This is hardly surprising; the reels that we enjoy are highly engineered tools featuring very sophisticated design and construction. Always take care of your reel – don't let multipliers, in particular, fall onto the sand, or long casting will become almost impossible. Keep your fixed-spool reel well oiled, and don't shrink from having it serviced once in a while.

◀ **MULTIPLIER (BAITCASTER) REEL**
The multiplier is the reel for really heavy work, especially lure casting. The line capacity of the multiplier is huge, perfect for a big running fish like sturgeon or mahseer.

◀ **FIXED-SPOOL (SPINNING) REEL**
This type has made casting vast distances really easy for everyone. In fact, no reel could be easier or more effective to use. The clutch is particularly sensitive and a delight to play a running fish upon.

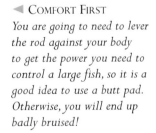

◀ **THE FLY REEL**
Fly reels need not be very sophisticated in design, since they are simply reservoirs for the fly line. However, lightness and reliability are important, and it pays to buy the best that you can afford.

▲ **CENTERPIN REEL**
Long trotting on rivers involves sending a float anything up to 330 ft (100 m) downstream. For this job, a traditional centerpin reel is hard to beat.

▲ **A GOOD CLUTCH**
It is at moments like this, when the pike is close in to you and sets about a final flurry, that your clutch really must give line without any hindrance.

LURES, FLIES, & BAITS

OF ALL THE DECISIONS in fishing, choosing the right morsel, real or artificial, with which to tempt the fish must be among the most important. It is also an aspect of fishing that brings the angler closest to the natural history of his quarry. The range of possible baits is truly vast, and the key lies in knowing when each should be used and how to present it.

PLUGS

EACH OF THE FOUR basic types of lure has its own way of working: soft-plastic lures imitate wildlife; spinners rotate; and spoons wobble *(see p. 174)*. A plug is a wooden or hard-plastic lure designed to look and move exactly like a small prey fish. An advantage of plugs is that you can choose one for whichever depth of water you wish to explore.

Just pick up a rod and line, take a bag of plugs and tackle, and roam at will. The secret lies in believing that the bait is alive – not a piece of wood or plastic but a frog, mouse, duckling, or an injured fish. Convince yourself of this, and you'll be surprised just how efficient your fishing can be. And it's fun!

▲ SUCCESS WITH A PLUG
Fish will not be attracted to your plugs if you retrieve doggedly, without imagination. Keep varying the action of the plug, and use every shred of your imagination.

◀ THE PLUG-FISHER'S WORLD
Anglers packing for a trip anywhere in the world will check their plug kit first. Plugs are the foremost lures for any predatory fish. But take enough with you – there are no tackle dealers in the back of beyond!

◀ DECEIVED
It is amazing that a predator can be tricked into mistaking a piece of wood or plastic for food, but fish intelligently and it can happen. Constant experimentation is the key.

▼ TWO SHALLOW DIVERS
These are two examples of lures that are designed to work in the surface layers as enticingly as possible. The jointed lure has an especially appealing wiggle!

SHALLOW DIVERS

Shallow divers generally work from just under the surface down to two yards or so. These have a particular place in shallow European waters, especially in the summer when weed growth is at its height. Shallow divers tend to have a sharply angled lip and are not too heavy, so they may float before retrieval. A lifelike action is important because in the top layers of water a wily predator will see anything amiss. Small, imitative divers are popular for bass, chub, and asp. Team them up with an ultralight rod and reel for a really challenging lure trip.

JOINTED LURE

SHAD RAP

FLOATING PLUGS

Floating plugs (also called top-water plugs) work exactly where their name implies, right on the surface, where they churn those calm bays into a foam! Here we're talking about crawlers, chuggers, stick-baits, prop-baits, and plugs with wings, nose-plates, concave faces, propellers, or just about anything that will splash and vibrate to give them as much impact as possible. There is no form of plug-fishing that is more exciting.

Floating plugs are generally the tool for warm spring and summer days, in shallow, clear water where there are plenty of lily-pads about. Once again, work that plug as though your life depended upon it, and put every ounce of thought into every retrieve. And don't imagine that the plug should be constantly on the move. Remember that some fish will take when the plug is at rest or just floating with the stream.

SPUTTERBUG

HEDDON TORPEDO

HULA POPPER

▲ FLASHERS AND SPLASHERS
Try fishing any of these at night when the water is warm and calm and there is a moon up. You will be surprised at how active predators can be in summer.

▼ THE STRIKE
If you can see that a predator is following your surface plug, do not slow down the retrieve! The take is less likely once the plug has been studied.

DEEP DIVERS

Deep divers work at depths greater than 6 ft (2 m) and go down to 40 ft (12 m) or beyond. They are used mostly in deep lakes in North America and central Europe, where weed growth is minimal. Rapala, one of the leading names in the deep diver market, concentrates on lures that search out predators that keep well down. Lake trout, pike, muskie, and bass can be tackled with these lures. Deep divers rely on a big lip at a shallow angle to force them nearly vertically downward.

HELLBENDER

BIG-LIPPED MINNOW

WEIGHTED JERKBAIT

▲ THREE DEEP DIVERS
These lures are all designed to work in deep water. Notice the big lips on the Hellbender and the Minnow, while the jerkbait is weighted with lead.

▲ GETTING DOWN DEEP
Once the weather has turned cold and the temperature of the water has begun to drop, it is vital to get that plug right down to the bottom where the predators will be lurking. Check out every snag and feature.

Soft-plastic lures, spoons, & spinners

Soft-plastic lures are made of rubberized plastic and come in all shapes and sizes. They are excellent for catching bass, perch, chub, trout, pike, zander, walleye, and asp – I have even caught rudd with them!

You can buy soft-plastic worms, lizards, crawfish, grubs, curl-tails, twin-tails, triple-ripples, tender tubes, toads, talking frogs, swamp rats, and just about anything else you can think of. They have lifelike actions and are light, so they make minimal noise as they enter the water – essential when pursuing crafty species such as chub or perch.

▶ IMITATING NATURE
What is more likely to tempt a pike on a hot summer's day than a frog swimming idly between the pads? Well, now you can imitate nature with a soft plastic from the tackle bag. Just watch those flippers go!

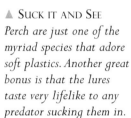

▲ SUCK IT AND SEE
Perch are just one of the myriad species that adore soft plastics. Another great bonus is that the lures taste very lifelike to any predator sucking them in.

▶ FATAL ATTRACTION
Soft plastics like this really cause a stir down deep. Here, a whole school has flocked to see what is new in town!

Spoons

Spoons are lures made of shaped sheet metal. When cast and retrieved from boat or bank, or when trolled *(see pp. 84, 85, 117),* their shape makes them wobble in the water, and their bright colors or shiny finish attract the attention of predatory fish.

A standard, heavy spoon is really effective for searching out predators that live in deep water. A fixed-spool reel *(see p. 171)* is best for this kind of fishing. Cast the spoon out, and when it hits the surface leave the bale arm (the winding mechanism of the fixed-spool reel) in the open position until line has ceased to leave the spool. When you are sure the spoon has hit bottom, close the bale arm and slowly retrieve the spoon.

Like most lures, the spoon is attached to a swivel at each end of the wire trace (the final section of the line). The swivel must be of good quality, or your line will twist badly.

▲ CATCH THE LIGHT
The best spoon will be nicely polished and kept really bright and glinting. Use big, highly reflective silver spoons when the sun shines, so that the light really bounces off through the water and pulls in the predators. A big vibrating action also helps.

HERON

ATLANTIC

HEDDON MOSS BOSS

◀ THREE SPOONS
A good spoon is colorful enough to be highly visible and gives out a thumping vibration that enables the predator to home in upon it. You will need to build up a collection of spoons of different weights and sizes, enabling you to fish different depths in all waters.

SPINNERS

A spinner is a lure with either an angled blade or a propeller mounted on its shaft. When an angler retrieves a spinner, or trolls it, water resistance makes it rotate and flash, attracting predatory fish.

The angle of the blade, rate of retrieve, and flow of the water itself control the spinner's rotational speed. Success is affected by these and by the choice of color (silver, gold, and copper are common) and finish (smooth, polished, hammered, fluted, or pointed).

The spinning action sends out vibrations. Sensing these *(see p. 17)*, the fish home in and find the lure itself. The revolving, flashing lure mimics the appearance of a twisting, turning crayfish, triggering the predator's instinctive strike response. Spinners can be made more effective by adding red wool, hair, real or plastic worms, rubber skirts, and even thin strips of fish to the treble hook.

FLYING CONDOM   SPRAT (DEVON MINNOW)   GOLD WING

▲ THREE SPINNERS
The Flying Condom has revolutionized salmon fishing. Its soft-plastic tail, also available in red, is hugely attractive, as is that of the Gold Wing. The Devon Minnow is one of the most traditional of all spinners and has accounted for more salmon than any other lure.

▼ EXPERIMENT WITH SPINNERS
Choosing the right spinner can be difficult, so buy a couple of each of the basic patterns, try them out, and build up experience.

UNLIMITED INVENTION

The world of the lure fisherman is a magical one in which thousands of inventors have exercised their imaginations over centuries. The result is a bewildering array of artificial beasties that mimic virtually every creature that a predator might find in nature.

You can buy plastic crickets and rubber shads, eel-type lures, and hairy, floating plugs that look like rats. You can make them yourself. This can be real sci-fi stuff, and the satisfaction of fooling a fish with one of the weirder creations is immense – especially if you made it at home on a winter's night.

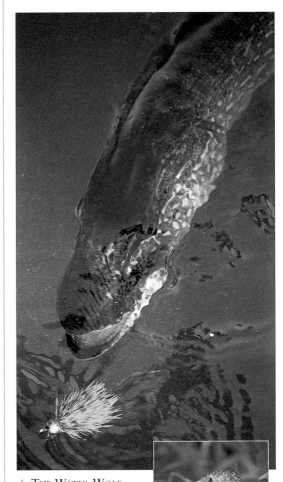

▲ THE WATER WOLF
It is heart-stopping to catch a big predator on the surface with a lure that imitates a small, scuttling creature. Takes are explosive, even if you don't always connect. The predator gets as excited as the angler and can miss the lure in its frenzy.

▲ MOUSE TRAP
Pike, muskie, trout, chub, taimen, asp, bass – any big predator will engulf an artificial mouse. Keep it moving, creating a strong wake, and fish around snags.

Flies

You would doubt whether concoctions of fur, feathers, and tinsel would fool any fish, let alone a creature as eagle-eyed as a trout. They certainly do, however, and a well-tied fly can prove to be virtually irresistible when properly presented. In broad terms, flies tend to be divided into two categories – the "attractors," which simply goad an investigatory or angry, attacking response, and the "deceivers," which try to imitate a natural food form.

Streamers

Streamers are large, gaudy flies, often tied in such unnatural colors as pinks, oranges, and neon blues. They generally have long, floating tails and big, built-up, even goggle-eyed, heads. Most importantly, they work!

To some degree, streamers imitate small fish, and they work particularly well with bass species at spawning, when the males chase them aggressively from the area. Don't fish a streamer on a light leader, or a grab-and-smash take is virtually guaranteed.

◀ **Attention to Detail**
Even though streamers are big and bold, tying them is still an art. Look at those lifelike eyes and the bright, fishlike tail.

▲ **Deceived!**
And the streamer actually works in action at the waterside. Perhaps it was that eye that did the trick and goaded this panfish into such an aggressive take!

Nymphs

All nymph patterns are deceivers, cunningly designed and tied to look as much like a natural insect as possible. The fly fisher will use small flies to resemble water boatmen, all manner of beetles and snails, caddis larvae, and the whole tribe of creatures that appear on the trout's day-to-day menu. The great point about the nymph is that, even if it does not resemble the food item exactly, the skillful fly fisher will nonetheless work it to make it seem lifelike. The working of the fly in the water is just as much the key as is the tying. Nymph fishing is all delicate, neat stuff that demands practice and skill.

Longshank Pheasant Tail

Marabou Nymph

Suspender Buzzer

Shrimp

▲ **Nymph Examples**
The flies above are all examples of deceivers. Look at the little artificial shrimp and imagine how enticingly that will work along the fringe of a weedbed, being twitched to rise and fall with a natural movement.

▶ **Got Him!**
A nymph has been worked with skill and patience, and the trout has made its one great mistake close to the bank after following for a good few yards. As the nymph rose to the surface, it made its last dash.

▲ **Closing In**
On every water, trout will follow flies over and over again, often just a body's length or less behind, checking them out, curious, and yet wary of making a mistake. In bright light and clear water, it may only be one trout in 10 that finally commits itself.

DRY FLIES

Generally, dry flies are also tied as deceivers, trying to copy the natural, hatching
insect. A perfect example would be the
mayfly, and today there are scores of mayfly
patterns, each designed to mimic the
natural. The range of dry flies is immense,
from huge craneflies down to tiny midges
not much bigger than a matchhead.

Dry flies are generally fished upstream
towards a rising fish, so that the angler is
not spotted and there is less chance of drag.
Accuracy in casting is important, and the fly
must float in a perky way toward the fish.

▲ WHAT THE FISH SEES
*Both of these flies (above
and below) are photo-
graphed from underwater,
as seen by the fish.*

HAWTHORN FLY   BLACK KLINKHAMMER

HARE'S FACE MIDGE

◄ DRY FLY EXAMPLES
*It is very important to
try to match the hatch
as closely as possible,
and for this reason most
dry fly enthusiasts are, to
an extent, entomologists.*

▲ MINUTE INSPECTION
*In a crystal-clear river like this one,
a rainbow trout will often take its time
and come very close indeed to the fly,
taking a careful look before making
any decision whatsoever. And, in most
cases, that decision will be negative.*

▲ SKILLFUL DECEPTION
*This fly is a realistic
imitation of a long-
legged cranefly. Like all
dry flies, it is held up on
top of the water by the
surface tension.*

WET FLIES

Wet flies are very much the weapon of the
quick-water, hillstream angler. They can be
either attractors or deceivers. Some are just
little bits of flash that imitate nothing but
attract the fish as they sparkle in the rushing
water, while others are tied to look like
aquatic insects.

Wet flies are often fished in teams of two
or three, and they are cast down the river
and then worked across the flow. Takes tend
to be sharp, very quick, and easy to miss.
Fishing a team of wet flies requires watercraft,
investigating all the calm little pockets of
water behind boulders or fallen trees.

BUTCHER   INVICTA

SOLDIER PALMER

▲ WET FLY EXAMPLES
*The Butcher, like many wet flies,
is a very old pattern indeed,
originally tied for the mountain
streams of the British Isles.*

▲ WET FLY BOX
*The fly box of a stream
fisherman will probably
contain a mixture of
wet flies and nymphs,
including gold-headed
ones with just that extra
bit of weight to help
them reach the bottom.*

◄ FISHING A WET FLY
*Heronlike, the angler
works his way downstream,
investigating every pocket
of water where he thinks
a trout may be concealed.*

BOTTOM BAITS

ALL ANGLERS THINK THEY want a bait that no fish can resist, and, sadly, every now and again a bait is discovered that really does sweep all before it. I say sadly because, in truth, the odds are almost too much in the angler's favor already. Just think. If every time you threw in your bait you caught a fish, where would the challenge be then? Let's make sure our baits are as good as we can make them, but be thankful that the fish is free to take or leave them as it chooses!

PARTICLE BAITS

Maggots, casters *(see opposite)*, and hempseed are traditional forms of particle bait, which simply means a small bait that is cast in very large quantities. Modern angling has exploited other seeds, and especially corn, as particle baits.

Indeed, it was the discovery of corn as a bait, during the 1970s, that brought particle baits to the forefront of angling in Europe and America. Carp, tench, bream – virtually all the nonpredatory species – went wild for the sweet yellow kernels.

The main problem with particle baits is presentation. The baits are tiny, and a large hook stands out clearly, so many particle baits are fished on a hair rig *(see opposite top)*.

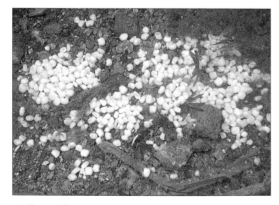

▲ FRESH CORN
A carpet of corn on the lake bed is a magnet for any passing fish. The color and the scent draw carp, tench, or bream in from many yards away. Sometimes, when hempseed is being used as the hookbait, a handful of corn can be used over a carpet of hempseed to make the hooked grain look less conspicuous.

DISTRIBUTING PARTICLE BAIT

Apart from presentation, the other problem with particle baits is distributing them a long way from the bank. They are too small and light to be cast any useful distance.

Using a slingshot is one answer, but even then you are restricted to a range of around 65–100 ft (20–30 m). This method involves rolling up a quantity of particle baits into a sizable ball of groundbait.

Swimfeeders follow this principle too: they are canisters that are packed full of particle baits and groundbait and cast out with the hookbait at the end of the fishing line. Casts of up to 300 ft (100 m) can be achieved.

Other ways of casting particle baits over long distances include freezing them into lumps that have the necessary weight, or packing them into a bag made of PVA, which dissolves in water – but remember to use dry bait, or the bag will dissolve in mid air!

▲ BARBEL ON A FEEDER
Here you can see clearly that the swim-feeder does work! This barbel was caught on a couple of kernels of corn, but it was attracted into the swim and encouraged to start feeding by a "free offering" of kernels delivered in the feeder and scattered around the hookbait.

◀ SMALL SWIMFEEDER
This is a new type of feeder. The concept is that the bait is mixed in with bread and packed tightly around the central core. The hookbait can also be pushed into the package, so that it is right in the middle of the baited area when the fish arrive.

◀ CAGE SWIMFEEDER
This kind of swimfeeder takes maggots (seen here) or any other particle bait mixed in with traditional groundbait. Pack it firmly so that the contents do not fly out during the cast but seep out once the swimfeeder has hit the bottom and the groundbait has become soaked.

◀ SLINGSHOT CAST
Here is an underwater shot of particle baits that have been cast in groundbait by slingshot. As the firmly packed mass breaks down in the water, a carpet of groundbait spreads over the lake bed, amid an enticing cloud of fine particles

HOME-BOILED BAITS

Home-boiled baits are better known to anglers in the British Isles as boilies. They are simply balls of nutritious, highly scented, very tasty concoctions that have been boiled to give them a hard skin. The idea is that the hard outer shell will prevent smaller, nuisance fish from nibbling them away, so they remain intact until the targeted carp or tench comes along. The ingredients of boilies exercise the minds of the best carp anglers, and there are literally thousands available. Every boilie has a base mix – often soy – and eggs are essential to bind the ingredients together. Coloring, flavoring, and as many as a score of different ingredients are added. Many anglers spend the winter months getting them ready for a summer blitz!

▶ THE TRAP IS SET
A scattering of free offerings is nearly always essential if the fish are to take the hookbait. In some cases, prebaiting with a particular type of boilie can begin weeks before fishing, so that the carp or tench have no suspicion of them whatsoever.

▶ HAIR RIG
This is the rig that transformed carp fishing. At first nobody would believe carp could be caught on a bait that was not even on the hook, but this is now the standard rig worldwide.

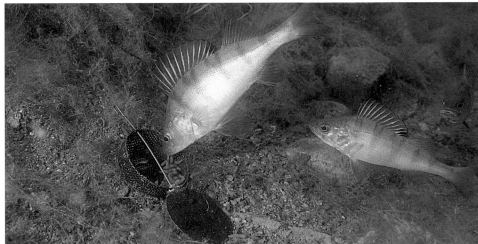

▲ DISSOLVING THE PROBLEM
Here is a PVA bag in action! It was filled with boilies, including the hookbait, and was cast out 260 ft (80 m) into the swim, where it sank 7 ft (2 m) to the bottom and began to disintegrate, spilling its contents out over the required area. Perfect!

MAGGOTS AND CASTERS

These have been used in Europe since the last century, long before anyone started calling them particle baits. Before the advent of sophisticated tackle shops, anglers would breed their own maggots or even search the bins in the butcher's back yard! There is hardly any fish that can refuse maggots: even predators like small pike will accept them readily. Maggots and casters are the constant baits for the match angler, and they have won more competitions than any other bait.

▶ BLOCK-END FEEDER
This is the perfect tool for getting loose-feed maggots out into the swim. Depending on the weight of the feeder, the maggots can be cast up to 330 ft (100 m). Block-end feeders are useful in both still and running waters. Vary the weight according to the current speed in rivers – the faster the flow, the heavier the feeder needs to be.

▲ BAIT DROPPER
A bait dropper will get maggots and casters to the bottom, especially in a river. As soon as it hits the bottom, it springs open and releases its contents.

◀ CARP ON THE PROWL
Cruising fish are usually hungry fish, and a carpet of bait will generally pull them down from midwater and encourage them to start feeding.

ACCESSORIES

IT IS IMPORTANT TO HAVE the right bits and pieces with you for those critical moments when they are needed. I divide them into three kinds: accessories for watching, hunting, and releasing fish. However, it is equally important not to get bogged down in attention to tackle alone. Remember, the very best tackle will never land you a fish without your own angling ability.

▲ GOOD STUDS
As I stand in water above my knees in a really speedy current, it is vital to know that my feet will not slip beneath me. Studs make sure that my soles will grip the bed, whether this is of mud, gravel, or smooth rock.

ACCESSORIES FOR WATCHING FISH

THE WHOLE PHILOSOPHY of this book has been that the key to successful fishing lies in understanding the waters, getting to know the fish, and recognizing all the clues that are placed before you. This means that you need to spend time beside the water, or even in it, minutely watching everything that happens above and below the surface.

Every little thing can tell an important story: a flat piece of water out in a ripple suggests that a fish has turned just beneath the surface and has given you a clue to its location. A dimpling of fry in the margin says that a predator might have gone past. The audible sip of a feeding trout tells you that it is taking one sort of fly rather than another. Go with the flow, immerse yourself in the freshwater world, open all your senses to what you are being told or shown, and your fishing will come alive. However, as an angler, you need to be able to respond quickly and effectively to what your senses are telling you.

This is where your accessories come in. Here we will be looking at the kinds of tools that the fish-watcher needs to make those precious hours by the waterside really count.

◄ TESTING THE WATER
Knowing whether the water temperature is rising or falling can give you invaluable insights into where the fish may be lying and what they could be feeding on.

WATCHER'S FOOTWEAR

In very cold conditions, you really must have truly warm, insulated boots, or the pain will set in, your concentration will go, and you will be back home within hours. On the other hand, in the summer, when conditions are dry and you want to tread softly and walk for miles, do you need waterproof footwear that will prove hot, clammy, and comparatively heavy? A better solution may be to wear light shoes and carry thigh waders or, even better, chest waders that will give you far more adaptability. But always take care when walking in a river or lake! Never tread in areas where you are uncertain of the bottom, and always wear buoyancy aids.

▲ GETTING CLOSE
A fisherman creeps through undergrowth to approach a pond in which some carp are basking in the warmth of the spring sun. His lightweight sneakers make virtually no vibrations on the bank.

BELT STRAP
Clipped onto a belt or waistband, a top strap keeps the lightweight, upper part of the boot upright.

▲ THIGH BOOTS
Good for pushing through wet undergrowth as well as wading, thigh boots that fold down are a good idea in summer because they are light and relatively cool.

WALKING BOOT

WALKING BOOT WITH STRAP-ON SOLE

▲ WALKING BOOTS
It is a good idea to take a variety of strap-on soles with you if you are to wade safely on different types of riverbed. Felt soles provide grip on smooth rocks.

USING BINOCULARS

Binoculars are an invaluable aid to the angler in hundreds of situations. The one task above all others in which they will help you is that of locating fish. The best anglers are hunters and not ambushers, and that means that they actively pursue their quarry. Locating it in the first place is therefore critical. Things that seem insignificant to the naked eye become hard evidence when seen through binoculars.

Even for relatively close-in work, a pair of binoculars can be a great boon: perhaps you will use them to see what kinds of insects are hatching in the foliage on the far bank, or to detect when that carp you are pursuing has finally taken your floating bait between its lips.

▶ WHAT YOU SEE
Sometimes rings at the surface can simply be the effect of marsh gas, but my binoculars revealed that the rings shown here were made by fish swimming and feeding close to the surface.

▼ RISING AND SETTING
Binoculars are useful throughout the day, but they are particularly helpful at dawn and dusk. When the naked eye is struggling, the lenses amplify the available light, enabling you to make an early start or stay late.

▶ THE RIGHT CHOICE
Ideally, you need lightweight binoculars that you can hold for long periods. Go for the highest quality of lenses that you can afford for a bright, clear view. It may also be worth considering binoculars that float!

MINIMIZING GLARE

One of the greatest problems a fish-watcher encounters, whatever the season of the year, is the glare of the sun reflected from the surface of the water. At certain angles it will be impossible to see into even the clearest of rivers and pools, and what you cannot see you cannot know. The fish-watcher must do something about this, and the first step is to invest in a good peaked hat and a top-quality pair of polarizing glasses.

◀ ESSENTIAL EQUIPMENT
Polarizing glasses are the greatest aid of all. They cut out reflected light, allowing the angler to see through the surface glare to what is happening beneath. Buy the best you can afford — and don't leave them on the bank.

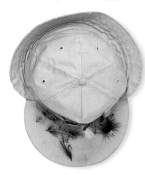

◀ SUN VISOR
A peaked hat is invaluable in sunny conditions, since it shades the eyes and prevents you from needing to squint. Choose a hat that is lightweight, cool, and neither too tight nor too brightly colored.

▲ BLINDED BY THE LIGHT
With a bright sky reflected in the water, you can look as carefully as you like with your unaided eye and you are unlikely to see anything that is significant. The water is still, and there is the odd stick floating in the shallows.

▲ SEEING THROUGH THE SURFACE
Put on your polarizing glasses and the whole picture becomes clear. Suddenly you are aware of this 4 lb (2 kg) pike hanging motionless in the margins, well camouflaged, and prepared to spring on its prey.

FISH-HUNTERS' ACCESSORIES

ONE LOOK AT A MAJOR mail-order catalog will give you some idea of the thousand and one items available for the angler. Some are absolutely vital, some are just useful, and others are designed to catch the angler's cash rather than the fish themselves! Nonetheless, an all-around angler does need quite a variety of items if he or she wants to be ready for every unexpected eventuality and be able to bring the very best out of every situation. One tip – get the very best quality you can afford. This is well worthwhile when you consider not only that good gear can last a lifetime but, equally importantly, that it will never let you down, whatever the test. Let us look at some of the things that I would not be without in my own angling life.

DRESS FOR THE SEASON

Remember that, if you are uncomfortable, you cannot concentrate on the job in hand – fishing! It is obvious, though often enough ignored, that if you are feeling cold in the winter or hot in the summer, you will not be fishing at full capacity. Get the clothing right and you are halfway to fishing properly, too. Remember that, even in summer, a light waterproof can be useful, because nothing chills you more than a sudden shower.

► SUMMER WEAR
A simple but well-made vest like this is perfect in summer. It carries a great deal of gear but doesn't wear you out or bake you!

▲ WARM LINING
Thermal linings mean that no properly equipped angler need be bothered by the winter's cold – a real boon in northern latitudes.

▲ WINTER INSULATION
With the range of materials on the market now it is possible to cocoon yourself against every vagary of the weather. When I was a child, it was a question of nylon anoraks and simple plastic wellingtons, and life could be very uncomfortable.

SEARCHING LARGE WATERS

On large waters – still or flowing – you need to be mobile if you are to find the fish, and a boat is essential. And so is an echo sounder. These pieces of high technology can provide you with all the information that you need in just a few hours, rather than seasons. Echo sounders are very precise instruments, giving accurate depths as well as showing underwater features. Most modern models can even pick out individual fish.

▲ FULLY FITTED OUT
These chest waders are made of the best of modern materials. Despite being waterproof, the material breathes, allowing you to walk for miles in complete comfort without melting inside them.

▲ A PERFECT SETUP
There's nothing better than knowing that you are fishing in a really efficient way. The boat is good, the engine is throbbing, the lures are working, and the echo sounder is heading you toward success.

◄ HUNTING OUT STEELHEAD
To explore steelhead rivers fully, a tough, shallow-draft boat and a reliable engine are absolutely indispensable.

TACKLE CONTAINERS

There are hundreds of types of bags and boxes on the market today, for every type of fishing situation. However, there are some basic considerations that you should take into account before making a final choice. First, you should aim for a tackle container that is going to suit you for most of your fishing life. If, for example, you are a European match angler, then you will want something that has the capacity of a trashcan to take all your tackle and the comfort of a living-room chair to accommodate your bottom! If, on the other hand, you are a more mobile type of angler, then you merely need something to sling on your shoulder to hold the minimum amount of gear that you will need for the day. Your tackle container will need to be tough as well as light so that it won't break apart when you are leaping from rock to rock across a stream or chasing frantically after a runaway fish.

▲ LARGE OR SMALL?
It is generally best to go big rather than small — there is nothing more frustrating then needing to leave essential items at home. A wicker basket like this one will last for years.

▶ WAIST BAG
A waist bag like this can simply be slung over your shoulder and taken everywhere. It is tough, relatively waterproof, and has several compartments for all the different types of gear. Some also have a removable waterproof inner bag.

▲ FLOAT BOX
A float box is essential if your floats are not going to get chipped, clipped, and broken. The best floats, especially hand-made ones, are very expensive nowadays. Look after them.

USING AN INNER TUBE

The great advantage of the inner tube is the extraordinary mobility that it gives you, allowing you to hunt among the reedy margins where the bass or trout lie, previously safe from the angler.

However, do take great care when using your tube, especially for the first few times. Don't venture out into a river, and avoid days with a strong wind. Set out against any current so that your journey home is easier. Always be aware of any rocks or snags that could become a problem, and keep your eye open for a safe beaching area.

STARTING OFF
Enter the water in the shallows, walking backward and against the wind, so that at worst you will simply be blown inshore.

TECHNIQUE
Allow the wind to drift your line through the water, across the taking fish.

DIRECTION OF WIND

▼ ULTIMATE MOBILITY
It is possible to drift for a long distance, testing out all sorts of areas. Use a short-handled landing net to scoop out any hooked fish. Watch for changing weather conditions.

FISH SIGHTING
In hot weather, bass and trout are likely to be at lower levels, and a sinking lure or fly will be needed.

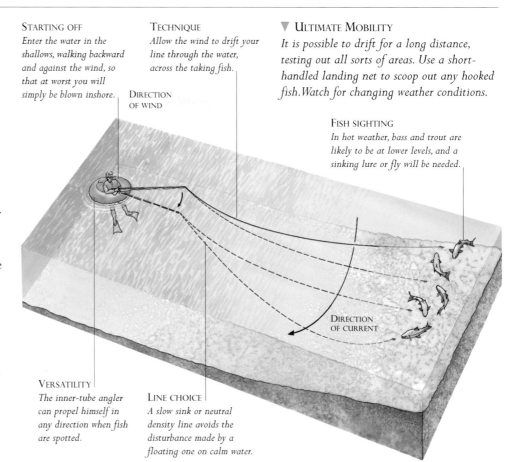

DIRECTION OF CURRENT

◀ LOCOMOTION
You will need to wear flippers for propulsion and maneuvering. To begin with, restrict your sessions to an hour or so.

WARM AND FLEXIBLE
Neoprene is the perfect material for wearing in cold water.

VERSATILITY
The inner-tube angler can propel himself in any direction when fish are spotted.

LINE CHOICE
A slow sink or neutral density line avoids the disturbance made by a floating one on calm water.

FISH-RELEASING ACCESSORIES

CONSERVATION IS BECOMING an important issue all across the world of angling. There is a growing realization that fish are creatures and not simply objects placed there for our own pleasure. This burgeoning new attitude is a mixture of both sense and sensitivity. It is common sense to realize that stocks of good fish are limited and that the existing fish stocks need to be looked after.

Sensitivity simply makes us all better anglers. We need to remember how delicate even the toughest looking bass or pike can be, especially when it is taken out of its natural element. It is hardly surprising, really – how tough would any of us be if we found ourselves beneath the surface without scuba gear? We should bear in mind that fishing is not nearly as much fun for the fish, so we owe it to them to get them back into the water as quickly as possible.

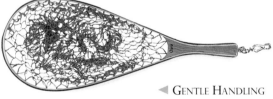

◀ GENTLE HANDLING
If you are going to use a net, make sure it has the softest possible mesh and that the fins will be safe against any knots. Also consider whether a net is needed at all – perhaps you could simply draw the fish into the shallows for unhooking.

▲ HANDLED WITHOUT STRESS
Make use of natural features like weed or lilybeds to provide a temporary rest for your fish. These have a soft, moist texture and are more friendly to the fish's flanks than dry grass, sand, or gravel.

HOOKS AND UNHOOKING

For decades now there have been major debates about the damage that barbed hooks can do. Do we actually need barbs on our hooks at all? If the pressure is maintained on a hooked fish, then it is very unlikely that the barbless point will ever come away. And when it comes to unhooking, there is no doubt that barbless hooks win over barbed on every occasion, since they are so much more easily removed.

We also need to consider the question of treble hooks on lures. Big trebles very often cause damage to fish, especially loose hooks outside the fish's mouth, because they can fly around and catch the fish's eye. Never use more trebles on a lure than you think are really necessary, and always make sure that the hooks are no larger than they need to be.

▶ REMOVING HOOKS
Large, trigger-handled, spring-loaded pliers are ideal for big hooks and predators. A smaller pair of surgical forceps is the right tool to slip the hook from a carp, bass, or trout. Never be without these items.

▲ HOOKS WITHOUT BARBS
Barbless hooks are now commercially available in every possible size and shape. Alternatively, you can simply flatten the barb down with a pair of forceps at the waterside to achieve pretty much the same effect.

▼ HOW TO UNHOOK
If possible, avoid taking the fish from the water when you are unhooking it. Lay it on its side in the shallows, where it will have water around it. Don't hold the fish too firmly, because vital organs could be damaged. Use forceps to slip the hook out then, once the hook is removed, return the fish to the water, facing it into any current.

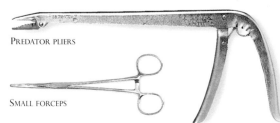

PREDATOR PLIERS

SMALL FORCEPS

PHOTOGRAPHING THE CATCH

Once upon a time, all fish that were caught were killed and eaten. Then came the days when angling was for sport rather than for food, and all big fish were killed, then mounted by the taxidermists.

Now, in what are hopefully more enlightened days, we can keep our records on film. Choose a tough, rugged camera, because the bankside is a great tester for all equipment, and there will inevitably be times when your bag is dropped, kicked, or crushed.

Do make sure that everything is prepared for the photograph before the fish is taken from the water. Speed is of the essence, so have the exact spot marked out where the fish is to lie or be held. If the size is what you want to record, have some kind of scale in position. Get the focusing and the exposure all sorted out beforehand. Hold the fish with wet hands or place it on wet weed.

A motor drive on your camera is a valuable aid, because it enables you to shoot quickly without winding manually. A polarizing filter helps if you take photographs of fish just beneath the surface.

▲ CLOSE TO THE WATER
When you are photographing your fish, always hold it either in the water or very close to it, just in case it leaps from your hands. A fall onto gravel or rocks can hurt the fish and may even be fatal.

▶ IN THE WATER
Perhaps the best shots of all are those taken of fish in their own environment, visibly being washed over by the water. Remember, too, that water enhances the natural colors of the fish.

FILM SPEEDS
Always think carefully when choosing your film speed: fast for low light, and as slow as possible for sunny days.

▲ A SUITABLE CAMERA
Most anglers who are serious about their photography will use a tough SLR type of camera, which will take excellent photographs under all conditions and is generally very tough and reliable.

▲ TAPE IS KINDER THAN SCALES
Inevitably, weighing a fish takes more time and is more stressful than simply laying a tape measure from head to tail.

▶ A GOOD TIME TO MEASURE
The best time to measure a fish is when it is lying in very shallow water. Measurements might not be totally exact in these situations, but they are usually quite adequate.

MEASUREMENT AND RELEASE

The whole issue of weighing fish, taking measurements, and keeping records is a very thorny one. Of course, big fish, especially historically huge fish, should be accurately recorded, but do we really need to take the measurements or weights of much smaller fish? Okay, take time over a personal best or a lake record, but put the rest back quickly.

In Britain, weight is still the key factor, but placing a fish in any kind of net or sack always runs the risk of damaging it. In other parts of the world, measurement of length is much more important. It is generally a lot quicker to measure a fish than to weigh it, and it is a great deal kinder. If at all possible, measure the fish lying in very shallow water. Put a stick into the silt or sand at its tail and another at the tip of its snout, and then measure the distance between them when the fish is on its way home.

INDEX

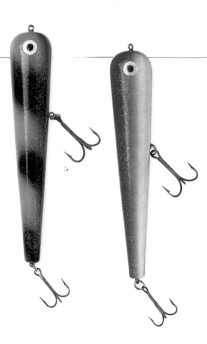

ACKNOWLEDGMENTS

AUTHOR'S ACKNOWLEDGMENTS
I WOULD LIKE TO EXTEND MY WARMEST THANKS TO:

Sylvia Hollingworth for typing the manuscript so magnificently, often at times of severe pressure from deadlines.

Johnny Jensen, Simon Channing, Nick Giles, and Michael Reiter for their help in the form of photographs, useful advice, and general support.

Jim and Shirley Deterding, Tom Cook, Pauline Harrold, and Michael Taylor for their help with photographic locations.

Peter and Catherine Smith at Caer Berris Manor in Wales for the loan of their water for fishing and photography, their marvelous hospitality, and their general support through thick and thin.

Petr, Radim, Franta, and all at Ingol for their help on some of the more exotic locations.

All who supplied tackle for our photography sessions, namely all at Sportfish for their magnificent support and hugely helpful advice; Richard Carter for his floats, reels, and general support; Chris and Sue at the Harris Angling Company, who have been particularly helpful and whose advice on lures has been unparalleled; Gary and Peter at Drennan International, who have been their usual towers of strength; and what on earth would I have done without all the help from Craig Brew at Shimano?

All at John Partridge and all at Musto – without your clothing I am quite sure I would have perished long ago on some wild, wet waterside!

Steve Knowlden and Ian Whitelaw, who were inspirational in moving this book from base camp; Ian, indeed, has gone on to prove himself the most excellent of fishermen and friends.

Kevin and Edward, for taking up so capably where Ian and Steve left off.

The thousands of anglers with whom I have fished over the last 20 years or so, and whose help, advice, and friendship will never be forgotten.

Finally, let me not forget my wife, who has sat so stoically on so many river banks in so many countries in so much evil weather . . . and who has never uttered a word of complaint!

PUBLISHER'S ACKNOWLEDGMENTS
The publishers would like to thank the following for permission to photograph fish, and for help at photography sessions:
NATIONAL SEA LIFE CENTRE, BIRMINGHAM:
Graham Smith and Sally Reynolds.
SEA LIFE CENTRE, GT YARMOUTH: Mitchel Hird.
CHALK SPRINGS, ARUNDEL: Jonathan Glover.

PHOTOGRAPHIC CREDITS
The publisher would like to thank the following people and agencies for their kind permission to reproduce photographs:
a=above, c=center, b=below, l=left,
r=right, t=top
Gillian Andrews 57br, 64br. **Animals, Animals** E R Degginger 18cra. **Ardea** 177bc. **John Bailey** 11br, 12b, 15t, 23tr, 23br & bc, 26bl, 31t & c, 34br, 39br, 42c & tr, 45cra, 48clb, 49clb, 53 tr & bl, 62cb, 64tr & cr, 70tr & cr, 71cr, 72cra, 73crb, 74cla & clb, 75tr, tc & br, 76 cr & bl, 77tc, 84tr, 88tr, 94tr & br, 99 (all), 100 tr & c, 101 cr, 104clb, tr & cr, 105 (all), 106tr & c, 107tc & clb, 108 cl, 109 clb, 111bl, 112 tc & cr, 114tr, 115cr & tc, 116c, 118 (all), 119 tr, c, bc & br, 121tl, tr, bl, cl & br, 122tr & bc, 124–5 (all), 128c, 130cl & crb, 132br, 133tr, cl, c, cb & cr, 134tr, 140br, 144 (all), 145c, 147tr, 148tr, 149cl, 150tr, crb & bc, 151c, 152clb, 154br, 156cr, 160cl & tr, 161br, 163cra, 171cb, 172c, 178tr, 180bc, 182, 183bc, 184tc, 187tc & bl. **Richard T Bryant** 46br & bl, 55tr & ca, 83tr, 114c, 117bc, 145cr, 158cr, 159tr, cl & cb. **Simon Channing** 56br,

57tr, cl, cr, & bl & 65cra, br & clb, 68–9 (all). **Bruce Coleman** Jeff Foot 86–7, 93bl; Johnny Jensen 93cr; Hans Reinhard 139c. **Kevin Cullimore** 8–9, 11tr, 16tr & bc, 20cr, 23tl, 34bl, 43tr & cr, 48c, 62br, 83cb, 107cr, 109tr, 129 (all), 179bc. **E R Degginger** 164tr. **Getty Images** Larry Goldstein 13bl; Bob Herger 38–9t; Peter Stef Lamberti 37br. **Nick Giles** 89cla, 122br, 123ct, 157cla, 187cr. **Heinz Jagusch** 17br, 25br, 44, 122c, 126–7, 140bl, 141bl & br, 146br, 147c, 164bl, 169bc. **JPH Foto** Erwin & Peggy Bauer 45cr; E Bauer-adi 172tr; Johnny Jensen 18cb, 46c, 48bc, 52t & br, 58tr & clb, 59cl & tc, 60tr & clb, 61tr & cb, 62clb, 73bl, 80cl, cb & bc, 81tr & cl, 85c, bc & crb, 90cra & br, 91cra & br, 94bl, 110, 112tr, 113, 116clb, 117cl, 120clb & bl, 121bc,123bl, 130tr, 131tc, bl & br, 137 (all), 146tr, 147tl, 150bl, 151tr & br, 154tr, br & cr, 155 (all), 164bc & cr, 165 (all), 168bl, 169br, 170br, 171br, 172bl, 173bl, 175bl & br; Doug Stamm 40–1, 176bl, 185, 186bl. **Natural History Photographic Agency** Agence Nature 55bl; G I Bernard 89cr; Daniel Buclin 139bc; Robert Erwin 20bl; T Kitchen & V Hurst 93br, 101cl, 130bc, 158c; Stephen Krasemann 92tr; Mike Lane 131cr; Lutra 115br; Peter Pickford 24tr & 59br; Kevin Schafer 92c; G E Schmida 56c; Hellio and van Ingen 19t. **Oxford Scientific Films** Doug Allen 73tr; Jack Dermid 71tr; John Downer 131clb; Max Gibbs 158clb, 159cr; Andreas Hartl 18tr; Philippe Henry 66clb; Roger Jackman 138cr; Tom Leach 82c; R Leszczynski 54br; Colin Milkins 18br, 128bl, 157crb; Peter Parks 26tr; Wendy Shattil & Bob Rozinski 65c. **Pictor International** 28–9, 45t, 47, 90bl, 142–3, 144 (all), 145cb. **Planet Earth Pictures** Richard Cottle 88c; Geoff du Feu 148c; D Robert Franz 92clb; Nick Greaves 145br, 77c; Martin King 34tr, 71tc; Ken Lucas 73c, 115cl; Mark Mattock 132tr; Linda Pitkin 12r; Mike Read 82tr; G van Ryckevorsel 2–3, 27b, 72br, 89cr, 97tl, 98b, 119bl; Tom Walker 21b, 93tr; A Zvoznikov 72ca. **Studio Schmidt-Luchs** 56b, 111br, 116cra, 123ca & crb, 138t. **TCL Stock Directory** D Norton 36–7. **Telegraph Colour Library** 90cl. **John Wilson** 146bl, 160br, 183crb.

COMMISSIONED PHOTOGRAPHY
PRINCIPAL PHOTOGRAPHER Steve Gorton
UNDERWATER PHOTOGRAPHY Kevin Cullimore 1, 6, 13tc, tr & br, 15br, 19bc, 21tr, 22tr, 25t, 27tr, 46tc, tl & bc, 48tr, 49tc, tr & bl, 50cl, 54cla, clb & bc, 55cl & c, 56c & tr, 58cb, 59c & tr, 61cr & br, 63bl, bc & br, 66cr & br, 67 (all), 78br, 80tr, cr & br, 83c & cr, 84tr, 97c, 102bl, 103tr, bl, bc & br, 108br, 109bc, 140tc, 149tc, cra & crb, 152tr, 153bc, 156tr, 158tr, 162cl, 163c, bc & br, 167clb, 173br, 174c, ca, tr & cr, 175br, 176cl, tr & br, 177tr & cr, 178br, c & bc,179ct, cra & cr, 192. ADDITIONAL PHOTOGRAPHY Ashley Straw 15c, 22b, 33tl, 102cr & tr, 103tl, 177tc & cr; David Rudkin 24b, 181c & cr; and also Peter Gathercole, Dave King, Colin Keates, Philip Gatward

ILLUSTRATORS
DIAGRAMS David Ashby 136; Carl Ellis 16, 17bl, 50bl, 52bc, 53br, 58br, 61cl, 69tc, 71br, 81b, 84br, 95br, 116br, 117bt, 139tr, 162cr, 184bl & br.
FISH Colin Newman 17cr, 43cr, 45b, 55tc, 56cl, 62tr, 76bc, 77tr, 82c, 83tc, 88bl, 90tc & c, 91tc & c, 92bc, 100bl, 101tc, 107ca & cb, 114bl, 115cl, 119tc, 123tr, 129cr, 145cr, 148c.
FISH MOTIF Caroline Church 3, 7, etc
MAPS Stephen Conlin 50,78, 96–97, 98, 102, 120, 124, 134, 136, 152, 160.
UNDERWATER SCENES John Barber 31, 32–33, 35, 36–37, 38–39.

DESIGN ASSISTANCE Anna Benjamin, Helen Diplock
EDITORIAL ASSISTANCE Tracie Lee, Ian Whitelaw
INDEX Julie Rimington
JACKET DESIGN Jo Houghton